Empirical Philosophy of A.J. Ayer

Empirical Philosophy of A.J. Ayer

Dr. Anjana Pathak

ADHYAYAN

ADHYAYAN PUBLISHERS & DISTRIBUTORS
New Delhi-110002

Published by
ADHYAYAN PUBLISHERS & DISTRIBUTORS
4378/4B, 105, J.M.D. House, Murari Lal Street
Ansari Road Darya Ganj, New Delhi - 110002
Ph.: 011-23263018, 011-23277156, Fax: 23280028
Email: adhyayanpublishers@yahoo.com

Empirical Philosophy of A.J. Ayer

Edition 2011
ISBN 978-81-8435-303-7

Printed in India

Published by Harish Chandra Yadav for Adhyayan Publishers & Distributors, Delhi. Laser Typesetting at Jain Computers and Printed at Tarun Offset Printers. Delhi

Foreword

Empirical Philosophy of A.J.Ayer is a lucid and Critical Assessment of Ayer's Philosophy. His *Language, Truth and Logic* is the most valuable book as it popularized the main tenets of logical positivism in the English speaking Countries of the Word. It is an analytical approach to Philosophical problems which combines the tradition of British empiricism with a continental method formulated by the continental Vienna Circle led by Moritz Schlick. It divided all meaningful discourse capable of being true or false into two categories-one is of the necessarily true propositions found in mathematics and logic, the other that of the contingently true propositions of sciences and everyday discourse. The former are held to be true in virtue of the meaning of the words which are used to express them, and the latter by agreement with our sense-experience. Underlying this division is the verifiability criterion of meaning which rejects all the putative propositions as nonsense which are neither analytic nor verifiable by sense-experience. What is said in morals, aesthetics, theology and especially metaphysics are declared to be cognitively meaningless. A place was found for moral statements as expressing our approval or disapproval. His second book *Foundations of Empirical Knowledge* offers a linguistic approach to the traditional problem of sense-data as the basis of what we perceive. In his later work *The Problem of Knowledge* Ayer moves away from his earlier position and does not fully endorse the verification principle of meaning.

He modifies but does not totally reject his empirical Philosophy. The modifications are more clearly pronounced in his *The Central Questions of Philosophy* and *Philosophy in the Twentieth Century.*

In the first Chapter of her book Dr. Anjana Pathak traces the main features and development of empirical philosophy as it is found in ancient Greek thinkers, Classical British philosophers, Comte and J.S. Mill. After the historical empiricism she considers the principal theses of Ayer. She analyses and examines the verification principle in different forms, the elimination of metaphysics and concludes that these attempts are not successful. She also considers the function of philosophy and nature of philosophical analysis as given by Ayer. Her treatment of the difficulties inherent in analysis which reduces object statements to phenomenalistic language is commendable. She also discusses Ayer's account of necessary propositions and its defects as pointed out by Quine and others. In order to make her study exhaustive she examines Ayer's views on personal identity and value judgements. In all her discussions Dr. Pathak also considers the gradual changes that Ayer made from time to time.

Like in other areas philosophy too has its fashion and fashions change in every age. It is true that logical positivism is no longer in fashion, but some of its principles are still relevant and so long as empiricism is alive in some form, Ayer's contributions cannot be ignored. Dr. Pathak has done a great service to philosophy by writing a book on one of the most important philosophers of the twentieth century.

- D.N. Dwivedi

Preface

The title of the present book is **"Empirical Philosophy of A.J. Ayer"**. The reason why I have selected such a subject is that I have always taken a keen interest in the questions concerning the source, validity and limits of our knowledge, and the way in which empiricist philosophers deal with these questions, attracts me very much. It is always important, as well as, interesting to know about the spirit of free inquiry, a natural-scientific view of the universe that takes place in the history of philosophy and proceeds further. The zeal for investigation extends to all sorts of problems and invades every field of study and prepares the way for a greater era. The spirit of independent thinking, logical inquiry and criticism are the characteristics of logical empiricism, which still remains influential in later philosophical views.

This book could not have been possible without the co-operation of a few people, and I would like to take this opportunity to acknowledge their invaluable contribution. I would like to start by thanking from the core of my heart, Prof. D.N. Dwivedi, former Head, Dept. of Philosophy, University of Allahabad, and an eminent scholar in his own right. It was he who suggested to me the subject for this book and also its present title. He is indeed a vast reservoir of knowledge and wisdom. He would always be next to me in person, or on phone, whenever I needed his time to clear a few conceptual issues. Working under his guidance has been a truly cherished experience, which has enriched my understanding and knowledge of various aspects of the subject. He has been generous enough to even write the foreword for this book, for which I am profoundly thankful. Needless to say, this book could not have seen the light of the day without his inspirational motivation.

I would also like to express my heartfelt gratitude towards Prof. J.P. Shukla, former Vice Chancellor, Rani Durgavati University, Jabalpur, Madhya Pradesh, as also Prof. Sabhajit Mishra, (Retd.) Dept. of Philosophy, Deen Dayal Upadhyaya University, Gorakhpur, U.P., both renowned scholars of Philosophy, for making invaluable suggestions to me about the concerned subject from time to time.

I am also deeply indebted to my teachers in the Dept. of Philosophy, University of Allahabad, namely Prof. Gauri Chattopadhyaya, Head of the Department, as also Prof. Narendra Singh, Prof. Mridula Ravi Prakash, Prof. J.S. Tiwari and Prof. H.S. Upadhyaya, for teaching me the subject during my formative years and giving me important tips towards the writing of this book.

I would also like to thank Dr. B.B. Tripathi, Principal, and Dr. Mukti Vyas, former Principal respectively of Allahabad Degree College, Allahabad for their constant support and encouragement during the entire period of writing this book. In this context, I would like to make a special mention of Dr. Ram Murti Pathak, Head, Dept. of Philosophy, Allahabad Degree College, Allahabad who helped me immensely by his deep insights and experienced inputs at every stage of writing this book. My thanks also extend to all my colleagues in the college, who have been very supportive of my endeavour to write this book.

I would also like to express my gratitude towards Dr. Sanjay Shukla, Associate Professor, Ewing Christian College, Allahabad, Dr. Rishikant Pandey, Associate Professor, University of Allahabad, Allahabad and Dr. K.C. Pandey, Associate Professor, University of Lucknow, Lucknow, who provided me books and other materials for purposes of research into this topic. I would also like to thank Dr. D.D. Dwivedi, Assistant Professor, Dept. of Defence Studies, Ishwar

Saran Degree College, Allahabad for lending a helping hand during the process of publication of the book.

I would like to thank the staff at the following libraries - I.C.P.R. Lucknow, Central Library of the University of Delhi, Jawaharlal Nehru University and Delhi School of Economics, for helping me out with a wide range of books on A.J. Ayer and other related topics.

I cannot forget the invaluable moral support and unending encouragement that all the members of my family gave to me during the hard and grinding days of writing the book. Here, I would like to make a very special mention of my late father - Dr. Chandra Prakash Pathak. The innumerable trips that I made with him for miscellaneous reasons associated with writing the book, are part of my cherished memories. I would like to express my deep gratitude towards my mother Smt. Malti Pathak who has been a source of immense strength and encouragement. She took care of my daily needs so that I could concentrate on writing the book. This book could not have been possible without her love and blessings. I would also like to thank other members of my family, especially my little nephew Aditya, who gave me endless reasons to laugh at the end of a strenuous day of writing.

And lastly, but not in the least, I would like to thank Adhyayan Publishers and Distributors, New Delhi, especially Mr. Harish Chandra Yadav who took great pains to ensure that the book was devoid of errors and flaws to the maximum possible extent, and that it is aesthetically pleasing to the visual senses.

Finally, I would like to mention to the readers of the book that though painstaking efforts have been made to ensure that there are no spelling or other errors, it is still possible that a few may have inadvertently crept into the book, for which I may be kindly forgiven. I sincerely hope that my book shall be accepted by one and all, from within and outside the realm of Philosophy, and shall benefit scholars and students alike.

Happy reading!

2nd February, 2011 **Dr. Anjana Pathak**

Introduction

Epistemology is the study of human knowledge -what we can know, how we can know and what we can not know. In order to have knowledge, the empiricist appeals to his experience. Empiricism, in one sense or another is a major thread, a chain, running through western philosophy since seventeenth century, including logical positivism and much of the philosophy of today. And Ayer's empiricism, that is, logical empiricism is a very important link of this chain.

The movement 'logical positivism' also known as 'logical empiricism' originated in 1920s among philosophers and scientists of the 'Vienna Circle', under the leadership of Moritz Schlick. The British philosopher A. J. Ayer attended its meetings in 1933 and made its ideas widely known in the English-speaking world.

The members of this movement had their resolution to combat the rise of irrationality in Europe. Fanaticism was on the rampage. These philosophers, virtually all of them were German or Austrian (Ayer joined them later) sought a place of refuge and sanity from which to explode the pretensions of absolutist fascism and relativism alike. That place of refuge was science, and most of the Vienna-circle was composed of scientists and philosophers of science.

Being a logical positivist, Ayer too has these tendencies. And with such scientific attitude, he presents his theories.

The present study is aimed to understand Ayer's philosophy in a historical background with the comments made by the contemporary philosophers, on it.

The study has been divided into eight chapters.

In the first chapter, which is *'A Brief History of Western Empiricism'* we shall take a look at the empirical tradition in the history of philosophy. It is found from the very beginning. In the Greek age, the philosophies of the Atomists and Sophists can be called empiricism. Then comes the classical British tradition, where Locke, Berkeley and Hume present their empiricist philosophy. And in 1920s, the movement known as 'logical Empiricism' formulates an entirely new and revolutionary conception of philosophy.

The second chapter *'The Elimination of Metaphysics'* deals with the proper concern of Ayer's philosophy, which is to be held with meaning. As having distaste for metaphysics, he proceeds towards its elimination of metaphysics by using the criterion of factual meaningfulness, which is known as verification principle. Through this criterion, Ayer condemns the statements of metaphysics as literally non-sensical. But Ayer fails in the successful formulation of this verification principle and faces a lot of criticism.

The third chapter is about *'The Function of Philosophy'*. It shows Ayer's view that if philosophy claims to make a special contribution to the stock of our knowledge, it must not attempt to formulate speculative truths, or to look for first principles etc. According to Ayer, he must confine himself to works of analysis, the logical clarification of language.

The fourth chapter *'The Nature of Philosophical Analysis'* is the most important one of the entire book. It records the views of Ayer about philosophical analysis. Ayer adopts reductionsim, according to which the statements about physical objects are reducible into equivalent statements about sense-data, as physical objects are logical constructions out of sense-data. Ayer illustrates the method of philosophical analysis and presents four preliminary definitions, which are, direct and indirect resemblance, and, direct and indirect continuity. But it is shown that according to critiques, Ayer's analysis is seriously flawed in its initial and its subsequent steps.

The fifth chapter, which is *'The Problem of Perception*

of the Physical World' takes an account of this problem presented by Ayer. Ayer presents the sceptic's claim that our perception of a physical object is always indirect. Again, Ayer talks about naive realist's belief that physical objects can be directly perceived. This chapter shows how Ayer replies both of them and points out their mistakes. This chapter also shows a new development in Ayer's thoughts.

The sixth chapter ***'Ayer's Distinction Between A Priori and A Posteriori'*** shows how Ayer Presents his distinction between a priori and a posteriori truths. Ayer shows that a priori truths are analytic, they are true by definition. They are necessary and certain because they cannot be confuted in experience as they lack factual content. The truths of mathematics and logic are necessary. On the other hand, a posteriori or empirical propositions are hypotheses which may be conformed or discredited in actual sense-experience. These synthetic propositions are only probable. According to Ayer, any genuine proposition must be either analytic or empirically verifiable. This chapter shows how Ayer's view is criticized by Blanshard and Foster.

The seventh chapter is ***'The Problem of Personal Identity and The Knowledge of Other Minds'***. This chapter deals with these two problem. First, it describes the traditional mind-body problems. After having the concept of a person it comes to the question of personal identity. From Descartes and Locke to Hume and Kant, the focus is on self-consciousness as the sole key to personal identity. Ayer establishes that the soul is a logical construction out of sense experiences. He defines personal identity in terms of bodily identity and bodily identity is defined in terms of the resemblance and continuity of sense-contents. This chapter also discusses our knowledge of other minds. Three main theories are presented here as solutions to this problem, that are, the behaviouristic theory, the criteriological theory and the argument from analogy. Ayer accepts argument from analogy to solve this problem, but since this argument remains open to the objections, he makes a change here.

The eighth chapter is ***'Ayer's Analysis of the Judgements*** *of Ethics and Theology',* which describes 'emotive theory' presented by Ayer. According to Ayer, ethical terms are emotive or at any rate, non-descriptive. They are expressions of feelings. They are designed both to express and to evoke the feelings of others. They are neither true, nor false. He calls the statements of theology as metaphysical utterances. Ayer accepts no criterion for determining the validity of these judgements. He makes a distinction between the activity of a moralist and that of a moral philosopher. But this theory faces criticism and is not found acceptable by many philosophers.

The book ends with a conclusion which takes an account of Ayer's philosophy and makes an assessment of Ayer's contribution to contemporary philosophy.

Contents

	Foreword	v
	Preface	vii
	Introduction	xi
1.	A Brief History of Western Empiricism	1
2.	The Elimination of Metaphysics	16
3.	The Function of Philosophy	56
4.	The Nature of Philosophical Analysis	78
5.	The Problem of Perception of the Physical World	109
6.	A. J. Ayer's Distinction between A Priori and A Posteriori	124
7.	The Problem of Personal Identity and the Knowledge of Other Minds	158
8.	A.J. Ayer's Analysis of The Judgements of Ethics and Theology	194
	Conclusion	217
	Bibliography	221
	Index	227

1

A Brief History of Western Empiricism

In this chapter, we shall take a look at the empiricist tradition in the history of western philosophy. Whether we can go beyond sensations and know any reality behind them is just one of those problems which we have to discuss and solve in philosophy. In fact, philosophy is not a matter of dogmatic assertions only. The conflict of different dogmatic systems makes philosophers suspicious about all philosophical theories. It fosters a spirit of critical enquiry among philosophers. The result is that all philosophical ideas and theories are subjected to a searching examination and nothing is accepted on trust.

Now what the proper method of philosophy should be, depends largely on what philosophy itself means. As we know the word 'philosophy' literally means love of wisdom and knowledge. But one can raise the question - Wisdom and knowledge of what? It may be the wisdom and knowledge of the physical world or it may be the wisdom and knowledge of the ultimate nature of existence and the ultimate categories of experience like space, time causality, substance and quantity, the individual and the universal. As Herbert Feigl writes, "There will always be those who find this world of ours, as cruel and deplorable as it may be in some respects, an exciting, fascinating place to live in, to explore, to adjust to, and to improve. And there will always be those who look upon the universe of experience and nature as an unimportant or secondary thing in comparison with something more fundamental and more significant. This tendency of thought may express itself theologically or metaphysically.[1]

Empiricism, Skepticism, Naturalism, Positivism, and Pragmatism are typical thought movements of the worldly, tough minded variety. Respect for the facts of experience, open- mindedness, an experimental trial and error attitude, and the capacity for working within the frame of an incomplete, unfinished world view distinguish them from the more impatient, imaginative, and often aprioristic thinkers in the tender-minded camp. Among the (1) latter are speculative metaphysicians, intuitionists, rationalists, and absolute idealists. One considers the other muddle-headed and the other thinks the one simple-minded. Again Feigl writes, "This fairly epitomizes the history of philosophy, that grandiose "tragicomedy of wisdom". Plato and Protagoras, St. Thomas and William of Ockham, Spinoza and Hobbes, Leibniz and Locke, Kant and Hume, Hegel and Comte, Royce and James, Whitehead and Russell are in many regards, though of course not in every feature, outstanding examples of that basic difference."[2]

A method of philosophy is a systematic and consistent way of attaining philosophical knowledge. Hence if philosophy is to give us true knowledge about real facts, or about sensible phenomena or about the physical world, then it has to depend on science itself for a correct analysis and formulation of both the special and general laws and concept of the physical world. Thus, we can see that the task of philosophy is not radically different from science, as science formulates not only the particular laws and concepts of our experience of the physical world, but also its most general and universal laws and concepts.

So, the method of philosophy should be, in principle, identical with the method of science. This method of philosophy is generally known as emphiricism. Taken strictly, empiricism is the theory which holds that all human knowledge comes from sense-experience, there being no innate ideas in the mind, and that whatever cannot be verified by sense-experience is unreal.

Empiricism is not a new streme of thought in philosophy. We find it from the very beginning of philosophical thinking, when different philosophers attempt to give scientific solutions to the problems concerning world, man, knowledge etc. If we look back, we find a sort of empiricism in the philosophy of the Atomists, Leucippus and Democritus. According to them, there is no reason or intelligence in the world. On the contrary, all phenomena and all becoming are completely determined by blind mechanical causes. Thus the atomists explain the world without introducing the notion of purpose or final cause. Things are explained by the purpose they serve. According to them there are two ultimate realities-atoms and empty space. Everything, even the soul, is composed of atoms. At death the soul atoms are scattered, and hence, there is, of course, no question of future life. Atoms by colloision, produce vortices, which generate bodies and ultimately worlds. A world may be destroyed by colloision with a larger world. Democritus puts forward a theory of perception, according to which objects project into space images of themselves composed of atoms. These images strike against the senses. Like atoms are perceived by like. Like Locke, democritus believes that such qualities as warmth, taste, colour are not really in the object, but are due to our sense organs, while such qualities as wight, density and hardness are really in the object; democritus is a thorough going materialist. He disbelieves in popular gods and popular religion. He explains that belief in god is due to fear of great terrestrial and astronomical phenomena, such as volcanoes, earthquakes, comets and meteors. thus we find that the attitude of the Atmists, in the main, is genuinely scientific whenever it does not merely embody the prejudices of their age.

It can be said that the empiricist tradition begins with the philosophy of sophists. Sophists have the main problem of the position of man in the universe. The earliest known sophist is Pratagores, who says, "Man is the measure of all things, of what is, that it is, of what is not, that it is not".[3] It means each individual man is the standard, the sensations and impressions of each man. Thus Pratagores denies the distinction between objective truth and subjective impression. He believes that there is no objective truth. Truth is identified with subjective sensations and impression. The doctrine is presumably based on the 'deceitfulness' of the senses. The earlier Greek philosophers make a clear distinction between sense and thought, between perception and reason, and believe that the truth is to be found, not by the senses, but by reason. But protagoras denies this distinction. Reason is universal, sensation is the particular element in man. Reason is communicable, sensation is incommunicable. One's sensations and feelings are personal to oneself, and can not be imparted to other people.

Gorgias is another sophist who shows the impossibility of knowledge. He attempts to prove three propositions-that nothing exists, that if anything exists, it can not be known, that if it can be known, the knowledge of it can not be communicated. Here, Gorgias makes use of the dialectic of Zeno. Since all existence is self contradictory, it follows that nothing exists. His second and third propositions follow from the identification of knowledge with sense perception, and ignore the rational element, since sensation is what cannot be communicated. Thus, we see that extreme subjectivity is the principle of the age. Individualism is the dominant note. Though it follows the scientific development of the nineteenth century and sophists are the founders of the science of rhetoric. But we see that to make the cultivation of individuality an end in itself, and to put exclusive emphasis on this, is wrong. The existence of an objective standard of truth is necessary.

Subjectivism visually ends in scepticsm. Scepticism means the doctrine, which doubts or denies the possibility of knowledge. Sceptical spirit is expressed in the thoughts of Pratagoras and Gorgias. But Pyrrho is the first to introduce a thorough going skepticism. According to him we can be certain of nothing, not even of the most trivial assertions. Therefore we ought never to make any positive statements of any subject. We only know how things appear to us, but of their inner substance we are ignorant. We may have opinion, but certainty and knowledge are impossible. He maintains that there can never be any rational ground for preferring one course of action to another. Scepticism regards all assertions as equally ill-grounded. The holding of any positive opinion whatever is by it regarded as dogmatism. Arcesilaus attacks especially the doctrine of the criterion of truth presented by the stoics. There is no criterion of truth, either in sense or in reason. although certainty and knowledge are impossible, probability is a sufficient guide for action. Carneades and Clitomachus develop a constructive doctrine concerning degrees of probability. Probability should be our guide in practice, since it is reasonable to act on the most probable or possible hypothesis. This view is one with which most modern philosophers would agree. Carneades says that nothing can ever be proved and it is impossible to know whether ideas of an object are true, whether they resemble the object because we can not compare our ideas with the object itself. We can only see the copy. The Philosophical sceptic says, "nobody knows, and nobody ever can know". But it is this element of dogmatism that makes the system vulnerable. Sceptics deny that they assert the impossibility of knowledge dogmatically but their denials are not very convincing.

Francis Bacon and to a less extent Hobbes (Partly because they are Englishmen with the British love for practical experimentation in their methods) are empiricists, that is, philosophers who believe that the primary source of all knowledge is the experience of the senses, and that generalizations from sense data should be derived inductively from observation and experiment. Bacon, as an empiricist, believes that human knowledge begins with sense-experience and can be enlarged by careful observations and experiments. From these, inferences must be made slowly and carefully, it will not do to leap from a few facts to some sweeping generalization. Nothing must be left out of account.

After that we come to the Philosophy of John Locke who follows the British empirical tradition and his task is to make a careful inventory of the knowledge immediately delivered by the senses and the Philosophy of the period is closely allied with Psychology and Physiology. At that time, due to the influence of the rationalist tradition, the mind was supposed to know all sorts of things a priori, Lock's thorough going empiricism was therefore a bold innovation. And in this sense, he may be regarded as the founder of empiricism. His Philosophy turns to the theory of knowledge and undertakes an examination of the nature, origin, and validity of knowledge. And in this sense, he may be regarded as the founder of empiricism which is the doctrine that all our knowledge is derived from experience. There are not innate or a priori principles of knowledge which we know from our birth and independently of all experience. Locke rejects innate ideas and gives a largely Psychological account of the manner in which we acquire ideas through experience. The mind, in its first state, is a tabula rasa, without any ideas. He explains that our ideas are derived from two sources-first is sensation, through which the mind is furnished with sensible qualities, and the other is reflection, or internal sense, which supplies the mind with ideas of its own operations. According to Locke, knowledge is the perception of the agreement or disagreement of two ideas. Since we can only think by means of ideas, and since all ideas come from experience, it is evident that none of our knowledge can antidote experience. In the third book of the essay, Locke shows that what metaphysicians present as knowledge about the world is purely verbal. Locke tells us that we have three kinds of knowledge of real existence. Our knowledge of our own existence is intuitive, our knowledge of God's existence is demonstrative and our knowledge of things present to sense is sensitive. Thus we see that as an empiricist Locke holds that all knowledge comes from experience, and yet he concedes that we have a real knowledge of substances underlying sensible qualities of matter, soul and God.

Then comes Berkeley who pushes empiricism further than Locke had done. Berkeley believes that all reality is known through experience, that is, through sensation and reflection. Everything that exists is either perceived, that is, an idea, or else it is a mind that perceives ideas. There is no such thing in reality as matter. We are not aware of any material substratum in which sense qualities inhere, they have no existence except in our own mind, or in the minds of other spirits. So called material thing is mere collection of ideas which is made up of some sense qualities like certain colour, taste, smell, figure, consistence etc. Berkeley rejects abstract ideas. He believes that it is impossible to arrive at any abstract idea that appears neither in sensation nor in reflection, and that any word used to designate common features of particular objects of our experience can only be a name, and that it cannot describe any real fact. Many introspective Psychologists agree with Berkeley here. Again, Berkeley rejects Locke's distinction between primary and secondary qualities. But Berkeley believes as thoroughly in spiritual substance, or the self, as Locke. Berkeley affirms that we have a notion of ourselves as a matter of direct experience, and that we are warranted by inference in forming notions of other selves, or other finite persons and of God, and he implies that notions are somehow different in nature from ideas. However, nearly all philosophers since his time, with the exception of Hume, admit that we actually are aware of our own selves, and that this awareness is different from our consciousness of our sensations and of external objects. According to Berkeley, all the ideas that we attribute to the outer world are purely passive, it is impossible for any idea to do anything or be the cause of anything. From this doctrine of the passiveness of ideas of the outer world, Berkeley shows influence of Melebranche and perhaps of other occasionalists, and makes God the cause of such ideas because neither any quality or combination of the ideas themselves nor material substance can be the cause of these ideas. Thus Berkeley explains the constancy and regularity of the involuntary ideas, popularly called the objects of the outer world, by attributing them to the activity of God. While voluntary ideas are produced by our own imaginations. The involuntary ideas have greater vividness, steadiness, order and coherence and this regularity enables us with foresight to plan our actions in the practical conduct of life, the description of them is the work of science. Berkeley's position is often classified as a form of empirical idealism or subjective idealism. A much better though not so common designation is mentalism, since Berkeley claims that all that is real is mental-minds and their contents. "To be is to be perceived" says Berkeley. He does not question that the things we see with our eyes and touch with our hands really exist. They are involuntary ideas, given us by God, who maintains them in accordance with the constant and regular laws of nature. All that Berkeley rejects is the material substance of Philosophers like Locke. He thinks that the removal of matter from the world eliminates all ground for skepticism and makes knowledge possible. In his Philosophy atheism is overthrown, and the existence of God is made absolutely certain. He establishes the natural immortality of the soul as the motions and changes, decays and dissolutions cannot affect an active, simple, uncompounded substance or the soul. Thus the consequences that Berkeley Claims for his Philosophy are to some extent epistemological and metaphysical, but mostly theological. In Barkeley's later works, his views change considerably, and in the siris, his thought largely departs from the interpretation of British empiricism which makes him the connecting link between Locke and Hume, and becomes a modified Platonism or neo-Platonism in some respects, and an anticipation of nineteenth century Kantianism and Hegelianism in others. Extreme empiricists who continue in the tradition of John Stuart Mill believe that Berkeley advances a step beyond Locke, and prepares the way for Hume. From their standpoint Berkeley is right in believing that reality consists of groups of sensations, as well as in his general Psychological approach. He is wrong in continuing to believe in spiritual substance, against which the same objections apply which he opposes to material substances, as Hume is later to establish.

Locke accepts that we have certain knowledge of our ideas, demonstrative knowledge of God and of morality, and practically certain knowledge of the external world of bodies. Berkeley denies the existence of a material world and limits our knowledge to ideas, relations, and spiritual beings. David Hume is a more thorough going empiricist than either Locke or Berkeley and insists more rigorously that all our knowledge is restricted to the data of sensation and reflection. He accepts the empirical theory of origin of knowledge and the Berkeleyan view that esse-percipi. He believes that our knowledge is limited to the world of Phenomena, we know nothing of ultimates, substances, causes, soul, ego, external world, universe. And if all we can knew are our own impressions we have no right to assert the reality either of material or of spiritual substances. We find no impressions that justify the assumption of any kind of substance. Like Berkeley, Hume believes that we have no evidence for the existence of matter. The objects of all our knowledge are impressions and ideas derived from them. All we can do, then, is to limit ourselves to the world of experience, to our impressions and ideas. Hume rejects Berkeley's claim of having a notion of a spiritual substance or self, something of which we have no direct impression. Our selves are, so far as we can observe our experience, "nothing but a bundle or collection of different perceptions, which succeed each other with any inconceivable rapidity, and are in a perpetual flux and movement.............There is no simplicity in it at one time, nor identity in different (times)."[4]

So, Hume believes that there is no empirical evidence for the existence of an immaterial, indivisible, imperishable soul substance. Finally, Hume says that we cannot demonstrate anything concerning the nature of God, his attribute, his decrees, his plan of providence. According to Hume, rational cosmology, rational psychology and rational theology are impossible. Humeagrees with Descartes, Hobbes and Locke in requiring that genuine knowledge must be self-evident, but he finds no such knowledge anywhere except in mathematics, which merely analyzes its own concepts. We can know only what we experience, and we can reach only probability in this field. Thus we see that Hume is consistent with his skeptical empiricism both in affirming that human knowledge either of the self or of the outer world cannot go beyond perceptions and also in denying the existence of all substances, spiritual as well as material. Again Hume shows that the empirical method of investigation can be employed in ethics and the social sciences. The significance of Davie Hume in the history of Modern Philosophy consists in his development of the knowledge (epistemology) to its logical conclusions. Hume's skepticism horrifieces Kant, who effectively refutes it by a new theory of knowledge, which conserves what is of real merit in Hume's empiricism. On the other hand, Hume's empiricism is found more satisfactory by Comte and J.S. Mill, who develop positivism.

The remarkable development of the natural sciences in modern times, especially in France, suggests the scientific method as the one to be followed in the new undertaking. The sole object of science is to discover natural laws and this can be done only by observation and experience. Knowledge thus acquired is positive knowledge, and only such knowledge can be successfully applied in the various fields of human practice. Comte is a positivist and his ideal is the reform of society. Comte sides with the thinkers of the empirical school, he belongs to the chain of Philosophers in which Hume and Diderot are important links. Comte agrees with Hume that it is impossible for us to discover underlying causes or substances. We can observe only the facts that are manifested to our senses. We can take note of the circumstances under which phenomena occur, and so formulate the laws of Phenomena. Comte is as skeptical as Hume in regard to the possibility of gaining any knowledge of the unknown causes of sensations, but Comte sees more clearly than Hume did that after all science can tell us a great deal. In contrast to skepticism which calls attention to what we cannot know, positivism bids us accumulate all the knowledge that actually is accessible to us, and use it for the advancement of mankind. Positive knowledge is Comte's ideal. He says that the term 'positive' means real, useful, certain and indubitable, exact, it means the opposite of negative, positive knowledge is not mere negation or criticism. One of Comte's fundamental doctrines is the law of the three stages, the theological, metaphysical and positive stages. Both theology and metaphysics believe in the possibility of absolute knowledge and of explaining the innermost essences of things. In the stage of positivism the attempt to discover the inner essences of things is abandoned as futile and replaced by the effort to discover the uniform relations existing between phenomena. The question asked is not why? But how? Laws of nature are substituted for absoluted causes. Mind or soul is a metaphysical entity and does not exist for positivism. We cannot observe mental process subjectively, introspection being impossible. Comte does not believe literally in personal immortality. Rejecting all metaphysics, it is impossible for come to accept the existence of God as an agency behind the Phenomena. According to Comte, metaphysics should be excluded from positive science. Comte thinks that at least one of the chief tasks of a philosopher should be to ascertain the methods common to the different sciences, and to organize their results into some kind of synthesis. This task is becoming increasingly difficult with the growing complexity of the sciences, but it is no less desirable.

Owing to the progress of the natural sciences, however, and the rise of positivism in France, the empirical conception again comes to occupy the leading place in British thought near the middle of the nineteenth century. It develops from the doctrines of Hume and Hartley and attains its high form in the logic of John Stuart Mill. There is much in common between French Positivism and latter day English empiricism. The same attitude of mind characterizes both views, both emphasize the value of facts and of scientific method, and both in principle, opposed to metaphysics, both aim at social reform and make the happiness and development of humanity the ethical ideal. Mill is an empiricist, following the tradition of Bacon, Locke, Hartley and Hume. All knowledge comes from experience, experience ultimately resolves itself into sensations, the latter, combined by the law of association, constitute our knowledge of the world. He formulates the principles of an empirical logic more thoroughly than had ever been done before, reveals its possibilities more adequately, and unconsciously discloses its limitations. According to Mill, the only ultimate source of knowledge is sensation; we can not know things in themselves. Mill gives an psychological explanation of our belief, based on memory, expectation, and the laws of association. The external world is, "a permanent possibility of sensation." Our belief in the continued existence of external objects can be accounted for psychologically, without entering into metaphysical speculations regarding the real nature of the outer world independent of our sensations. There is no evidence for believing with Berkeley in a permanent spiriticual substance. Mill is aware of the difficulties in Hume's treatment of the self. Mills is willing to accept the fact of self-consciousness, but thinks it impossible to give a further account of it. Mill denies that there are any truths known a priori. All knowledge consists ultimately of inductions from experience. Even the principles of logic and mathematics are generalization from experience. So far as they are true their truth is confirmed by actual experience. But after all we see that as a thoroughgoing empiricist, Mill's views incline toward positivism as he believes that what we know are phenomena, and it is useless to speculate about ultimates.

In this sequence, we look at the Philosophy of logical positivism. Logical positivism or logical empiricism is one of the most influential movements in recent Philosophy. Warnock says, "The slightly political suggestion in the word 'movement' is not inappropriate since, for a time at any rate, the Philosophers of this group had much of the deliberate cohesion of a political party, and even a definite programme, platform, or creed."[5]

The movement originated in the 1920s among Philosophers and scientists, who organized themselves into a Philosophical group at Vienna in 1928. The group became known as 'Vienna Circle' (Der Wiener Krcis), under the leadership of Moritz Schlick, professor at the University of Vienna. The circle organized its first international congress in 1929, attracting sympathizers from many countries. In 1930 it took over a journal, renamed 'Erkenntenis', for the publication of its ideas. On the philosophical side, its leading members, apart from Schlick himself, were Friedrich Waismann, Rudolf Carnap, Otto Neurath, Herbert Feigl and Victor Kraft, on the mathematical side. Hans Hann, Karl Menger and Kurt Godel.

The movement gradually spread, and Prague, Warsaw and Lwow became some of its active centres. Hans Reichenbach founded a centre also in Berlin. In America also it found some sympathizers like E. Nagel and C.W. Morris.

At Oxford, the movement found an able advocate in A.J. Ayer. The British Philosopher A.J. Ayer attended its meetings in 1933 and made its ideas widely known in the English Speaking world with the publication of 'Language, Truth and Logic' in 1936.

An important influence was that of Wittgenstein, though he was not a member of the circle. He maintained close personal relations with Schlick and Waismann, and the group was very much influenced by his ideas. His 'Tractatus-Logico-Philosophicus, appeared in 1921, and to a considerable extent it set the pattern which, at least in its early days, the Vienna Circle followed.

In logical positivism we find united in a peculiar way the skeptical empiricism of David Hume, the positivism of Comte, the scientific conventionalism of Mach and Poincare, and the logical analysis of the type indicated at Cambridge by Moore, Russell, Wittgenstein and whitehead and on the continent by Frege. Logical empiricism has the advantage of indicating the affinity of the circle's ideas with those of the empiricist tradition begun by Locke in the seventeenth century, and later represented by such thinkers as Moore and Russell.

"The term 'logical' indicates a primary interest in language and meaning as opposed to knowledge. The main questions for such philosophers, as Locke and Descartes had been about the sources and extent of knowledge, and the empiricist Locke Claimed that sense-experience was the only source. In the new empiricism, by contrast, the primary question is not "How do we know that P.?" but 'what does "P" mean."[6]

Logical positivists formulate an entirely new and revolutionary conception of Philosophy. According to them Philosophy is concerned with the discovery of the Speculative truths and ultimate concepts of science. Nor is it concerned with the knowledge of transcendent realities like God and the Self.

From the very beginning, logical positivists have two principle aims, to provide a secure foundation for the sciences, and to demonstrate the meaninglessness of metaphysics. They present the verification principle and they adopt the method of logical analysis, specially of language for realizing this double aim. According to verification principle, there are only two kinds of meaningful statements. They are empirical statements, verifiable by observation, and there are statements, such as those of logic and mathematics, whose truth can be known a priori, but these are regarded as not presenting 'new' knowledge, but merely on analysis of what is known already. Other statements are to be dismissed as meaningless 'pseudo-statement'. Metaphysical propositions about transcendental realities are not verifiable in sense-experience and are, therefore, non sensical.

The proper function of Philosophy is the logical analysis of the propositions of science. It is this method which mainly distinguishes this new movement from the positivism and empiricism of earlier times. It is distinguished from the empiricism of Hume by the fact that while Hume bases his Philosophy on the Psychological analysis of experience, these new empiricists base their theories on the logical analysis of it. Again while earlier positivists object to metaphysical speculation either because it is unprofitable or because its truths cannot be proved, the new positivists object to it because logical analysis of metaphysical language convinces them that all metaphysical propositions are meaningless. The antimetaphysical attitude of logical positivism is, therefore, more radical. It dismisses metaphysical questions themselves as nonsensical so that the question of their solution does not at all arise.

Thus we can say that according to logical positivism, philosophy is a criticism of scientific propositions to determine their interrelation and significance in terms of sense-experience. Some logical positivists go further and maintain that Philosophy is the analysis of sentences and words, scientific or otherwise, in order to disclose their meaning and significance. If they have any use, if they describe a situation, they have meaning, if not, they are meaningless.

References

1. 'Twentieth Century Philosophy' Living Schools of Thought Edited by Dagobert D. Runes, Philosophical Library, New York, 1943, p. 373).
2. Ibid, p. 374.
3. 'A Critical History of Greek Philosophy', p. 112.
4. David Hume, 'A Treatise of Human Nature,' Bk I, Pt. IV, Sec. 6.
5. G.J. Warnock, 'English Philosophy Since 1900', p. 34.
6. Oswald Hanfling 'Logical Positivism' taken from 'Philosophy of Science, Logic and Mathematics in the Twentieth Century, p. 195.

2

The Elimination of Metaphysics

The problem of metaphysics is the discovery of ultimate principles of reality. How shall we explain the world, what is its essence? Metaphysics in Aristotelian sense is definable as a science which investigates the nature of being, that is, a substance. The term 'metaphysics' means no more than 'after-physics.' There is the suggestion that metaphysics is intended to deal with questions which physics leaves unanswered. As Coplesten says, "metaphysical philosophy begins, in a sense, where science leaves off."

Logical positivism has two main features-on the one hand an extreme respect for science and mathematics, and on the other, an extreme distaste for metaphysics. Its main aim is thus to devise some clear criterion by the use of which science and mathematics can be proved acceptable, and metaphysics by contrast can be condemned.

Being a logical positivist, Ayer begins by criticising the metaphysician. By metaphysics, Ayer means theory of reality lying beyond experience- The fundamental postulate of metaphysics is that there is a super (or hinter) phenomenal reality......... it is the aim of metaphysics to describe a reality lying beyond experience and therefore, any proposition which would be verified by empirical observation is ipso facto not metaphysical.[1]

Ayer says that the view that philosophy begins where

science leaves off is perfectly alright if it means that the philosopher takes the results of the scientist, analyzes them, shows the logical connection of one proposition with another, and so on. But if it means that it leaps into a quite different realm, the realm which is described as the 'transcendent', then it is not acceptable. Though Ayer finds it possible to be a metaphysician without believing in a transcendent reality, because many metaphysical utterances are due to the commission of logical errors, rather than to a conscious desire on the part of their authors to go beyond the limits of experience. But he begins by criticising the metaphysician who claims knowledge of transcendent reality by enquiring from what premises his propositions are deduced. Must he not begin, as other men do, with the evidence of his senses'. He may say that he knows through intuition. Consequently one cannot overthrow transcendent metaphysics by criticising how it arises, but by criticism of the actual statements which comprise it.

Logical positivists make the claim that they notice something about existing and traditional philosophy, which will completely overturn it and render it largely otiose. Carnap raises the question- "Can it be that so many men, of various times and nations, outstanding minds among them, have devoted so much effort, and indeed farvour, to metaphysics, when this consists of nothing more than words strung together without sense?"

But if we go back to different philosophical systems, we find that metaphysics has always been an important part of those. The first problem to which the early Greek philosophers like Thales, Anaximander, Anaximenes and then the Pythagorians, Heraclitus etc. address themselves, is the problem of substance. Parmenides shows a firm belief in reason. According to him, the world of sense is an illusion. Reality is conformable to reason and what is contradictory to thought cannot be real. Russell, in 'A History of Western Philosophy' says, "Parmenides' reasoning is the first example in philosophy of an argument from thought and language to the world at large."

There are metaphysicians who maintain the belief that the world is really very different from what it appears and thus wish to downgrade the material world by comparison with the transcendental, spiritual world. Plato says, the world made apparent to us by our senses is contrasted with an intellectually apprehensible world of ideas or forms. The sense-world is reduced to the status of phenomena or appearances of the real world. Aristotle regards the particular objects or individual beings as real substances. There is a plurality of individual substances.

The seventeenth century rationalist philosophers Descartes, Spinoza and Leibniz share the idea with Plato that knowledge of the way things really are, is to be obtained through the exercise of pure reason and not through sense-perception. Ayer says, "Of the three, Descartes is, in modern terms, the least metaphysical, since the picture of the world to which his reasoning led him could just as well have been the product of the study of contemporary physics." Descartes is a dogmatist in the sense of believing in the competence of reason to attain certain knowledge. Ayer says, "His peculiarity lays in supposing that he could reach these scientific conclusions by purely logical deduction from self-evident premisses."[3]

Leibniz says, "Our ideas of space, figure, motion and rest have their origin in the common sense, in the mind itself for they are ideas of the pure understanding, which, however, have reference to the eternal world."[4]

The aim of Kant is to show, against the Leibniz–Wolffain "dogmatists" that we cannot have knowledge of the supersensible in metaphysics, that metaphysics in this sense is a pseudo-science. But he holds that categories are imposed by us upon the world as a prior condition of its being accessible to our understanding. Ayer says, "Thus, for Kant, the world that we know is partly our own creation. We can infer that there is a raw material upon which we go to work. But what things are in themselves, independently of our processing of them, is something that we can never know."[5]

Hegel represents the history of the world as a spiritual

progress, the necessary ascent of what he obscurely calls the absolute idea.

Bradley accepts that metaphysics in an attempt to know reality in contrast to mere appearance...........

Ayer says, "No statement which refers to a 'reality' transcending the limits of all possible sense-experience can possibly have any literal significance, from which it must follow that the labours of those who have striven to describe such a reality have all been devoted to the production of non-sense."[6]

In fact, the rejection of metaphysics as such is not a new phenomenon which occurs for the first time in the present century. We can see even in the ancient period the skeptics and the empiricists consider the gaining of metaphysical knowledge to be impossible. In the modern era, the attempts made by some philosophers are very important. Before logical positivism. Hume and Kant also condemn transcendent metaphysics, but the grounds are different. Hume and Kant make it on epistemological grounds. The criteria, they use, is 'what can we know?" And both of them try to show that we cannot have the knowledge of transcendent realities.

Hume says that if all we can know are our own impressions, we have no right to assert the reality either of material or of spiritual substance. Our knowledge is limited to the world of phenomena. We know nothing of ultimates, substances, causes, soul, God, ego, external world, universe. We can know only what we experience and we can reach only probability in this field. The human mental world is the only legitimate sphere of science and enquiry. We must limit our enquiries to such subjects as are best adapted to the narrow capacities of the human understanding. We can never hope to attain any satisfactory knowledge with regard to the origin of our impressions or the ultimate constitution of a universe behind our impressions and ideas. Metaphysics, in the sense of knowledge of the ultimate origin and nature of the universe is impossible.

Kant also says that we cannot transcend our experience or have a priori knowledge of the supersensible, of things-in-themselves. We can know only what we can experience. Percepts and concepts constitute the elements of all our knowledge. In sense-perception, we know only the way things appear to consciousness, not what they are in themselves. According to Kant, things-in-themselves exist, we can think them but not know them as we know the facts of the empirical world. Nor can they be perceived or intuited by the intellect, we do not possess intellectual intuition. So, the thing-in-itself is essentially unknowable, but the concept of a thing-in-itself is not self-contradictory. Kant demonstrates that reason is bound to lose itself in contradictions if it ventures beyond the limits of possible experience. Hence, a speculative or rational metaphysics embracing cosmology, theology and psychology is impossible. We cannot have a metaphysics that transcends experience, a metaphysics of things-in-themselves, a metaphysics, that can offer us genuine knowledge of a non-phenomenal world in which reside free will, immortality and God. Metaphysics in this sense is a pseudo-science. But here the question is- if it is possible to know only what lies within sense-experience, how it can be asserted that things lie beyond. As Wittgenstein says, "In order to draw a limit to thinking, we should have to think both sides of this limits."[7]

A truth which Bradley ingeniously twists in maintaining that anyone ready to prove metaphysics impossible is a brother metaphysician with a rival theory of his own.[8]

In fact, Kant does not show the logical impossibility of transcendental reality, but he shows that the factual knowledge of transcendental reality is not possible. Thus, he makes the impossibility of a transcendent metaphysics a matter of fact, not a matter of logic as logical positivists do. This is the basic difference between them which we shall see later on.

Comte rejects metaphysics as a stage on the road to positive science, which the world has now outgrown. But though the rejection of metaphysics is not a new thing, its grounds are always different. Most of the earlier objectors maintain that metaphysics is practically impossible or worthless because we cannot test the truth or falsity of its statements, but its statements are at least intelligible. The grounds offered for its rejection by the logical positivists are substantially novel. Now, the objection is made that metaphysical questions and answers are one and all nonsensical, metaphysics is not worthless, idle speculation, but pseudo-speculation. This emphatic, clear-cut distinction between idle speculation and nonsense disguised as speculation is not made before the twentieth century.

In order to understand the anti-metaphysical attitude of logical positivists, it is necessary to consider the positivists conception of meaning. Ludwig Wittgenstein first develops this conception through the logical analysis of language and experience in his celebrated earlier treatise 'Tractatus-Logico-Philosophicus.' According to it, language is the symbolic representation of facts experienced. It can be analysed into significant assertions called propositions, and all propositions can be shown by further analysis to consist of some elementary propositions. Every elementary proposition, Wittgenstein holds, is a picture of some atomic fact experienced. 'The proposition is a picture of reality.'[9]

By a fact, he means 'what the case is', that which makes a preposition true. And "An atomic fact is a combination of objects." Logical analysis of the world of experience as pictured by propositions asserting the existence of the world brings us thus to facts as the ultimate constituents of the world. The sense of a proposition requires that it should at least refer to possible empirical facts. And thus the ultimate referents or objectives of propositions are empirical facts. A proposition which does not refer to 'any state of affairs', any fact of experience, is, therefore, no proposition at all, it fails of its purpose by failing to express any sense. It is then a nonsensical expression, a pseudo-proposition.

Here comes the point that if all statements are truth functions of elementary propositions which report observations, then they will all be either empirical themselves or else tautologies or contradictions. But metaphysical statements do not seem to be classifiable under any of these heads. In Tractatus, he says, "Most propositions and questions, that have been written about philosophical matters are not false, but nonsensical. We cannot, therefore, answer questions of this kind at all, but only state their senselessness. Most questions and propositions of the philosophers result from the fact that we do not understand the logic of our language .... and so it is not to be wondered at that the deepest problems are really no problems."

Thus, Wittgenstein is the basic source for the anti-metaphysical attack.

Urmson talks about its reaction. He says, "The general reaction in England was to take the line that metaphysics was legitimate provided that it was critical and not speculative. Wittgenstein's own metaphysics was regarded as critical, it was therefore, regarded as in principal at least, acceptable, and his characterization of it as nonsense was rejected. But in Vienna, where, the old positivist tradition was strong, Wittgenstein s rejection of metaphysics was accepted. The members of Vienna Circle accept the anti-metaphysical strain in Wittgenstein. They call themselves logical positivists or logical empiricists and accept the view of Wittgenstein that metaphysics is not merely outdated, as the old positivism had it, but is a logically impossible enterprise, being excluded by the essential nature of language, it is positivism on logical grounds."[10]

We see that Logical Positivists have two principle aims, to secure a firm foundation for the sciences and to demonstrate the meaninglessness of metaphysics. For achieving these aims, they want to establish some clear criterion by the use of which science and mathematics can be proved acceptable, and metaphysics by contrast can be condemned. Logical Positivists are not, as philosophers, concerned with the truth or falsehood of scientific statements, as they consider it the affair of the scientists. Their proper concern is held to be with meaning. The criterion they devise is to be a test of meaningfulness or significance, a test which the sciences can pass and metaphysics cannot.

Positivists construe metaphysics as covering such allegedly philosophical enterprises as the attempt to describe reality as a whole, or to find the purpose of the universe, or to reach beyond the everyday world to some supra-sensible spiritual order. they condemn it not as being unduly speculative, or even as being false, but as being literally non-sensical.

The criterion they present to achieve their aim is known as 'Verification Principle'. Before we see its formulation, it is important for us to know that logical empiricists recognize two, and only two, kinds of meaningful statements. They are, first and mainly, empirical statements, verifiable by observation. Second, there are statements, such as those of logic and mathematics, whose truth can be known a priori, but these are regarded as not presenting 'new' knowledge, but merely an analysis of what is known already. Any other statements are to be dismissed as meaningless 'pseudo-statements'.

The verification principle is first formulated by Wittgenstein, but its most frequent use occurs in the writings of Schlick. Wittgenstein and Schlick, both formulate the principle as "The meaning of a proposition is the method of its verification."

According to Wittgenstein, to understand a sentence is to know what atomic facts must obtain for it to be true, and to know this is to know how to verify it. He says, "to understand a proposition is to know what is the case, if it is true", that is, what facts it stands for, which can be expected to be observed or experienced if the proposition is true. But the method of verifying the proposition is also to observe such facts. Hence, the very experience which can verify a proposition is also that which constitutes its sense.

Moritz Schlick, the leader of the group of philosophers and mathematicians, calling themselves the Vienna Circle, says that whenever we ask about a sentence, 'what does it 'mean', what we expect is instruction as to the circumstances in which the sentence is to be used, we want a description of the conditions under which the sentence will form a true proposition, and to those which will make it false."

We see that the verification principle logically follows from Wittgenstein's conception of proposition as a pictorial representation of experienced facts. "As well as providing an answer to the question 'What is meaning?' the principle is intended to provide a criterion to distinguish what is meaningful from what is not."[11] Thus, if there is no method of verification- no way of verifying the proposition- then it must be meaningless.

But there are a number of difficulties with the principle, corresponding to the terms- 'proposition', 'is' and 'method of verification'. The original German word for 'proposition' is Satz, and the straight forward translation of this is 'sentence'. But sentences cannot be treated as objects of verification, because a sentence cannot be regarded as true or false in itself. Therefore, the term. "Proposition"has been used, which means, roughly, what is asserted by means of a declarative sentence. And it is propositions that are true or false. But if this is so, then the question of meaningfulness has already been decided in using the term 'proposition', for only what is meaningful can be described as true or false. Then it would be self-contradictory to speak of a meaningless proposition. One way of overcoming this is to put 'putative' before proposition, another is to use the word 'statement'. And we can ask of a statement both whether it means anything and, if so, whether it is true.

The second difficulty is about the word 'is'. How are we to understand this identification? 'Meaning' and 'method' are concepts of different types. 'One can sensibly talk about using a method, but (not) "using a meaning".

The third difficulty is about 'method of verification'. What can be the relevant method in the case of the statement 'it is raining'? One may verify this by putting his hand out of the window. But this act may serve to verify all sorts of statements, and, on the other hand, all sorts of methods may be used to verify the statement.

After all, there is something right about the verification principle, that there is, at least, an important connection between meaning and verification. Thus, if we are unsure what someone means by his words, we can often find out by asking how one would verify what he said. And sometimes, at least, the admission that there is no conceivable method of verification will lead us to conclude that what was said is meaningless.

After Schlick, we see what Carnap says about the principle. He accepts that all significant propositions are ultimately reducible to protocol statements, that is, simple propositions which are immediately derived from and verifiable in experience, no proposition which is not so reducible to empirically verifiable protocol propositions can possess any significance. Again he says. "But there is always the theoretical possibility of continuing the series of test observations. Therefore, here....... no complete verification is possible but only a process of gradually increasing confirmation."[12]

He continues, for such a simple sentence as 'There is a white thing on this table' the degree of confirmation, after a few observations have been made, will be so high that we practically cannot help accepting the sentence. But even in this case there remains still the theoretical possibility of denying the sentence."[13]

Carnap says that metaphysical propositions (including some epistemological and ethical ones) by their very nature ultimately rest upon some propositions which purport to assert the existence of unverifiable, trans-empirical entities. They do not, therefore, possess any sense. Such propositions are really not propositions at all.

He says there are two chief sources that give rise to meaningless sentences. Either the component words of a sentence lack meaning, and the sentence, as a whole, becomes nonsensical. For example "twas brilig and the slithy fores'. Or it may be that the constituent words are all individually capable of expressing meanings in other contexts, but in the particular context the words taken together do not yield any sense. Like—"Caesar is a prime number." Carnap says that the metaphysician indulges in the second kind of nonsense experience.

Now, we look into how Ayer interprets this principle of verification. According to him, any genuine proposition must be either an a priori truth or empirically verifiable. It means that, apart from those whose truth can be established a priori, the only significant assertions we can make-the only assertions which can properly be said to be true or false-are the ones which are open to empirical verification.

Ayer begins by formulating the principle as follows- "We say that a sentence is factually significant to any given person, if, and only if, he knows how to verify the proposition which it purports to express- that is, if he knows what observations would lead him, under certain conditions, to accept the proposition as being true, or reject it as being false.[14]

It may seem curious that Ayer should count as a way of verifying a proposition evidence which leads one to reject it. But in fact, he often uses the term 'verify' as short for 'verify or falsify', and this is one such occasion. He is `prepared to count both empirical verifiability and empirical falsifiability as sufficing for factual, and hence, literal significance. And in this respect, at least, he is surely right. For, sentences which are devoid of literal significance do not express propositions at all and hence do not express anything true or false. All one needs to add is that Ayer should, in a similar way, allow significance to sentences whose negations are analytic (or can be established a priori), though there is no indication that he is willing to do this.

One obvious defect in this formulation, as it stands, is that it assumes that a person's evaluation of his observational evidence is always rational. It assumes that someone has actually verified (or falsified) a proposition if his observations lead him to accept (reject) it. And this assumption is clearly false. As Ayer himself points out in his much later 'the central questions of philosophy.'

Someone may be disposed to accept a proposition on the basis of observations, which do not genuinely support it. For example, someone who prays for rain and sees it subsequently fall may treat his observation of the rainfall as a reason for accepting the proposition that God exists.[15]

This defect is, of course, easily corrected. Instead of speaking of the observations which induce acceptance (or rejection), we have to speak of those which justify it. And, in fact, the defect gets corrected, in his subsequent elaboration.

Ayer tries to derive the principle of verification from an analysis of understanding. The content of the statement consists of a range of situations, experiences, that would substantiate or refute it. And the statements to which no situations are relevant one way or the other are ruled out as non-factual. Ayer describes the philosophical assertions and questions which his criterion eliminates as 'metaphysical'. He explicitly defines a 'metaphysical sentence' as one which 'purports to express a genuine proposition, but does, in fact, express neither a tautology nor an empirical hypothesis.'[16]

Ayer says that the truth or falsehood of so-called transcendent statements does not make the slightest difference to anything that anyone experiences. As metaphysical statements are not testable by observations, logical positivists hold they are not descriptive of anything, so that a sentence only qualifies as metaphysical if it fails to satisfy the criterion.

Ayer says if in a case no observation leads us to answer the question, then the sentence under consideration does not express a genuine question, However, strongly its grammatical appearance may suggest that it does. The sentence may be emotionally significant to one but it may not be literally significant.

We can say that verification principle is the criterion of factual meaningfulness. The purpose of this criterion is to delimit the type of expression which has possible reference to fact from the other types which do not have this kind of significance, the emotive, the logico-mathematical, the purely formal and if, there should be such the completely non-significant.

The emphasis here is on the word 'factually'. It is not denied that language has other uses besides that of imparting factual information. Nor is it maintained that these other uses are unimportant, or that metaphysical statements may not serve them. They may, for example, express an interesting and challenging attitude to life. All that is claimed is that they are not capable of stating facts.

According to Urmson the verification principle is not

essentially a very novel or obscure doctrine except in its traditional formulation. If we go back, we find that Hume is an ancestor of this. According to him, to know the meaning of a word is to know with what type of impression it is linked by ostensive definition. And we can now see the verification principle as involving a corresponding reformulation of Hume's epistemological thesis that all meaningful words must be ostensibly definable.

The old empiricism, with all its difficulties, was plausible, but the new version is much more plausible. For the minimum self-contained unit of speech is the sentence, Hume could not explain plausibly how such words as 'all', 'and', 'is', 'but' have a meaning, but now we can see that a word has a meaning if it does a job in a sentence, whatever job that may be. The verification principle, it appears, can explain what it is for a sentence or a word to have a meaning.[17]

In order to describe the principle of verification, first of all Ayer draws a distinction between verifiability in practice and verifiability in principle. He describes it that we all understand and in many cases believe propositions which we don't even try to verify. Many of these are propositions which we can verify if we feel the necessity of it and if we take enough trouble and make different attempts to verify it. In such cases, we are in a condition where we have practical means to verify a proposition. For instance. 'There are total ten students in my class' is an example of practical verifiability. We can verify it by counting the number of students.

But, it is asked, how is it possible to understand the meaning of statements about objects not yet perceived? Or of historical statements, about the past, or of statements about other minds or about interperceptual states of physical objects, none of which can ever be actually observed. Faced by these difficulties some positivists admit that by 'verification' should be meant verification in theory or principle, and not necessarily in practice.

Ayer says, that there remain a number of significant propositions, concerning matters of fact, which we can not verify even if we choose, simply because we lack the practical means of placing ourselves in the situation where the relevant observations could be made. Ayer presents an example which is given by Schlick, which is, there are mountains on the farther side of the moon. Schlick considers it significant. It is not improbable that no human being will ever be able to verify or falsify it, but which philosopher would be bold enough to declare the sentence to be devoid of meaning. Since there is no theoretical impossibility in thinking of a man, with sufficient improvement of the necessary mechanisms, being able to observe the object and test the proposition.

Ayer says, "No rocket has yet been invented which would enable me to go and look at the farther side of the moon, so that I am unable to decide the matter by actual observation. But I do know what observations would decide it for me, if, as is theoretically conceivable, I were once in a position to make them. And therefore, I say that the proposition is verifiable in principle, if not in practice, and is accordingly significant.[18]

It means the possibility of its verification should remain always. Thus verifiability in principle too determines the literal significance of a proposition.

On the basis of this distinction, Ayer shows that metaphysical propositions are verifiable neither in practice nor in principle. A metaphysical pseudo-proposition as 'the absolute enters into, but is itself incapable of, evolution and progress', is not only in practice, but even in principle unverifiable. For one cannot conceive of an observation which would enable one to determine whether the absolute did or did not, enter into evoluation and progress. Ayer says it is possible that the author of such a remark is using English words in a way in which they are not commonly used by English speaking people and whatever he intends to assert could be empirically verified. But until he makes us understand how the proposition that he wishes to express would be verified, he fails to communicate anything to us. And if he admits that the proposition expressed by him is neither a tautology nor it is capable, at least, in principle, of being verified, then it has no literal significance even for himself.

After that, Ayer makes a further distinction between the 'strong' and the 'weak' sense of the term 'verifiable'. He explains, "A proposition is said to be verifiable, in the strong sense of the term, if, and only if, its truth could be conclusively established in experience. But it is verifiable, in the weak sense, if it is possible for experience to render it probable."[19]

Each of these have its attractions and its drawbacks. If we accept the epistemological correlate of the extreme atomistic hypothesis held by Wittgenstein, according to which the only facts are particular atomic facts, and there are no general facts, then we shall hold the strong verification principle. It alone is compatible with a thorough going truth functional view of language. Every proposition is a truth function of a set of simple statements all of which could in principle be checked, and the truth or falsehood of the proposition thus conclusively established. Urmson says that, "epistemologically, we can say that as to know the meaning of a statement is to know the method of its verification then to the extent that it can not be verified it cannot be understood. How, if a statement is only partly verifiable, are we to understand it in so far as it is not verifiable. so, if one holds the verification principle at all one must hold it in the strong version."[20]

But we can see there are some difficulties, and formidable ones, for the strong version of the verification principle. If the meaning of verification is taken by the positivists in the sense of conclusively proving some proposition to be true or false, it would make the general propositions of science meaningless, as it is not possible to prove conclusively or exhaustively the truth of a general statement by any limited series of sense perceptions.

Ayer Argus that, 'if we adopt conclusive verifiability as our criterion of significance...... our argument will prove too much,[21] since many significant empirical statements cannot, even in principle, be conclusively validated or confuted. He focuses on the example of generalizations of law such as 'arsenic is poisonous' and 'a body tends to expand when it is heated', 'all men are mortal'. Such statements cannot be conclusively verified, since we can never check through the potentially infinite number of cases to which they apply. Then, if only conclusive verifiability is accepted as the criterion of significance, it will be a logical obligation to treat these general propositions of law as the statements of metaphysician are treated or as meaningless.

Logical atomism faces a great difficulty presented by general propositions which it seems impossible to regard as truth functions of atomic propositions. While Russell considers himself obliged to recognize the existence of general facts, Ramsay denies that so-called general prepositions are propositions at all. He says, "If not truth-functions of elementary propositions, then not propositions."

Now we see the views of Moritz Schlick concerning this division. He accepts only strong verification. He does not accept it in its weak version. He says, "If not conclusively verifiable in principle, then not propositions. "According to him, "Natural laws do not have the character of propositions which are true or false but rather set forth instructions for the formation of such propositions. ...... Natural laws are not general implications because they cannot be verified for all cases, they are rather directions, rules of behaviour for the investigator to find his way about in reality, to anticipate certain events........ We should not forget that observations and experiments are acts by means of which we enter into direct connection with nature. The relations between reality and our selves frequently stand in sentences which have the grammatical form of assertions but whose essential sense consists in the fact that they are directions for possible acts."[22]

Schlick meets this situation by the rather heroic and embarrassing confession that these general propositions are really nonsensical, only they are an 'important type of nonsense'. But here the introduction of the term 'important' is simply an attempt to hedge. Ayer rejects Schlick's view because it renders the criterion of meaning self-stultifying. Again this difficulty is not restricted to the case of general propositions of law, we find it in the case of propositions about the remote past. Historical statements may have strong evidence in their favour, their truth can never become more than highly probable. Indeed, no proposition, other than a tautology, can possibly be anything more than a probable hypothesis. And if this is correct, the principle which demands only conclusive verifiability to consider the factual significance of a sentence is self-stultifying as a criterion of significance. For it leads to the conclusion that it is impossible to make a significant statement of fact at all.

This situation makes Karl Popper remark that, "Logical Positivism destroys not only metaphysics but also natural science."[23]

Popper, in his "Die Logik der Forschung', suggests that falsifiability, not verifiability, is the mark of a scientific proposition. He tries to save the situation by suggesting that even a limited number of crucial observations can conclusively confute (falsify) if not establish a general proposition, and that a sentence should be allowed to be significant if it expresses something which can be confuted by experience. Thus, he presents the principle of falsifiability, not as a criterion of meaning, but as a method of demarcating scientific statements from those that he calls metaphysical.

Some positivists, without Poppers agreement, interpret the requirement of falsifiability as a general test of meaning. A sentence should be allowed to be factually significant if, and only if, it expresses something which is definitely confutable by experience. This view has the advantage that unlike the strong verification principle, it can treat natural laws as genuine propositions. Since 'All As are B' is conclusively falsified by a contrary instance.

But this criterion of falsifiability has its own disadvantages and Ayer does not accept it. He rejects Poppers view because even the confutation of a hypothesis by crucial observation is not conclusive and absolutely certain since it rests upon some presuppositions about the circumstances under which observation takes place. He says "for when we take the occurrence of certain observations as proof that a given hypothesis is false, we presuppose the existence of certain conditions. And though, in any given case, it may be extremely improbable that this assumption is false, it is not logically impossible."[24]

Again, as a general test of significance, this view has a corresponding disadvantage. For just as universal propositions are conclusively falsifiables but not conclusively verifiable, so existential propositions are conclusively verifiable but not falsifiable. The proposition that there are abominable snowmen is probably false, but it cannot be strictly falsified, since we cannot search the whole of space at every moment of its existence.

Ayer says, "these anomalies are not so disturbing as they would be if the criterion of falsifiability were put forward as a criterion of meaning, but one might think that they made the class of empirical statements unduly narrow."[25]

Urmson says that, "we can in fact easily construct a statement which is neither conclusively falsifiable nor conclusively verifiable by making it contain both the unverifiable 'all' and the unfalsifiable 'some', an example would be the statement that every person who walks under a ladder will meet with some misfortune."[26]

So, Ayer thinks that a hypothesis cannot be conclusively confuted anymore than it can be conclusively verified. His response is to make factual significance depend, not on conclusive verifiability, but merely on the possibility of favourable or unfavourable evidence. He says, "Accordingly, we fall back on the weaker sense of verification. We say that the question that must be asked about any putative statement of fact is not, would any observations make its truth or falsehood logically certain? But simply, would any observations be relevant to the determination of its truth or falsehood? And it is only if a negative answer is given to this second question that we conclude that the statement under consideration is nonsensical.[27]

It is at this point that Ayer starts to run into difficulties. He regards this formulation of the verification principles as insufficiently clear. In his later 'Introduction' the reason he gives is that the word 'relevant', as it occurs in the phrase 'relevant to the determination of truth or falsehood', is 'uncomfortably vague' (L.T.L., 11), a remark which is itself uncomfortably vague.

Ayer says, "A proposition is verifiable, in the weak sense, if it is possible for experience to render it probable."

To make his position clearer, Ayer formulates it in another way. He says, "Let us call a proposition which records an actual or possible observation an experiential proposition. Then we may say that it is the mark of a genuine factual proposition, not that it should be equivalent to an experiential proposition, or any finite number of experiential propositions, but simply that some experiential propositions can be deduced from it in conjunction with certain other premises without being deducible from those other premises alone.[28]

Ayer gives reason for why only the weak sense of the term is required by his principle of verification. Ayer feels that these (strong and weak) are not two genuine alternatives as he says that all empirical propositions are hypotheses which are continually subject to the test of further experience, and from this it follows that it is impossible for any one to establish the truth of any such proposition conclusively. According to Ayer, it is only a priori or analytic propositions which can be demonstrated to be certain or verifiable in the strong sense. But no empirical or synthetic proposition can be verifiable in the strong sense. It is verifiable only in the weak sense. Hence only in this sense a synthetic proposition can be said to be significant.

According to most positivists ostensive or protocol propositions based on immediate experience do not stand in need of any further verification as we feel immediately certain of their truth. But Ayer rejects this view of the positivists. He does not admit that "any synthetic proposition can be purely ostensive" and can be absolutely certain. All synthetic propositions, without exception, are only probable and verifiable in the weak sense. this position of Ayer commits him to relativism. He accepts it and further makes some corrections in his view. In the second addition of L.T.L. (1946)

he expressed it. He now thinks that there is a class of empirical propositions of which it is allowable to say that they can be verified conclusively. Ayer calls them 'basic propositions', which refer solely to the content of a single experience and "what may be said to verify them conclusively is the occurrence of the experience to which they uniquely refer."[29]

Ayer agrees with those who say that propositions of this kind are 'incorrigible' because it is impossible to be mistaken about them except in a verbal sense. Ayer says, "my being in pain will verify the proposition that I am in pain......... when I say 'I am in pain' I mean I am in pain, and if P, then P".[30]

According to Ayer, except these basic statements, all empirical hypotheses are verifiable only in the weak sense of the term.

Ayer interprets his criterion that a statement is 'weakly' verifiable, and therefore, meaningful, if 'some possible sense experience would be relevant to the determination of its truth or falsehood.

But Ayer realizes, this itself requires interpretation, for the word 'relevant' is uncomfortably vague. The notion of relevant evidence is too broad to serve Ayer's purposes. Accordingly, Ayer puts forward a second version of his principle. Making a slight difference, now, in the place of experiential proposition', he uses the phrase 'observation-statement' to designate a statement 'which records an actual or possible observation.'

In this version, the principle is that, "a statement is verifiable and consequently meaningful, if some observation statement can be deduced from it in conjunction with certain other premises, without being deducible from those other premises alone.

Ayer's reason for putting it in this way is to make provision for hypothetical propositions and for generalizations of law which can not be simply equated with any finite set of statements of particular fact. But this criterion is liberal enough to allow meaning to any statement whatsoever.

Sir Isaiah Berlin points it out for the first time. He shows that if 'O' is an observation statement, then whatever statement 'S' may be, 'O' follows from the conjunction of 'S' with 'if S then o' without following from 'if S then o' alone. Thus the statements 'the Absolute is lazy' and 'if the Absolute is lazy, this is white' Jointly entail the observation statement 'this is white' and since 'this is white' does not follow from either of these premises, taken by itself, both of them satisfy this criterion of meaning. Furthermore, this holds good for any other piece of nonsense that one care to put, as an example, in place of 'the Absolute is lazy' provided only that it had the grammatical form of an indicative sentence. But a criterion of meaning that allows such latitude as this is evidently unacceptable.[31]

Ayer says that the same objection applies to the proposal that we should take the possibility of falsification as our criterion. For, given any statement 'S' and any observation statement 'O', 'O' will be incompatible with the conjunction of 'S' and 'if S then not O'.

Another difficulty which Ayer overlooks in his original attempt to formulate the principle of verification is that most empirical propositions are in some degree vague. Though any such statement is tested by making observations which consist in the occurrence of particular sense contents, but there is always an indefinite number of other tests, differing to some extent in respect either of their conditions or their results, that serves the same purpose. And this means that there is never any set of observation statements of which it can truly be said that precisely they are entailed by any given statement about a material thing.

Ayer says that, 'when we speak of the 'entailment' of observation-statements, what we are considering to be deducible from the premises in question is not any particular observation statement, but only one or other of a set of such statements, where the defining characteristic of the set is that all its members refer to sense contents that fall within a certain specifiable range."

After that Ayer thinks of the more serious objection that

his criterion allows meaning to any indicative statement whatsoever. To meet this, he makes further amendment in his criterion. He says that, "I propose to say that a statement is directly verifiable if it is either itself an observation statement, or is such that in conjunction with one or more observation statements it entails at least one observation statement which is not deducible from these other premises alone; and I propose to say that a statement is indirectly verifiable if it satisfies the following conditions : first, that in conjunction with certain other premises it entails one or more directly verifiable statements which are not deducible from these other premises alone, and secondly, that these other premises do not include any statement that is not either analytic, or directly verifiable, or capable of being independently established as indirectly verifiable. And I can now reformulate the principle of verification as requiring of a literally meaningful statement, which is not analytic, that it should be either directly or indirectly verifiable, in the foregoing sense.[32]

So, in case of the other objects which by their very natures cannot be directly observed, verification is possible in an indirect way, by observing the perceptible consequences they follow if the given proposition is true. "For example, we can determine the presence of an electric current by observing either the heat produced in the conductor or the deviation of a magnetic needle, or the quantity of substance separated from an electrolyte etc."[33]

Similarly, statements about past facts can be verified by observing their present consequences, and those about other minds by their observable external manifestations.

Describing the conditions of indirect verification, Ayer says that the 'other premises' may include analytic statements, because in this way he intends to allow for the case of scientific theories which are expressed in terms that do not themselves designate anything observable. A 'Dictionary' may be provided by means of which they can be transformed into statements that are verifiable, and the statements which constitute the dictionary can be regarded as analytic, without accepting this provision, the distinction between such scientific theories and those which are declared and dismissed as metaphysical will not be possible. Ayer says that the statements of the metaphysician do not describe anything that is capable, even in principle, of being observed, but also that no dictionary is provided by means of which they can be transformed into statements that are directly or indirectly verifiable.

Russell says, "Every proposition which we can understand must be composed wholly of constituents with which we are acquainted."[34]

Ayer makes a comparison between the criterion of his own and that of the old empiricists. He says, "Metaphysical statements, in my sense of the term are excluded also by the older empiricist principle that no statement is literally meaningful unless it describes what could be experienced, where the criterion of what could be experienced is that it should be something of the same kind as actually has been experienced." Thus Ayer shows that his criterion, the principle of verification is more liberal than of the older empiricists as it tries to maintain the meaningfulness of scientific theories while the other imposes too harsh condition upon the forms of scientific theories which cannot be fulfilled and thus rules out them.

Professor Stace argues that the principle of verification 'rests upon' the principle of observable kinds, but according to Ayer this is a mistake. Ayer says it is true that every statement that is allowed to be meaningful by the principle of observable kinds is also allowed to be meaningful by the principle of verification, but the converse does not hold.[35]

After his definition of direct and indirect verification, Ayer, in the 'introduction' (L.T.L., 2nd ed.) says that sometimes his critics assume that he takes the principle of verification to imply that no statement can be evidence for another unless it is part of its meaning, but this is not the case. Actually Ayer means to say that, even though a factually significant statement must be open to observational evidence, there can be forms of observational evidence, which are extraneous to its factual meaning. He sees it as a consequence of his principle of verification that, 'although its generality may prevent any finite set of observation- statements from exhausting its meaning', a statement about a material thing 'does not contain anything as part of its meaning that cannot be represented as an observation statement.' Likewise, he sees it as a consequence that a theological statement 'does not have any other factual meaning than what is contained in at least some of the relevant empirical propositions'.

The meaning of a statement, the factual meaning, consists in the range of ways in which there could ('in principle') be observational evidence relevant to the determination of its truth of falsity Ayer is endorsing this thesis, though with one qualification, 'the meaning of the statement does not consist in this range, but, rather, is wholly contained in it.

Ayer hopes that his formula is so minutely worked out that it is now free from, all difficulties. It can be said that this is an ingenious proposal and elegantly expressed. But unfortunately it does not work. Its failure is first demonstrated by Alonzo Church, who points out that even in its emended form, this criterion still allows meaning to any statement, whatsoever. To show it, Church presents a complex formula 'Either (not O_1 and O_2) or (O_3 and not S)', where 'O_1', 'O_2' and 'O_3' are (or strictly, express) observation statements which are logically independent of one another and 'S' is any statement one can choose. Since in a conjunction with 'O_1' it entails 'O_3', and since ex hypothesi 'O_1' alone does not entail 'O_3', this formula qualifies as directly verifiable in Ayer's sense. But this means that 'S' qualifies as indirectly verifiable, since in conjunction with the formula it entails '$O\text{-}_2$', which is not deducible from the formula alone. Since 'S' can be any statement, it turns out that any statement whatsoever, counts as significant on Ayer's new criterion as on the old.

Finally many attempts are made to amend the criterion to escape Church's counter example but none of these is successful in the purpose.

Now, we come back towards the aim, to which this

criterion tries to achieve. The whole point of the criterion is to expose forms of nonsense which, unlike the gibberish, are not explicit. A sentence has literal significance if, and only if, it expresses something which is either tautologous (analytic) or empirically verifiable. The distinctive feature of sentences which lack literal significance in Ayer's sense is not that they are wholly unintelligible (though some of them will be), but that, while assertoric, they are not semantically equipped to say anything true or false, and it is in this sense that they fail to express genuine proposition.

Ayer uses his criterion of significance to dispose, in the most summary fashion, of much of what passes as genuine philosophy. Ayer describes the philosophical assertions and questions which his criterion eliminates as 'metaphysical.' He explicitly defines a 'metaphysical sentence' as one which 'purports to express a genuine proposition, but does, in fact, express neither a tautology nor an empirical hypothesis (L.T.L., 41), so that a sentence only qualifies as metaphysical if it fails to satisfy the criterion.

He claims that many of the assertions made by philosophers are shown to be nonsensical, being neither tautologies nor empirically verifiable, and that many of the questions which have formed the traditional subject-matter of philosophy are shown to be pseudo-questions, since they demand nonsensical answers.

Through many examples, Ayer tries to show the meaninglessness of such metaphysical propositions as no observation is relevant in their verification. One of them is the world of sense experience is altogether unreal. No doubt, we are, sometimes, deceived by our senses but it is further sense-experience, and nothing else, that informs us of the mistakes that arise out of sense experience. Just because, our perceptual judgments, which are based on our sensations, are sometimes found to be erroneous, it does not mean that the world of sense experience is unreal. And indeed, no conceivable observation, or series of observations can have any tendency to show that the world is unreal. So it is literally nonsensical to deny the reality of the world.

Ayer takes of a controversy which lies between monists and pluralists concerning the number of substances that there are in the world. But there cannot be any empirical situation which can solve their dispute. Ayer says, "there are genuine logical and empirical questions involved in the dispute between monists and pluralists. But the metaphysical question concerning 'substance' is ruled out by our criterion as spurious."

Similarly there is another controversy between realists and idealists, in its metaphysical aspect. And no possible experience is relevant to the solution of this dispute as hear the term 'real' is in the sense in which it is opposed to 'ideal'. Consequently this problem is fictitious in its metaphysical interpretation according to this criterion.

Ayer shows that sometimes linguistic usages mislead the metaphysician and he makes some misconception because of them. There are some who employ the term 'substance' to refer to the thing itself and make it the grammatical subject of the sentences, but it does not follow that the thing itself is a 'simple entity' or that it cannot be defined in terms of the totality of its appearances. Actually whenever we talk of 'its' appearances we do not mean to distinguish the thing from the appearances that is simply an accident of linguistic usage.

After that, Ayer shows that a consideration of grammar leads to metaphysics and he takes the instance of the metaphysical concept of being. For instance, the sentence 'Martyrs exist' and 'Martyrs suffer' both have grammatically the same appearance and it leads one to assume that they are of the same logical type. But as Kant says that existence is not an attribute. When we ascribe an attribute to a thing, we covertly assert that it exists. If existence were itself an attribute, then all-positive existential propositions were tautologies, and all negative essential propositions self contradictory, and this is not the case.

Again there is a superficial grammatical resemblance between the sentences, 'Dogs are faithful' and "Unicorns are fictitious', and it creates the assumption that they are of the same logical type. Dogs must exist in order to have the property of being faithful, but it is plainly self-contradictory to say that fictitious objects exist. Again the assertion that fictitious objects have a special non-empirical mode of real being is devoid of all literal significance as there is no way of testing it.

Ayer is particularly concerned to expose as nonsensical the suggestion that there is, or may be, a reality transcending the empirical world of ordinary observation and scientific theory. He says that his difficulty is not in answering the question "Are there, or are there not, metaphysical realities?' but in understanding what usage is being given to the expression 'metaphysical reality'. Thus the assertion that the empirical world is really an illusion concealing an underlying reality in some quite different character, the assertion that the core of a material object is an in-itself-featureless substance in which the object's empirical properties inhere the assertion that a person's experiences are the acts of states of an immaterial substantival ego, and the assertion that there is a realm of objective values, to be discerned by some faculty of moral intuition, are all dismissed as nonsensical (devoid of literal significance) as assertions which purport to say something factual, about the nature of reality, but fail to achieve factual significance because they are unverifiable. There is no criterion for deciding whether they are true or false. He says, "It will be found that much of what ordinarily passes for philosophy is metaphysical according to this criterion, and, in particular, that it cannot be significantly asserted that there is a non-empirical world of values, or that men have immortal souls, or that there is a transcendent God."[36]

Ayer and other positivists consider these metaphysical assertions as mere gibberish. Metaphysical statements are not explanations, in any accepted sense of the term. Ayer says, "And as tautologies and empirical hypotheses form the entire class of significant propositions, we are justified in concluding that all metaphysical assertions are nonsensical."

Some philosophers speak of the metaphysician as a kind

of misplaced poet. His statements have no literal meaning, but they may have considerable value, as means of moral inspiration, or even as works of art. But Ayer does not accept this view. The sentences, produced by poets do have literal meaning. While the metaphysician lapses into nonsense through being deceived by grammar, or through committing errors of reasoning. But a poet does not makes mistakes of this sort. Ayer says, "And thus we see that the view that a number of the traditional 'problems of philosophy' are metaphysical, and consequently fictitious, does not involve any incredible assumptions about the psychology of philosophers."[37]

According to Ayer, it would be a mistake to reject these assertions by asserting their negations, for if the assertions are neither true nor false, so are their negations. It is not the business of philosophy to look into these questions, since there are no significant answers to be found.

Thus Ayer describes the philosophical assertions and questions which his criterion eliminates as 'metaphysical'. The criterion condemns as nonsensical much of what has traditionally gone under the title of 'metaphysics', and in Ayer's view, the criterion is correct.

Thus, the only important issues are whether the criterion really is correct and whether it really does condemn what Ayer thinks it condemns.

The only defence of the principle is that it yields intuitively acceptable results in the case of those putative propositions whose status is uncontroversial, and that, as far as he can see, no rival criterion can do as well.

Ayer says that there are some prima facie propositions which by universal agreement are given as significant and some expressions which are agreed to be meaningless. Trusting our criterion if it accepts the former class and rejects the latter, we apply it to such doubtful cases as that of the propositions of metaphysics and if they fail to satisfy if we pronounce them nonsensical......... if therefore, a philosopher maintains that our criterion is too narrow and that metaphysical propositions are significant, it is for him to put forward a more liberal criterion, one that allows the significance of metaphysical propositions yet is not so liberal as to allow the significance of expressions such as "jealousy pronoun live" or "siffle hip brim" which are agreed by all parties to be meaningless. In Ayer's view, this challenge cannot be met.

Schlick says that, "Metaphysics, as we stated before, consists essentially in the attempt to express context, i.e., in a self-contradictory enterprise, but it is by no means easy to see that a question inquiring into the nature of content is nothing but a meaningless arrangement of words. The difficulty of perceiving this is the real cause of all the troubles from which philosophical speculation has been suffering for about twenty five centuries."[38]

He says that if the nonsense in the typical metaphysical issues could be detected, then most of the futile discussions of the great thinkers would have been avoided.

Then, about the verification principle, Schlick says that this principle, or new or wonderful: on the contrary, it has always been followed and used by scientists as a matter of course, at least unconsciously, and in the same way it has always been acknowledged by common sense in everyday life, the only place where it has been neglected is in philosophical discussions. He says, "Science could not possibly act otherwise, because its whole business consists in testing the truth of propositions, and they cannot be tested except on the strength of our principle."[39]

But the principle of verification faces big criticisms. We see that various formulations are attempted by Ayer and others to escape the difficulties against the principle of verification, but they do not get success. The principle faces a lots of criticism by different philosophers.

It is said that the verification principle is itself not verifiable. Its application to itself shows it to be meaningless, because unverifiable. But here is an obvious confusion. Verification principle is not a theory because it is not offered as either true or false. It is put forward as a definition, not as an empirical statement of fact. And it makes no sense to discuss the truth or falsity of a definition. A. C. Ewing and stace, bath take the principle of verification to be an empirical hypothesis while Ayer wishes it to be regarded as a definition.

The first objection is that the principle of verifiability itself, on the face of it, is neither an empirical generalization nor a tautology. What, then, is its status?

The second objection is that we ordinarily inquire into the meaning of words or sentences. A proposition is what a sentence means, not something that has a meaning. On the other hand, it is proposition which we verify, describe as true or false. How, then, can verifiability be identified with meaning?

The other objection is that propositions may be unverifiable either because we cannot, for the moment, think of any way of verifying them, or because it is physically impossible to verify them, or because any attempt to verify them is ruled out for purely logical reasons. Which of these species of unverifiability carries meaninglessness with it?

Again it is said that the term 'verify' is ambiguous, it can mean 'prove the truth of' or 'test the truth of'. Are we to say that a proposition is meaningless unless there is some way of proceeding which, if successful, would prove it to be true, or is it demanded only that there should be some way of testing its truth? Furthermore, is this method of procedure, in either case, identical with the proposition's meaning, or merely a way of showing that it has a meaning?

The next is that the principle of verifiability leads towards ultimate verifies. If a proposition's meaning consists in what verifires it, these 'verifiers' cannot thereselves be propositions, or, alternatively, they must be propositions whose meaning somehow lies in themselves. What are they? And no answer is there.

Coplestan makes some criticism about the principle of verification. He says, if Ayer says that any factual statement, in order to be meaningful must be verifiable, and if by 'verifiable' he means verifiable by sense-experience, then he is presupposing that all reality is given in sense-experience. It means he is presupposing that there can be no such thing as a metaphysical reality. Thus Ayer is presupposing a philosophical position which cannot be demonstrated by the principle of verification. Thus, acceptance of the principle of verifiability implies the acceptance of philosophical positivism.

But this criticism that the positivist arbitrarily confines his notion of experience to sense-experience is partly true. For, some positivists include introspection also with experience, and Carnap in his recent writings does not overlook mystical experience. But no change in the basic outlook is noticed inspite of such recognition.

Ayer says that he does not wish to restrict experience to sense-experience. He does not at all mind counting what might be called introspectible experiences or feelings, mystical experiences etc. But then that people who have not have certain experiences won't understand propositions which refer to them. After that, Ayer is ready to believe that others have experiences different from him. But he says that the factual content of other's statements is determined by the experiences, which counted as their verifiers or falsifiers.

After that Capleston talks about a distinction made by Ayer between cognitive and non-cognitive. Copleston presumes that by cognitive statements Ayer means statements which satisfy the criterion of meaning of verifiability, and by non-cognitive statement, Ayer means statements which do not satisfy that criterion. When Ayer says that metaphysical statements are non-cognitive he is not saying much more than that statements which do not satisfy the criterion of verifiability do not satisfy the criterion of verifiability. And in this case no conclusion follows as to the significance or non-significance of metaphysical propositions, unless one has first assumed that they are non-significant.

Ayer accepts the fact that the word 'meaning' is commonly used in a variety of senses, but he claims that there is at least one proper use of the word 'meaning' in which it is incorrect to say that a statement is meaningful unless it satisfies the principle of verification. Ayer uses the expression 'literal meaning' to distinguish this use from the other, while applying the expression 'factual meaning' to the case of statements which satisfy his criterion without being analytic. He suggests that it is only if it is literally meaningful, in this sense, that a statement can properly be said to be either true or false.

Caploston makes his another argument that, if Ayer is applying the criterion of verifiability in his treatment of metaphysical propositions, then the significance of metaphysical propositions is ruled out of court a priori, since the truth of the principle of verifiability inevitably involves the non-significance of such propositions. In this case the application of the criterion to concrete metaphysical propositions constitutes a proof neither of the non-significance of these propositions nor of the truth of the principle.[40]

Now Coplestan says about the principle of verification that it shows only that metaphysical propositions do not satisfy a definite assumed criterion of meaning but it does not follow that one must accept that criterion of meaning.

Ayer accepts that it is open to anyone to adopt a different criterion of meaning. But he defends the use of the criterion of verifiability as a methodological principle and realizes that for the effective elimination of metaphysics it needs to be supported by detailed analysis of particular metaphysical arguments.

One more argument which Copleston presents is that Ayer seems to be demanding that in order for a factual statement to be significant one must be able to deduce observational consequences from it. But if he means directly observable consequences then he is demanding too much. In any case there are some propositions which are not verifiable, even in principle, but which are considered by most people to have meaning and to be either true or false. Copleston gives an example, "Atomic warfare will take place, and it will bloat out the entire human race."

Most people think that this statement has meaning, it means what it says. But it cannot possibly be verified empirically. If the prediction is fulfilled, there will be no one there to verify. As the last man cannot say with his last breath; "Capleston's prediction has been verified.' Thus, he tries to show the limitations of the principle of verification.

G. J. Warnock has also some objections against the principle of verification. He criticizes it by saying that if verification principle is regarded as really general criterion of significance that anything at all which fails by this test is to be declared to be meaningless. It then appears at once that not only metaphysics, not only theology but also every single moral and aesthetic judgment, any judgment of value of any sort, must be regarded as meaningless. For nothing in any of these fields can be verified solely by empirical observation.[41]

He shows the incompleteness of the principle of verification that it has no application at all to forms of words which is no way aspired to the condition of statements. It does not make sense to speak of the verification of commands, Prayers, premises, expressions of wishes, and so on, these cannot be verified but it does not impugn their linguistic respectability and does not imply that they are meaningless.

He further says that it is after all by no means arbitrary what we call a 'statement' and what we do not, it is not a mere matter of free linguistic choice.

Again, he says, there are some propositions, found in religious creeds, for example, which can only be statement, if they are anything at all and then they must either be empirically verifiable or meaningless. Every statement in religion, ethics, esthetics and every area of concern or value is neither verifiable nor falsifiable. Thus he is not satisfied with the principle of verification at all.

Warnock criticizes this principle by saying that can it really be that any two people ever mean or understand the same thing? Verification for one must occur in his experience, and for me in mine. Hence, what any statement really means must apparently be systematically different for each person who does or might hear or read, speak or write it. How then do we succeed in communicating with each other? What I mean, others can necessarily not understand.

Positivists say that this 'linguistic solipcism' does not matter, and the general intelligibility of language can be saved without denying it. Schlick's solution of this difficulty is to say that while the content of our experiences is indeed incommunicable, their structure is not.

In an article entitled 'metaphysics and meaning' which appeared in Mind (in October, 1935) Prof. W. T. Stace attacks the verificational theory of meaning by saying that it proves to much, that its use as a criterion of meaning lead not merely to the elimination of metaphysics, but also to the elimination of all statements about the past, and it condemns as meaningless any objective theory of value. Ayer says that it can be seen that this criterion denies meaning to metaphysical statements such as those which deny the reality of the sensible world or assert the existence of things-in-themselves. But this criterion does not deny meaning to all prepositions about the past. Ayer considers the example given by Prof. Stace which is 'I ate bacon and eggs for breakfast this morning'. Ayer does not say that such a proposition can be verified conclusively, but experiences may be there, which have some bearing on its validity either as substantiating or as discrediting it. And this is all that the principle of verification requires.

The next objection that Prof. Stace has about this criterion is that it rules out significant questions concerning the experiences of other minds. Ayer answers it by saying that logical positivists analyse it in terms of the observable behaviour of the people in question. Ayer explains that we define the qualitative identity and difference of two people's sense-experience in terms of the similarity and dissimilarity of their reactions to empirical tests.

The other objection stace makes is that the principle of verification rules out all objective theories of value. Ayer finds it misleading. He says that if it is not clear that what do people mean by such theories and they cannot indicate how it can be verified what they do mean, is surely justified holding that they have not provided with any significant information at all.

After that Prof. Stace argues that 'metaphysical propositions are not necessarily, and as such, meaningless' on the ground that 'the assertion of a reality which lies behind our experience, and which can never be experienced by us, may be meaningful provided it is conceived as the possible experience of some other mind which shares structure with our own.'[42]

Ayer finds it significant that there may be people who have experience which we do not have, but this does not imply that metaphysical utterances may be significant. Because this fact does not imply that anything which purports to be a description of these experiences will be intelligible to us. It will be so only if it is susceptible of verification in our experience. And this metaphysical utterances are not. It is said about logical positivist that, "One thing he can do, of course, is to act as a sort of intellectual policeman, seeing that nobody trespasses into metaphysics."[43]

Ayer talks about the criterion of meaning presented by Prof. Stace, according to which a statement can be said to have meaning if, and only if, every concept employed in it has empirical application. But Ayer finds an instance to show that this will not do. The concepts of 'density', 'death' and 'fatherhood' all have empirical application, but the sentence 'density death fatherhood' does not express a significant proposition. For a sentence to have a meaning it is not sufficient that each of the words comprising it should have a meaning. It is necessary also that they should be combined in a significant way.

Critics of logical positivism show many defects even in this modified conception of meaning. First of all, it is arbitrary to make meaning dependent on verifiability, seeing that the two concepts are by no means necessarily and directly related, since we can understand the meaning of a sentence without thinking in the least of its verifiability.

The absurdity of this conception of meaning is indirectly proved by the fact that if this conception is true, absurd conclusion will follow. For, a sentence like, "this circle is a square" will be quite significant according to this criterion as the falsity of this assertion can be shown by observation and the sentence is thus verifiable. On the contrary, a strong sentence like 'a king had four sons' will be meaningless as no question of verification can even arise here. A complete subversion of the ordinary meaning of 'meaning' thus follows.

A possible defence against this criticism is that the ambiguous word 'meaning' is used by the positivist in a special sense. By the meaning of a sentence he means other sentences which follow from it by implication and with the help of which it can be verified. We can see an approach to this special sense in common usages like 'Marriage means responsibility', 'Fear means weakness'. Meaning is, in brief, logical implication. Now 'this circle is a square' can be said to have meaning in so far as its truth has some implications for future experience, such as 'then it must have four right angles' which can be verified to be false. And a story sentence can be said to be meaningless, because we realize, that such a sentence implies no consequence which can possibly be observed.

But this defence suffers from at least two defects. It makes the positivistic theory confined to a particular special aspect of meaning which is not the primary sense of the term, and leaves the primary sense unaffected. Secondly, metaphysics can no longer be said to be meaningless in the ordinary and primary sense of 'meaning'. Positivism thus becomes considerably weakened.

The verificationists use such examples as Heidegger's statement 'the nothing nothings', and F. H. Bradley's talk about 'the Absolute' as in the statement, "The Absolute enters into, but is itself incapable of, evaluation and progress.' Ayer says, this is 'a remark taken at random' from Bradley's 'Appearance and Reality'. Ayer claims, it is, 'not even in principle verifiable', therefore, nothing more than a 'metaphysical pseudo-proposition.'

Oswald Hanfling writes that a sentence, plucked 'at random' out of its context, may strike the reader as meaningless. But it is not so because, it is unverifiable. In Bradley's argument, we can find there the means of assessing the truth of his statement. That will be the appropriate method of verification in this case. So, in taking the statement out of its context, Ayer denies us access to the relevant method of verification.

It is a question, that, is sense experience, the only kind of experience? Ayer speaks of 'mystical intuition'. But, he goes on, the mystic's statements, like others, 'must be subject to the test of actual experience'. But is not the mystic's experience itself a kind of 'actual experience'.

Again, How is their preference for empirical statements and empirical methods of verification, itself to be justified? The claim that all knowledge comes from experience cannot itself be derived from experience.

Thus we see that verification principle faces great criticism and ultimately does not get success in its systematic formulation. Then, to overcome the problems inherent in the verifiability theory of meaning, British analytic philosophy takes a new turn, still concerned with language and meaning but no longer restricted to the verifiability theory. Wittgenstein here revises his conception of language and its role in human life. Language remains central but now its primary role is no longer to describe and make scientific type statements but to define 'the forms of life' and particular uses of language, he calls "language- games'. Now this theory of meaning is 'the meaning of a word or sentence is its use." Wittgenstein says that all philosophical problems are due to :language going on holiday." He finds his task not to develop a 'theory of meaning' but rather to attend with extreme care to the everyday "games" we play with language and see how philosophers tend to abuse that language and get themselves in bizzare corners. Language however useful for science and description, is primarily a tool for doing things, for asking questions, making promises and for having uninformative but polite conversation. And ordinary language philosophy projects how we use language and how philosophers, by abusing ordinary language, raise problems that are not really problems at all.

Again, we see that the positivist flavour of their thought comes out most strongly in their hostility to metaphysics. Wittgenstein feels that sometimes we try to use language when there are no 'facts' at all. Then he say, "Whereof one cannot speak, thereof one must be silent', but positivists do not accept this 'keep silent' suggestion. When it comes to metaphysics, says Neurath, "One must indeed be silent, but not about anything.'

We see that verification principle is strongly criticized, but it does not mean that it is completely failed in its purpose of showing the meaninglessness of metaphysics. British metaphysics, however, could not again return to the old substance metaphysics and the illusory quest for "the way the world really is." The logical positivists borrow "Hume's fork" and turn it into a formidable weapon, every statement is either an analytic truth, or it is an empirically verifiable statement with specifiable tests for its truth or falsity. Everything else is meaningless.

It we look at Kant, he takes a middle ground between the natural scientist and the speculative, or visionary metaphysician. According to him, the philosopher can and should ask-what must be true of the world, is experience in and of the world is to be possible at all, what concepts are central in our experience of the world etc. We see that the task is conceptual, but in a sense descriptive, or analytical, rather than speculative. The philosopher is to take our concepts as he finds them, and work out the necessary condition of their empirical employment. And the leading metaphysical system builder P.F. Strawson shows that descriptive metaphysics is possible. The new metaphysics is modest. It claims only to be a comprehensive description of the way we conceive of our world through our use of language.

References

1. Philosophical Papers, Vol. II, (1935-36) Reidle, 1979, p. 270.
2. A. J. Ayer, "Demonstration of the Impossibility of Metaphysics", 'Mind', July, 1934.
3. A.J. Ayer, 'The Central Questions of Philosophy', p. 8.
4. Liebniz, 'A Letter to Queen Charlotte of Prussia', 1702, Trans. by Duncan in ' Philosophical Works of Liebniz'. p. 150.

5. A.J. Ayer, 'The Central Questions of Philosophy', p. 10.
6. A.J. Ayer, 'Language, Truth and Logic', p. 14.
7. L. Wittgenstein, 'Tractatus -Logico- Philosophicus', Preface.
8. F.H. Bradley, 'Appearance And Reality' 2nd Ed., P.I.
9. L. Winttgenstein, 'Tractatus-Logico- Philosophicus', p. 63.
10. J.O. Urmson, ' Philosophical Analysis', p. 105.
11. 'Philosophy of Science, Logic and Mathematics', Ed. by Stuart G. Shanker, p. 196.
12. Rudolf Carnap, "Testability and Meaning', Philosophy of Science, III, IV (1936, 1937).
13. Ibid, p. 426.
14. A.J. Ayer, 'Language, Truth and Logic', p. 35.
15. A.J. Ayer, 'The Central Questions of Philosophy', p. 26.
16. A.J. Ayer, 'Language, Truth and Logic', p. 41
17. J.O. Urmson, 'Philosophical Analysis', p. 108.
18. A.J. Ayer, 'Language, Truth and Logic', p. 36.
19. Ibid, p. 18.
20. J. O. Urmson, 'Philosophical Analysis', p. 111
21. A.J. Ayer, 'Language, Truth and Logic', p. 37.
22. Moritz Schlick, 'Die Kausalitat In Der Gegenwartigen Physik' trans-by Weinberg, 'Examination of Logical Positivism', p. 146.
23. Jeoergensen, 'Development of Logical Empiricism', p. 72.
24. A.J. Ayer, 'Language, Truth and Logic', p. 19.
25. A.J. Ayer, 'The Central Questions of Philosophy', p. 29.
26. J. O. Urmson, 'Philosophical Analysis', p. 113.
27. A.J. Ayer, 'Language, Truth and Logic', p. 38.
28. Ibid, p. 20
29. Ibid, p. 10
30. A.J. Ayer, 'Verification and Experience' Proceedings of the Aristotelian Society, Vol XXXVII, also in 'The Foundations of Empirical Knowledge', p. 80-4.
31. I. Berlin, 'Verifiability in Principle', Proceedings of Aristotelian Society, Vol. XXXIX.

32. A.J. Ayer, 'Language, Truth and Logic', p. 13.
33. Rudoly Carnap, 'Encyclopedia and Unified Science', p. 51.
34. Bertrand Russell, 'The Problems of Philosophy', p. 91.
35. W.T. Stace, 'Positivism', Mind, 1944.
36. A.J. Ayer, 'Language, Truth and Logic', Preface, p. 9.
37. A.J. Ayer, 'Language, Truth and Logic', p. 27.
38. Moritz Schlick, 'Meaning and Verification' in 'Essential Readings in Logical Positivism' Ed. by Oswald Hanfling, p. 36-37.
39. Ibid, p. 40.
40. A. J. Ayer, 'Logical Positivism- A Debate' From 'The Meaning of Life and other Essays', p. 39.
41. G.J. Warnock, 'English Philosophy Since 1900, p. 36.
42. W.T. Stace, 'Mind', p. 436.
43. The Revolution in Philosophy, Ed. by A. J. Ayer, p. 78-79.

3

The Function of Philosophy

As we have seen in the previous chapter that for the logical positivist, all cognitively significant statements are, either empirically verifiable statements of fact or tautological statements, depending on the structure of the language or other symbolic systems. Logical positivist rules out as meaninglesss, literally non sensical-almost the whole of metaphysics. The works of traditional philosophy are filled with statements which are neither empirical statements of fact nor analytic tautologies, and the positivists are prepared to select almost at random statements from the classical philosophers to illustrate their contention that metaphysics is largely non sense.

Now, a question arises here that if tall or most metaphysical utterances are relegated by the positivistic criterion to a limbo on nonsense, what is the function of philosophy? Of course the elimination of metaphysics does not mean for the logical positivest the abandonment of Philosophical activity. He disallows all Philosophical questions about super phenomenal reality on the ground of their meaninglessness. On the other hand he also regard all questions regarding the properties of empirical objects as falling properly within the domain of science. Yet Philosophy has a field of its own within the empirical sphere.

According to Ayer, logical positivism is not a system of philosophy. It consists rather in a certain technique-a certain kind of attitude towards Philosophic problems. One thing which logical Positivists tend to have in common is that they deny the possibility of Philosophy as a Speculative discipline. If Philosophy is to be a branch of knowledge, it has to consist in logic or in some form of analysis.

Ayer says, "We do not maintain that philosophy should 'entirely shut up shop'. For, when metaphysics is eliminated, analysis remains. And we claim that our conception of philosophizing as an activity of analysis accords at any rate with the general practice of the majority of the great philosophers of the past.[1]

According to Ayer, the analysis, or more broadly, the clarification of our concepts is the only legitimate business for Philosophy. And we can see that this, indeed, is a direct consequence of his criterion of significance, according to which any genuine proposition must be either a tautalogy or empirically verifiable. His criterion condemns as nonsensical much of what has traditionally gone under the title of metaphysics.

But the trouble, however, as Ayer himself reconizes, is that many of our non-Philosophical assertion made in the context of ordinary discourse or scientific theory, appear, on the surface, to involve metaphysical commitments of the kind he is seeking to eliminate. Thus ethical and arithmetical assertions seem, in their different ways, to make factual claims of a radically non-empirical kind, and assertions about the remote past or about the mental states of the other persons, while they concern the character of the empirical world, seem to be beyond the reach of adequate verification. Even assertions about the current state of one's physical environment, such as 'there is a table in this room' are problematic. For if, as Ayer accepts, the immediate data of snese-perception are purely phenomenal entitles, whose esse is percipi, it seems that, in trying to characterise what lies beyond the perceptual data, such assertions are unverifiable. Ayer's response is to try to save the threatened assertions by Philosophical analysis-by arguing that once we have understood what the assertions really mean, we can see that they are not condemned by the criterion. How this result is achieved varies considerably from case to case. As we shall see in later chapters that when he deals with ostensibly empirical assertions, such as those about the physical world, the past, and other minds, Ayer's analysis takes the form of a reduction: the problematic sentences are shown to be empirically verifiable by their equivalence to sentences about the (potentially) available sensory evidence. His treatment of arithmetical assertions is quite different, these he reconciles with the criterion, not by giving them empirical content, but by construing them (when true) as mere tautologies, which make no claims about matters of fact. His approach to ethical assertions is different again. For (at least in respect of their ethical content) these turn out, on Ayer's analysis, to be not genuine assertions, but expressions of feeling, and, as such, they fall outside the scope of the criterion.

Thus we see that analysis, here, is considered as the function of philosophy. But it can be asked that is it a new task for Philosophy or analysis has always been a proper function of it. When it is said that the activity of Philosophizing is essentially analytic, it does not mean that the each and every philosopher has actually been engaged in carrying out analysis. These modern logical empiricists, hope to have freed themselves from the naivete and dogmatism of the various nineteenth century materialists and monists. They are conscious of their Philosophy's role as a turning point in the history of critical thought. Nevertheless, they do not claim originality, for they are aware that the empirical and analytic trend in Philosophy is no less persistent than the speculative and intuitive approach, though it is admittedly less spectacular and popular.[2]

But it does not mean that each and every philosopher has actually been engaged in carrying out analysis. On the contrary, the maximum part of Philosophy is metaphysical in character. If we go back and see, we find that metaphysics has always been a very important, or the most important part of the Philosophy. Philosophers from the very start are attracted towards it. We can see that the first problem to which the early Greek Philosophers address themselves is the problem of substance. The Ionian or Milesian Philosophers ask the question of the basal stuff of which the world is composed. Thales declares water to be the original stuff, and water simply becomes other things-that things are produced by the transformation of water. Anaximander says that the essence of things is the boundless or infinite, conceived as an eternal, imperishable substance out of which all things are made and to which all things return. Anaximenes describes the emergence of the variety of things from the primary substance, air, as due to processes of condensation and rarefaction.

The Problem of substance is also the primary concern of the Pythagoreans, who advance an abstract number-theory, that numbers are the primary causes of things. They fix their attention not so much upon a concrete, sense-perceived substance, as upon the relations existing between things, the order, uniformity or harmony in the world. Things are the copies or imitations of numbers. The Pythagoreans make entities of numbers, just as many persons today make entities of laws of nature, speaking of them as though they are the causes of whatever happens.

Heraclitus chooses the most mobile substance, the ever living fire as his first principle. According to him, All things are exchanged for fire, and fire for all things. Man's soul is a part of the universal fire and nourished by it. Everything is in a state of flux. There is no real permanence in things. He also brings out the idea that there is a reason in the world controlling its happenings. According to him, sense-knowledge is inferior to reason the eyes and ears are bad witnesses. Perception without reflection does not reveal to us the hidden truth, which is discernible only by reason.

Parmenides, the metaphysician of the Eleatic School, believes that the principle of things must be Permanent, Unmoved and neverchanging. Thought and being are identical. Being or reality is a homogeneous, continuous, indeterminate mass. The world of science is an illusion. What we perceive by the senses is to confuse being with non-being. He shows a firm belief in reason. Reality is conformable to reason and what is contradictory to thought cannot be real. Parmanides shows that logical thought compels us to conceive the world as a unity, as unchangeable and immovable. Sense perception, reveals to us a world of plurality and change, this is the world of appearance and opinion. Russel in 'A History of Western Philosophy' says that parmenides is a victim of the linguistic fallacy of arguing from language to reality. Russell says, "Parmenides" reasoning is the first example in Philosophy of an argument from thought and language to the world at large. It cannot, of course, be accepted as valid, but it is worth-while to see what truth it contains the whole argument shows how easy it is to draw metaphysical conclusions from language, and how the only way to avoid fallacious arguments of this kind is to push the logical and psychological study of language further than has been done by most metaphysicians."

After that, we see that the greated pupil of Socrates-Plato establishes his theory of Ideas, according to which, the world made apparent to us by our senses is contrasted with an intellectually apprehensible world of Ideas or forms. This world of Ideas is conceived as an ideal realm transcending the particular things in space and time. In the sensible world, things come into being and pass away, they have different properties at different times. By contrast the forms exist eternally and do not change. The forms determine the character of perceptible things and these things partake of reality just to the extent that they participate in the forms. The sense world is reduced to the status of phenomena or appearances of the real world. He believes that the source of knowledge lies in reason and not in sense-perception. For Plato, the superiority of the forms consist in their immutability and also, in their being objects of the intellect rather than the senses. The Demiurge or God fashions the world after the pattern of the ideal world. The final cause of the whole world is the idea of the Good. Plato offers many arguments to establish the immortality of the soul. For Plato, substance is the universal, the type of form which he assumes to reside in a world apart, the eternal and transcendent world of ideas.

Then comes Aristotle who formulates the notion of substance in sharp contrast to the Platonic. Aristotle regards the particular objects or individual beings as real substances. But the essence of the particular concrete being is constituted by its form, by the essential qualities of the class to which it belongs. Every individual substance is an admixture of matter and form. Substances arrange themselves in as ascending scale, the limits of which are indeterminate matter at the bottom and God or pure form at the top, the whole array of substances lies between these two extremes. God is the final cause of the world. He is the goal towards which all thing strive.

The Stoic metaphysics is a partial reversion from the Platonic-Aristotelion Philosophy to the hylozoism of an earlier stage in the development of Greek thought, it combines materialism with rationalistic pantheism. The animating principle of things is reason-intelligent, purposeful and good. The universe is a cosmos, a beautiful, well-ordered, good and perfect whole. The rational principle is related to the world as the human soul is related to its body. All life and movement have their source in the logos, it is god, it contains the seeds of life.

In the modern age, we can see that Descartes establishes the idea that knowledge can be obtained through the exercise of pure reason and not through sense-perception. His aim is to reach clear and certain knowledge which cannot spring from the senses, for the senses do not reveal what things really are, but only how they affect us. The mind has its own standards or norms, which guide it in the pursuit of truth. The first part of true Philosophy, according to Descartes, is metaphysics, which contains the principles of knowledge, such as the definition of the principle attributes of God, the immortality of the soul, and of all the clear and simple ideas that we posses. So, he is interested in discovering a method of truth rather than in a detailed discussion of epistemological problems. Ayer says, " His peculiarity lay in supposing that he could reach these scientific conclusions by purely logical deduction from self-evident premises."[3]

Spinoza too believes that the goal of Philosophy is the complete knowledge of things, and this can be reached by clear and distinct thinking. He begins with definitions and axioms and proceeds to propositions which he demonstrates in the geometrical order, each proposition occupying the exact place in the argument appropriate to it. And Spinoza, by reflecting on the concept of substance, deduces that there can be only one substance, to which he gives the name of 'God' or 'Nature', who is the transcendent cause of nature. The attributes of thought and extension are perfectly corresponding of this single substance, and everything within nature is rigorously determined-Spinoza defines the substance as something that contains in itself the reason for its own existence. But Ayer says that what he means by a reason is a logical ground, and nothing that exists concretely can contain a logical ground for its existence, in the sense that the fact that it exists can be deduced merely from the description of its character. And it cannot be said that God is the one exception to this rule.

Leibniz also reflects on the concept of substance. He establishes that the world of bodies is composed of an infinite number of dynamic units or immaterial un-extended simple units of force. Everyone of which is a particular, individual substance. He calls these simple substances as metaphysical points, monads or units, which are external; Leibniz interprets the monads as spiritual or psychic forces. The same principle that expresses itself in the mind of man is active in inanimate matter, in planet and animal. The universe is composed of an infinite number of monads in a gradually ascending scale of clearness. Each of them mirrors the same universe from its own point of view, by a pre established harmony which is the work of God, the creator of the system. God has arranged his universe in such a way that it works without interference from him. "The source of mechanics lies in metaphysics" is the motto which Leibinz places at the head of his system.

His theory of knowledge rests on his metaphysical presuppositions. According to him, universal and necessary propositions cannot be derived from the senses, they must have their seat and origin in the mind itself. So called empirical truths are accidental propositions. Sense-perception does not see things in their true reality, as they are in themselves, that is, as active spiritual substances or monads, but perceives them obscurely and confusedly as phenomena, as spatial. Leibniz says, "Our ideas of space, figure, motion, rest have their origin in the common sense, in the mind itself, for they are ideas of the pure understanding which, however, have reference to the eternal world."[4]

The universe is a rational system in which nothing happens without a sufficient reason, it is conceived in analogy with a logical system, in which the propositions are rationally related. The problem of philosophy is to discover the fundamental principles or presuppositions of knowledge, which are at the same time the fundamental principles of reality.

Kant shows, against the Leibiz-Wolffian "dogmatists", that we cannot have knowledge of the supersensible in metaphysics, that metaphysics in this sense is a pseudo-science. But he holds that the world is bound to satisfy the very general concepts to which he gives the name of categories, they are imposed by us upon it as a prior condition of its being accessible to our understanding. But Kant leaves himself with nothing to say about the nature of things as they really are, so the distinction between things as they appear to us and things as they really are does not play an important part in Kant's system.

Then comes Hegel, who represents the history of the world as a spiritual progress, the necessary ascent of what he obscurely calls the Absolute Idea. According to Hegel, it is the business of Philosophy to know the world of nature and of human experience, to study and comprehend the reason in things, not their superficial, transitory and accidental forms, but their eternal essence, harmony and law. He says that things have a meaning, the processes in the world are rational, purposive, full of meaning, since reality is at bottom rational, a necessary, logical process of thoughts or notions, it can be known only by thought. Thus, the function of Philosophy is to understand the laws of necessary forms according to which reason operates. The universe is a process of involution, in which ends or purposes of universal reason are realized.

In this continuation, Hegel's English disciples, Bradley and MC Taggart retain the belief that reality is spiritual. Mc Taggart's view is that all reality is spiritual, and the composite parts of this spiritual reality are integrated selves. And what we misperceive as physical objects in spatio-temporal relations are really immaterial selves eternally contemplating one another with spiritual love. For Bradly, reality consists in the absolute, an undifferentiated whole of experience, which can be positively described only in the vaguest and most general terms, since any limited description, which abstracted only a part of it, would be false to its nature. He accepts that metaphysics is an attempt to know reality in contrast to mere appearance, or the study of first principles, or ultimate truths, or the effort to comprehend the universe, not simply piecemeal or by fragments, but somehow as whole. Man has an instinctive longing to reflect on ultimate truth, and to comprehend reality as adequately as his nature permits. Bradley regards the discursive intellect as incompetent to understand the world. By a critical examination of a number of typical ways of interpreting reality for example, in terms of relation and quality, space and time, substantive and objective, motion and change, causation and activity, and the self he reaches the negative result that they are self-contradictory. Bradley says that the things which we seem to perceive as spatio-temporally related have the degree of reality which occurred to them as appearances. They are not ultimately reals. Ayer says whatever may be in question is either real or not, there is no room for anything in between. So, it is not clear what does he mean by talking of degrees of reality. Ayer says it is plainly absured to say that space and time and matter are unreal. G.E. Moore points out that if these are unreal, it fallows that nothing ever changes or decays or grows, that a man's birth does not proceed his death, that nothing ever happens before or after anything else, that nothing ever moves, that a man's head is at no distance from his feet. If matter is unreal, then the stars, the sun and the earth and everything in it, including human beings themselves, are as mythical as unicorns or gorgons. If such theories are true, no body holds them. For, if matter is unreal, there are no metaphysicians, and if time is unreal, then no body ever makes a statement or acquires a belief. In the same way, if Zeno had been right in asserting that the concept of motion was self-contradictory, he could not have assert it, for whether he spoke or wrote, some part of his body would have had to move.

Thus we see that metaphysics plays a very important role in the history of Philosophy. And mostly, it is considered as the chief junction of Philosophy to search for the reality behind this perceptual world or for the transcendental truths. Therefore, to show that Philosophy has nothing to do with metaphysics, it needs a definition of Philosophy which should be in tune to some extent with the practice of Philosophers, and at the same time be accordant with the common assumption that Philosophy is a special branch of knowledge. Metaphysics does not satisfy this second condition so efforts are made to distinguish it from Philosophy: Though it is commonly reffered to as Philosophy. To show that Philosophy is a special branch of knowledge and metaphysics is not, this distinction is necessary.

We see that after making this distinction between them only, it can be made clear that what the function of Philosophy really is. Ayer tried to show that what exactly is the function of Philosophy. There are some view about it. Ayer takes them one by one and refutes them as the function of Philosophy.

There is a thought that it is the business of the Philosopher to construct a deductive system. Ayer does not say that deductive reasoning is of no use for a Philosopher or he can do his job without it. He accepts the utility of deductive reasoning for a Philosopher but he rejects the view that a

Philosopher has the right to posit certain first principles, and then offer them with their consequences as a complete picture of reality. To refuse this procedure, it is to show that there can be no such first principles. As these first principles provide a certain basis for our knowledge, they are not to be found among the so called laws of nature. Because the laws of nature are simple hypotheses which may be confuted by experience. Again these system-builders cannot choose inductive generalizations for their premises as these are merely probable. Here, Ayer talks about the system of Descartes. Descartes' aim is to find a body of certain and self-evident truths, such as everyone endowed with common-sense and the faculty of reasoning will accept. He feels that if such certain and self-evident truths can be discovered in philosophy as mathematics contains, like twice two is four, then there would be an end to countless dispute and controversies and it will be possible to prove the existence of God, the immortality of the soul, the reality of an external world and thus we may get success in laying secure foundations for the sciences. Descartes attempts to derive all human knowledge from premises whose truth is intuitively certain. Ayer says that probably Descartes realizes that a mere appeal to intuition is insufficient for his purpose, since all men are not ready to believe this, therefore Descartes tries to base all our knowledge on propositions which it would be self-contradictory to deny. Descartes thinks that he has found such a proposition in 'Cogito', which must not here be understood in its ordinary sense of 'I think', but rather as meaning 'there is a thought now'. Ayer says, in fact, he is wrong, because 'non cogito' would be self-contradictory only if it negated itself and no significant proposition can do this. But even if it is true that such a proposition as 'there is a thought now' is logically certain, it, still cannot serve Descartes' purpose. For if 'Cogito' is taken in this sense, his initial principle' 'Cogito ergo sum' is false. 'I exist' does not follow from 'there is a thought now.' The fact that a thought occurs at a given moment does not entail that any other thought has occurred at any other moment, still less that there has occurred a series of thoughts sufficient to constitute a single self. As Hume conclusively shows that no one event intrinsically points to any other. The existence of events, which are not actually being observed, are inferred with the help of general principles. But these principles must be obtained inductively. By mere deduction from what is immediately given one cannot advance a simple step beyond. And consequently, any attempt to base a deductive system on propositions which describe what is immediately given is bound to be a failure. Ayer says, if one still wishes to deduce all our knowledge from 'first principles', without indulging in metaphysics, the only other way for him is to take for his premises a set of a priori truths. But an a priori truth is a tautology and from a set of tautologies only further tautologies can be validly deduced. But it would be absurd to put forward a system of tautologies as constituting the whole truth about the universe. And thus it becomes clear that it is not possible to deduce all our knowledge from 'First-Principles'. Ayer says if someone still believes that, it means he is denying philosophy's claim to be a genuine branch of knowledge.

After it Ayer talks about the next conception. About Philosophy it is oftenly said that it is the study of reality as a whole. But this conception is not clear. If it is taken in the sense that philosopher has an ability to project himself outside the world and have a complete vision of it, then it is clearly a metaphysical conception. The special sciences gradually investigate the reality. They do it in stapes. They can't search it as a whole. There are some who assert that 'reality as a whole' is different from the reality explored in stages by these special sciences. But Ayer again considers it a metaphysical one. Ayer says, "But if the assertion that philosophy studies reality as a whole is understood to imply merely that the philosopher is equally concerned with the content of every science, then we may accept it, not indeed as an adequate definition of philosophy, but as a truth about it."[5]

Because when there is a discussion about the relationship

of philosophy to science, then philosophy, in principle, is not found to be related to any one science more closely than to any other.

Again, it is sometimes said that philosophy can be placed close by existing sciences, as a special department of speculative knowledge. Ayer means to rule out this supposition by saying that philosophy is concerned with each of the sciences in a certain way. There are some people who believe that there are some things in the world which lie beyond the domain of empirical science and are possible objects of speculative knowledge.They make this supposition. But this is a misbelief. There is no area of experience which cannot, in principle, be brought under some form of scientific law. And there is no type of speculative knowledge about the world which, it is, in principle, beyond the power of science to give.

Logical positivist disallows all philosophical questions about super-phenomenal reality on the ground of their meaninglessness. Yet Philosophy has a field of its own within the empirical sphere. It is not, as it may be supposed, the function of philosophy to piece together or synthesize the empirical results of the different branches of science into a world view, and thus play the proud role of the science of all sciences. Really these synthetic views are the work of poetic and aesthetic imagination, and do not admit of empirical verification, and do not, therefore, deserve to be called scientific or philosophical.

According to logical positivism, the function of philosophy is wholly critical. The question is, in what exactly does its critical activity consist? It may be said that it is the philosopher's business to test the validity of our scientific hypotheses and everyday assumptions. F. P. Ramsey says, "In philosophy we take the proposition we make in science and in everyday life, and try to exhibit them in a logical system with primitive terms and definitions, etc. essentially a philosophy is a system of definitions or, only too often, a system of descriptions of how definitions might be given".[6]

It represents a view of the subject. But this view, though

largely accepted, is mistaken. If a man decides to doubt the truth of all the Propositions he ordinarily believes, Philosophy has no such power to reassure him. Now, what Philosophy can do, apart from watching whether his beliefs are self-consistent, is to present the criteria which are used to determine the truth or falsehood of any given proposition. The sceptic realizes that his propositions can be verified by certain observations and he himself can make such observations and so consider his original beliefs to be justified. Here, philosophy only shows the role of experience to justify one's beliefs and it is not Philosophy which justifies his beliefs. Philosophy can just provide constituting sufficient evidence for the truth of any given empirical proposition.

Ayer talks about an another issue by saying that there is the superstition that natural science can not be regarded as logically respectable until philosophers have solved the problem of induction. The problem of induction is the problem of finding a way to prove that certain empirical generalalizations which are derived from past experience will hold good also in the future. It is first clearly posed by David Hume in his book 'A Treatise of Human Nature'. He says, "all reasoning concerning matters of fact seem to be founded on the relation of cause and effect." First he shows that the inference which is being put in question is not deductive. Then Hume says that since every effect is distinct from its cause, it cannot be logically contained within it. He denies that events can be connected by any relation of necessity which is not a logical relation. In other worlds, there is no such thing as natural necessity. If it is taken as a genuine problem then there are only two ways of approaching this problem. One may attempt to deduce the proposition which one is required to prove either from a purely formal principal or from an empirical principle. In the former case one commits the error of supposing that from a tautology it is possible to deduce a proposition about a matter of fact, in the latter case one simply assumes what one is setting out to prove. Thus, we find neither of these can lead to its solution. There are some who believe that 'uniformity of nature' or a 'principle of limited independent variety' justify induction. But, the principle of the uniformity of nature merely states misleadingly, the assumption that past experience is a reliable guide to the future, while the principle of limited independent variety presupposes it. In fact, any other empirical principle which is presented as a justification of induction fails in its purpose because such principles themselves are being believed on inductive grounds. Since all genuine problems have at least theoretical capability of being solved, the problem of induction is a fictitious problem because there is no possible solution of this problem. Actually, the only test of a scientific procedure is the test of its success in practice. As long as our procedure does the work which it is designed to do, that is, enables us to predict future experience, and so to control our environment, we can have faith in it. Of course there is no logical guarantee that it will continue to be so. But where such guarantee is logically impossible, there it is a mistake to demand such guarantee. And in spite of that, it is not irrational to expect future experience to conform to the past as 'being rational' for us entails being guided in a particular fashion by past experience.

Again, the task of defining rationality is clearly the sort of task that it is the business of philosophy to undertake, but in achieving this, it does not justify scientific procedure. A scientific procedure can be justified by the success of the predictions to which it gives rise, and this can be determined only in actual experience. By itself the analysis of a synthetic principle tells us nothing whatsoever about its truth. But the philosophers, concerned with the so-called theory of knowledge, generally overlook this fact. So, they commonly assume on the subject of perception that, unless one can give a satisfactory analysis of perceptual situations, one cannot believe in the existence of material things. But this is fallacious. One believes in the existence of a certain material thing because he gets certain sensations. We can say that the thing exists and we can say that such sensations are obtainable and it does not make any difference. Both are equivalent. And what a philosopher can do is to give a correct definition of material things in terms of sensations. But his success or failure in this task has no bearing whatsoever on the validity of our perceptual judgements. That depends wholly on actual sense-experience.

Ayer says it means that the philosopher does not have the right to despise the beliefs of common sense. If he does so, it means he does not know the true purpose of his inquiries.

Now, Ayer tells that if the philosopher claims to make a special contribution to the stock of our knowledge, he must not attempt to formulate speculative truths, or to look for first principles, or to make a priori judgements about the validity of our empirical beliefs. Ayer says, "He must, in fact, confine himself to works of clarification and analysis of a sort which we shall presently describe."[7]

Thus, Ayer shows that analysis is the function of philosophy. Wittgenstein says that philosophy is not one of the natural sciences. According to him, "All philosophy is "Critique of language".[8]

He says, "The object of Philosophy is the logical clarification of thoughts. Philosophy is not a doctrine but an activity. A philosophical work consists entirely of elucidations. The result of Philosophy is not a number of philosophical propositions, but to make propositions clear. Philosophy should make clear and delimit sharply the thoughts which otherwise are, as it were, apaque and blurred."[9]

F.P.Ramsey describes that, "Philosophy must be of some use and we must take it seriously, it must clear our thoughts and so our actions. Or else it is a disposition we have to check, and an inquiry to see that this is so, i.e., the chief proposition of philosophy is that philosophy is nonsense. And again we must then take seriously that it is nonsense, and not pretend, as Wittgenstein does, that it is important nonsense.

Ayer says that while the 'history of philosophy' contains some metaphysics, the majority of the great philosophers are primarily not metaphysicians but analysts. Ayer talks about locke that Locke, like G.E. Moore at the present time, puts forward a philosophy of common-sense. But he does not, any more than Moore, attempt to give an a priori justification of our common sense beliefs. He thinks that as a philosopher his business is only to analyse them. He says, "to be employed as an under labourer in clearing the ground a little, and removing some of the rubbish that lies in the way of knowledge." He devotes himself to the purely analytic task of defining knowledge, and classifying propositions, and displaying the nature of material things. The little of Locke which is not philosophical is not metaphysics, but psychology.

Again it is not fair to regard Berkeley as a metaphysician. He does not, in fact, deny the reality of material things but discovers that material things must be defined in terms of sense contents. Ayer says, "We know that it must be possible to define material things in terms of sense contents, because it is only by the occurrence of certain sense-contents that the existence of any material thing can ever be in the least degree verified".[10]

But in spite of this, unfortunately, Berkeley finds it necessary to postulate God as an unobservable cause of our 'ideas'. Again his conception of the nature of the self is not defendable.

Hume explicitly rejects metaphysics. Ayer says, "Hume does not, so far as I know, actually put forward any view concerning the nature of philosophical propositions themselves, but those of his works which are commonly accounted philosophical are, apart from certain passages which deal with questions of psychology, works of analysis." He has been accused of denying causation, whereas in fact he is concerned only with defining it. He lays the way open for the view that every assertion of a particular causal connexion involves the assertion of a causal law, that every general proposition of the form 'C cause E' is equivalent to the form 'whenever C, then E', 'whenever' refers to the infinite number of possible instances.

Ayer continues it by saying that when we consider Hobbes, Bentham and the best part of John Stuart Mill, we may claim that English empirical philosophy has been essentially analytic, while a more complete list of the analytic philosophers certainly include Plato, Aristotle and Kant.

Thus, efforts are made to prove that philosophy is totally independent of metaphysics. The critics suppose that the analytic method has a metaphysical foundation. They assume that, philosophical analysis is an activity of dissection, which finally shows that the whole universe is ultimately exhibited as an aggregate of 'bare particulars', united by external relations. But, Ayer says, this is a misleading concept.

Ayer says that Gestalt Psychologists talk about genuine wholes, in which the properties of every part depend to some extend on its position in the whole, but then it is an empirical fact that there exist genuine, or organic wholes. And if analytic method involved a denial of this fact, it would indeed be a faulty method. A philosopher, as an analyst, is not directly concerned with the physical properties of things. He is concerned only with the way in which we speak about them.

The propositions of philosophy are not factual, but linguistic in character, it can be said that philosophy is a branch of logic, concerned with the formal consequences of our definitions and not with questions of empirical fact. Therefore, Philosophical and scientific propositions can not conceivably contradict one another. The possibility of Philosophical analysis is independent of any empirical assumptions.

Ayer explains further that the propositions and questions which are really linguistic are often expressed in such a way that they appear to be factual and this fact creates a problem for the nature of analysis. A striking instance of this is the proposition that 'a material thing can not be in two places at once'. This looks like an empirical proposition, but critical inspection shows that it is actually linguistic. It simply records the fact that as a result of certain verbal conventions, the proposition that two sense contents occur in the same visual or tactual sense-field is incompatible with the proposition that they belong to the same material thing. And this is necessary fact. but it has not the least tendency to show that we have certain knowledge about the empirical propositions of objects.

Ayer tries to make it clear that philosophy is full of questions, which seem to be factual, but are not. Thus, to ask what is the nature of a material object is to ask for a definition of 'material object'. And this is to ask how propositions about material objects are to be translated into propositions about sense contents. Philosophical questions are requests for definition of a peculiar sort.

After that, Ayer says, although it is misleading to write about linguistic questions in factual language, it is often convenient for the sake of brevity. But it does not mean that the philosopher is engaged on an empirical or a metaphysical inquiry. We can say that he analyzes the facts, or notions, or even things. But these are just ways of saying that he is concerned with the definition of the corresponding words.

The systematic pursuit of the problem of meaning by means of a logical analysis of language distinguishes logical empiricism from the earlier, more psychologically oriented types of empiricism, Positivism and Pragmatism. The tradition they now represent has centered its chief inquiries around the two humble questions, "What do you mean?" and "How do you know? Runes writes, "The systematic pursuit of meaning by the Socratic method and the searching scrutiny of the foundations of knowledge are thus again declared the genuine task of philosophy, a task which differs from the quest for truth as carried on by science and yet is most intimately related to it.[11]

It is important to know that three disciplines are being developed to carry out this task of clarifying language and meaning. Pragmatics investigates the functions of language in its full biological, psychological and sociological setting. Here language in its relation to behaviour is the primary object of study. By two successive steps of abstraction the disciplines of semantics and syntax are arrived at Semantics analyzes the meaning of terms and expressions. Its studies center about the relation of designation and the concept of truth. While pragmatics is interested predominantly in the expression and appeal function of language, semantics explores the symbolic or representative aspect of language.

Syntax, finally, ignores even the meaning-relation and studies exclusively the connections of linquistic signs with each other. It systematizes the purely formal, structural rules for the formation of sentences and the transformation rules of logical derivation.

Granting that language as used in common life serves in a fusion or a combination of various functions, it seems imperative that some sort of theoretical separation of functions be undertaken for the sake of greater clarity and the avoidance of confusion. Again, many metaphysical "problems" and their "Solutions" depend upon the erroneous presumption of the presence of factual meaning in expressions which have only emotive appeals and/or a formally correct grammatical structure. And many an epistemological question has been obscured by mistaking logico-mathematical for factual meanings. The main contribution that philosophical reconstruction can make in this regard lies in the direction of an education toward maturer ways of thinking, thinking which possesses the virtues characteristic of science clarity and consistency, testability and adequacy, precision and objectivity.

Philosophical or logical analysis, in the sense of a clarification of the meaning of language, differs from philological analysis in at least three important respects. First, logical analysis concentrates on terms of basic importance for the representation of knowledge. The more general these terms the greater in the danger of various confusions due either to un-clarity in type of meaning or simply to vagueness or ambiguity of meaning. Hence the necessity and the value of such an analysis as a therapeutic measure. Second, the logical reconstruction is independent of the grammatical (and a fortiori the emotive) peculiarities of the specific language, living or lead, in question. Inasmuch as it is the cognitive meanings that we are interested in, idealized models, or in the extreme limit, an ideal language may be used. The tools developed in modern symbolic logic prove of utmost value for this purpose. Third, logical analysis is usually directed analysis. That is to say, it is either postulational codification (as in the mathematical and the exact empirical sciences) or epistemological reduction (the reconstruction of factual terms and propositions on a basis of observational evidence).

A characteristic difference between two types of procedure in logical analysis is worth observing. Wittgenstein, very much like G.E. Moore before him, and like the English analytic School on the whole, pursues the Socratic task in a Casuistic fashion, individual confusions are subjected to elucidation. It is the specific case that is treated, and the general theory of the treatment is not elaborated systematically. Carnap and his followers, on the other hand, proceeded with the development of a complete system, very much like whitehead and Russell in Principia Mathematica. A whole system is set up, and the theory of the machinery fully set forth. In the course of later developments this difference in procedure become associated with another one, in their choice of a basis for logical reconstruction. Wittgenstein, followed by Schlick, Waisman, and others, remained experientialistic, whereas Neurath, Carnap, Hempel and others become physicalistic.

"Throughout its history, philosophy has been the particular stronghold of verbal magic. By purely verbal means it has tried to explain things which only science could explain or which can not be explained at all. In the process it creates its own perplexities, and at its worst it attempts the "Solution" of these Pseudo-Problems, Problems arising only out of linguistic confusion, by means of Pseudo-techniques, more verbal magic. Analysis teaches us that all this is altogether unnecessary. Thus, Philosophy can be defined as the disease of which it should be the cure."[12]

References

1. A.J.Ayer, 'The Principle of Verifiability' an article in 'Essential Readings in Logical Positivism', Ed. by Oswald Hanfling, p. 60.
2. 'Twentieth Century Philosophy', Ed. by Dagobert D. Runes, p. 375.
3. A.J. Ayer, 'The Central questions of Philosophy', p. 8.

4. Leibniz, 'A Letter of Queen Charlotte of Prussia', 1702, p. 150.
5. A.J. Ayer, 'Language, Truth and Logic', p. 32.
6. F.P. Ramsey, 'The Foundations of mathematics', p. 263.
7. A.J. Ayer, 'Language, Truth and Logic', p. 37.
8. L. Wittgenstein, 'Tractatus-Logico-Philosophicus' 4-0031.
9. Ibid, 4.112.
10. A.J.Ayer, 'Language, Truth and Logic', p. 39.
11. 'Twentieth Century Philosophy', Ed. by Dagobert D. Runes, p. 376.
12. Ibid, p. 376.

4

The Nature of Philosophical Analysis

In the 'Tractatus', Wittgenstein says, "The right method of Philosophy would be this" To say nothing except what can be said, i.e. the propositions of natural science, i.e. something that has nothing to do with philosophy : and then always, when someone else wished to say something metaphysical to demonstrate to him that he had given no meaning to certain signs in his propositions. This method would be unsatisfying to the other-he would not have the feeling that we were teaching him philosophy- but it would be the only strictly correct method.'

In this Chapter, we shall see How Ayer and other positivists give the accounts of the nature of analysis. As we have seen that according to the logical positivists, analysis is a legitimate and, moreover, valuable activity without making any metaphysical statements. And on a great deal there is virtual unanimity amongst the positivists.

Logical positivists, like Hume, claim that all legitimate uses of language are either synthetic and a posteriori, i.e. empirical, or are tautologies. The empirical propositions are those of the natural sciences, understood to include the factual statements of everyday life, the tautologies are typically what we meet in the exact sciences, such as mathematics. Wittgenstein says, and the logical positivists agree that there are no special propositions of Philosophy, metaphysical or otherwise. Philosophy is not a science alongside the natural sciences. Therefore, the philosopher does not make empirical statements. Again analysis does not consist of empirical statements. The form of an analysis is the assertion of an equivalence between two expressions ; for examples, it can be said that "The present king of France is bald" is equivalent to 'There is one and only one thing which, & C'. But a statement of an equivalence is, if correct, a tautology, if incorrect, a contradiction. So, if a philosopher sticks to making analyses, he will avoid either infringing on the preserves of natural sciences or attempting to make a special sort of philosophical statement. Philosophy is therefore to be identified with analysis. Analysis is the one and only legitimate activity of philosophy.

J.O. Urmson writes, "The metaphysics of logical atomism and the conception of analysis which went with it had been complementary Roughly, the metaphysics had been the justification of the method of analysis, and the metaphysics had in turn determined the exact nature of the ideal to which analysis had to conform."[1]

It is always obscurely felt that analysis, which overtly consists in replacing one forms of words by another with the same meaning, is a proper philosophical pursuit, and that there is good reason for Preferring one form of words to another. But before that here come such questions as why analysis should be done? Why analysis is a proper pursuit? And then why one form of words is preferable to another? And then we can see the difference between these to thoughts. The logical atomist gives the justification that his analyses, if correct, has the verbal form of equivalence, but he says that the point of it is analysis of fact, the clarification of the structure and interrelationships of facts, and thus of the world. The new form of words better picture the structure of reality. But the logical positivists do not accept this. They can't give such an answer. According to them, Philosophy is the analysis and clarification of language as such, or, since the purpose of a language is that we may make scientific statements, the clarification of the language of science.

Ramsey explains the method of philosophy by saying that, "In philosophy we take the propositions we make in science and in everyday life, and try to exhibit them in a logical system with primitive terms and definitions, etc. Essentially a philosophy is a system of definitions, or, only too often, a system of descriptions of how definitions might be given.[2]

Of the alternatives that Ramsey offers, Ayer chooses the one in which philosophy is required to furnish definitions. He says, "It represents a view of the subject which was then coming into fashion and one that I adopted wholeheartedly."[3]

But this assertion that the function of Philosophy is to provide definitions does not show that it is the job of the Philosopher to compile a dictionary. Ayer takes philosophical analysis to consist mainly, if not exclusively, in the provision of what he calls 'definition in use.' Such definitions are contrasted with what he calls 'explicit definitions', such as one might find in a dictionary. He says, "We define a symbol explicitly when we put forward another symbol, or symbolic expression which is synonymous with it. And the word "synonymous" is here used in such a way that two symbols belonging to the same language canbe said to be synonymous if, and only if, the simple substitution of one symbol for the other, in any sentence in which either can significantly occur, always yields a new sentence which is equivalent to the old."[4]

The vast majority of the definitions which are given in ordinary discourse are explicit definitions. The process of defining 'Per genus et differentiam', to which Aristotelian logicians devote so much attention, always yields definitions which are explicit in the foregoing sense. As an example of an explicit definition, Ayer gives the difinition of 'oculist' as 'eye-doctor'. Thus, when an oculist is defined as an eye-doctor, it is being asserted that, in English, the two symbols 'oculist' and 'eye-doctor' are synonymous. But the philosopher is primarily concerned with the provision of definitions in use. Ayer says, "We dêfine a symbol in use, not by saying that it is synonymous with some other symbol, but by showing how the sentences in which it significantly occurs can be translated into equivalent sentences, which contain neither the definiendum itself, nor any of its synonyms."[5]

As an example of a definition in use, he gives Russell's theory of definite description, which purports to show how sentences containing referring phrases of the form 'the so-and-so' can be translated into sentences which do not employ such phrases or anything synonymous.

Thus the sentence 'The author of waverley was Scotch" is equivalent to 'one person, and one person only, wrote waverley, and that person was Scotch', and 'The round Square can not exist' is equivalent to 'No one thing can be both square and round'. These examples show us how to express what is expressed by any sentence which contains a definite descriptive phrase without employing any such phrase. And thus they furnish us with a definition of these Phrases in use.

In both cases, when Ayer speaks of two sentences as 'equivalent' he means, in effect, 'inter-deducible', though he expresses this in a more complicated way. He says,

> ".....we say that two sentences of the same language are equivalent if, and only if, every sentence which is, entailed by any given group of sentences in conjunction with one of them is entailed by the same group in conjunction with the other. And, in this usage of the word "entail", a sentence 's' is said to entail a sentence 't' when the proposition expressed by 't' is deducible from the proposition expressed by 's."

It might be objected that the author must already understand the sentences in order to be able to define the symbols which occur in them. But this initial understanding need not amount to anything more than an ability to tell, in practice, what sort of situations verify the propositions they express. Such an understanding of sentences containing definite descriptive phrases may be possessed even by those who believe that there are subsistent entities, such as the round square, or the Present king of France. Ayer says, "But the fact that they do maintain this shows that their understanding of these sentences is imperfect. for their lapse into metaphysics is the outcome of the naive assumption that definite descriptive phrases are demonstrative symbols."[6]

But this assumption is false. Nor can this end be achieved by an explicit definition of any descriptive phrase. Ayer says, "It is the purpose of a philosophical definition to dispel those confusions which arise from our imperfect understanding of certain types of sentences in our language, where the need can not be met by the provision of a synonym for any symbol, either because there is no synonym, or else because the available synonyms are unclear in the same fashion as the symbol to which the confusion is due."

John Foster writes, "Ayer thinks that philosophy is primarily concerned with the provision not of explicit definitions, but of definitions in use. One reason for this is that he takes a somewhat narrow, and surely a too narrow, view of what explicit definition can be expected to achieve."[7]

Thus, in considering such definitions, he focuses his attention exclusively on the sort of example we find in dictionaries, like that of 'oculist' meaning 'eye-doctor, and obviously it is not his sort of definition which it is the concern of Philosophy to provide. Again Foster says that, "He seems to forget that explicit definitions can also be of a deep and, so to speak, philosophically Pregnant kind, ones which express or reflect the resolution of philosophical issues."[8]

And, in the case of terms expressing philosophically crucial concepts, the quest for such definitions surely does constitute a major concern of analytical philosophy.

But we can see his own analysis of factual knowledge in his later book 'The Problem of knowledge' furnishes an example, for the analysis, in effect, yields an explicit definition of 'knows that' as 'has the true and justified conviction that'.

But probably the main reason why Ayer downgrades the

importance of explicit definition is that it is definitions in use which he particularly needs in the kind of analyses which most concern him, that is, in the reductive analyses which bring ordinary and scientific assertions in line with the requirements of the content-principle. For in all these analyses the move from 'analysandum' to 'analysans' involves a change in ontological perspective : sentences which are nominally about one class of objects (objects which are not directly observable) are translated into sentences about some other class of objects (objects which are directly observable).

Thus what leads Ayer to seek an analysis of our physical terminology is that, because, on the face of it, the entities which form the ontological subject matter of Physical discourse are external to, and logically independent of, the realm of sense-experience, it seems that the factual content of physical statements is not purely observational and that, consequently, such statements would not be factually significant under the strong version of the verification principle which he accepts. Clearly, this problem can not be met by providing synonymous expressions for each physical term, since by being synonymous, such expressions would preserve the original ontology. What is needed is an analysis in which all references to, and quantifications over, physical entities are eliminated, that is, an analysis which shows how sentence about physical entities are equivalent to sentences (or perhaps infinite truth-functional complexes of sentences) about something else. It is because such an analysis involves this change in ontological perspective that we think of it as, in a distinctive sense, 'reductive' (though an analysis which preserves the original ontology, but involves a sufficiently radical change in 'ideological' perspective, will also count as reductive).

Thus the old activity of analysis can go on undisturbed. Positivist maintains that Hume in his analysis of causation, Berkeley in his analysis of physical objects, even Plato in his analysis of knowledge in the Theaetetus do philosophy as the positivists conceive it, even if they make mistakes of comparitive detail in so doing and give a wrong account of what they do. The business is still the old reductive analysis, even if it is under new management.

Urmson Says, "Not merely is a new rationale of analysis being given, but the new talk, when doing analysis, is of words, sentences, and the like-is talk about language, whereas the old analysis used metaphysical pseudo-concepts such as 'thing', 'fact' and the like. It was nonsensical, surely, according to the new regime, and that indicates a big difference."[9]

Ayer notes that, equivalence, as he defines it, does not guarantee sameness of meaning in the ordinary sense. But he seems to think that if two equivalent sentences do differ in meaning, the difference is merely one of psychological effect and something which the philosopher can afford to ignore. He says, "It is possible for two sentences to be equivalent, by our criterion, without having the same effect on anyone who employees the language........... Accordingly, one should avoid saying that philosophy is concerned with the meaning of symbols, because the ambiguity of "meaning" leads the undiscerning critic to judge the result of a philosophical enquiry by a criterion which is not applicable to it, but only to an empirical enquiry concerning.... Psychological effect.... Such empirical enquiries are quite distinct from the logical enquiries which constitute philosophy."[10]

Now Ayer is clearly right in claiming that philosophical analysis need not preserve meaning in that Psychological sense, the sense in which he believes that the term is most commonly used. Where he goes wrong is in supposing that equivalence is enough. For example, we look for a set-theoretical analysis of arithmetical concepts and formulate rules for translating arithmetical sentences into equivalent sentences about sets-yielding the translation-manual T and we suppose that T meets all the intuitive requirements for analysis. Now, we consider the alternative manual T^1 which is exactly like T except that it reverses the translations of '2+2=4' and '9x7=63'. Since these two arithmetical sentences are analytically true, they are also equivalent to each other in Ayer's sense and thus equivalent to their new translations given their equivalence to the old. Consequently, if equivalence is all that is required for a successful analysis, T^1 serves as well as T. But obviously it does not. For given the difference in meaning between the two arithmetical sentences, it cannot be the case that the original translations and the reverse translations serve the purposes of analysis equally well. And since we have assumed the adequacy of T, we must infer the defectiveness of T^1. And as the arithmetical example shows, it certainly is not enough in cases where the sentences to be translated are analytically true or analytically false. Nor, in fact, is the point restricted to analytic sentences. The three synthetic sentences 'There is a table in this room', 'if 2+2=4, there is a table in this room' and 'If there is not a table in this room, 1+1=3' are equivalent. But it can hardly be said that, for the purposes of analysis, a good translation of one would be an equally good translation of all.

Still, for the purposes for which Ayer needs an analysis of ordinary and Scientific discourse, Ayer has to show that, contrary to initial appearances, certain sentences have factual significance under the content Principle. To show this, it suffices to show that these sentences are equivalent to sentences whose factual significance under that principle is already established. For, since equivalence is transitive and since a sentence is purely observational, if and only if, it is equivalent to a sentence, or to an infinite truth-functional complex of sentences, in an observational language, then obviously if two sentences are equivalent and one is purely observational, the other is purely observational too. So, Ayer's requirements for analysis are sufficient for his particular purposes.

It is important to know here that Ayer's Position with respect to physical statements is that of linguistic phenomenalism—the view that such statements are equivalent to experiential statements and the point of his analysis is to elaborate that position. But he does not offer a definition-in-use for every physical term or formulate rules of translation covering every type of physical statement. Rather, he contents himself with offering what he describes as an 'analysis of the notion of a material thing'.[11] And clearly Ayer regards this limited analysis as sufficing to vindicate his Phenomenalist Position and as indicating the general lines which an exhaustive analysis will take.

Linguistic Phenmenolism claims that statements about physical objects can be translated into equivalent statements about sense data, where the later statements make no explicit reference to Physical entities and are entirely devoid of any distinctively physical vocabulary. It also claims that the concepts employed in sensory statements are more basic than the physical concepts employed in the statements they translate, so that we are to see the rules of translation into the Phenomenal language as constituting an exhaustive analysis of physical concepts in sensory terms. If we want fully to understand the content of a physical statement, it is to its sensory translation that we must turn.

Now, we must know what these sense data are ? These sense data have some characteristic features, which are- that sense data are, in Pitcher's Phrase, 'ontologically distinct' from material objects or from their surfaces, that they are private to the individual who has them as part of his sensory field and that they are immediately or directly present to consciousness.

D.J. O' Connor writes that there are certain claims about sense data as-sense data are the atoms or building blocks of our sense experience, they are known directly and immediately in contrast to Physical objects which are hypothetical and problematic. Some times such claims are linked with a method of philosophical analysis.

According to O' Connor, it can always be said that in using the identifying mode of language one is identifying (or at least purporting to identify) a part of the physical world. But what he is describing may often be something which is patently not an item of the material world at all— an after image, a dream, the content of an hallucination, or some other demonstrably maverick inhabitant of a sensory field.

Ayer suggests that to accept the theory of sense data 'involves nothing more than a decision to use a technical language.' To believe in sense data does not commit us to accepting a new range of entities over and above the ordinary inhabitants of the world, it commits as merely to using a terminology in our talk about perceiving, that is, philosophically less troublesome than more ordinary ways of talking.

Again it can be said that sense data are genuine items of experience. But if they really are such, why is there any need of argument to establish their existence? The answer is that the argument is not needed to show that there are really such things but to show that certain recognisable features of our experience have properties which require these features to be emphasized as philosophically important.

Ayer says that interpretation of language depends on the 'meaning' ascribed to its symbols. It is possible for two sentences to be equivalent, by his criterion, without having the same effect on anyone who employs the language. For instance, 'P is a law of nature' is equivalent to 'P is a general hypothesis which can always be relied on' but the assertions of the symbol 'law' are such that the former sentence gives rise to belief in an orderly power 'behind' nature. This, Ayer suspects, accounts for the widespread reluctance to admit that the laws of nature are merely hypothesis, just as the failure of some philosophers to recognize that material things are reducible to sense-contents is very largely due to the psychological effect of the term 'material thing'.

Accordingly, Ayer says, one should avoid saying that philosophy is concerned with the meaning of symbols, because the ambiguity of their 'meaning' on different groups of people. But the deduction of relations of equivalence from the rules of language is a purely logical activity, and it is in this logical activity that philosophical analysis consists.

Ayer says that a complete philosophical elucidation of any language consists in enumerating the types of sentence significant in that language, and then displaying the relations of equivalence that held between sentences of various types.

But this is made complicated in language such as English by the prevalence of ambiguous symbols. for example- 'is' in the sentence 'He is the author of that book' is the same as that in 'A cat is a mammal'. But when these sentences are translated, the first is equivalent to 'He, and no one else, wrote that book', and the second to 'the class of mammals contains the class of cats.' 'IS' is an ambiguous symbol for existence, class membership, identity and entailment.

Again Ayer raises a question. "is there any problem about the meaning of such sentences as "This is an inkstand" or "Hens lay eggs". He takes these two of Moore's examples. Surely there is no difficulty about defining 'inkstand' or hens' or 'eggs' or the verb 'to lay'. The dictionary does it quite adequately. It is not in that sense that we do not know what is meant by the sentence in which these words occur.

Ayer says we do not know how to analyse these sentences. We know what is meant by the English Sentence 'This is an ink-stand', but we don't know what its correct analysis is. But how does 'knowing the analysis' differ from 'knowing the meaning'? Due to moore, there is a distinction, but he never explains it properly. One example is that 'brothers are male sibbilings' which one can certainly learn from a dictionary. The question what brothers are is not of any Philosophical interest, what is of philosophical interest is the more general question-how to interpret statements of identity, and how it comes about that they are not trivial. And here consulting the dictionary is not helpful.

Again the dictionary will not be helpful when it comes to analyzing sentences like, 'This is an inkstand'. And this not only because the inkstand is not appearing in its own right but merely as a specimen of a physical object. For looking up the dictionary definition of a physical object will not be of any use either. Ayar explains that when Moore asks for the analysis of sentences like 'This is an inkstand' Moore raises the question how physical objects are related to the sense data which he thinks that the demonstratives in such sentences are used to designate.

But there a great difference takes place between knowing

the meaning of the sentence and knowing its analysis. Again there is a question how to sense data get into the picture? What is going to count as a satisfactory analysis of sentences expressing perceptual judgments is a way of reformulating them which will show how these judgments can be known to be true. Thus sense data are brought in because of Moore's assumption that it is only through being presented with some sense datum that one can even know of the existence of a physical object.

Again to say that a symbol is constituted by signs, and that a sign is a sense-content, or a series of sense-contents, is not to say that a symbol is a collection, or system of sense-contents. For when we speak of certain objects b,c,d.......... as being elements of an object e, and of e as being constituted by b, c, d .... we are not saying that they form part of e. What we are saying is that all the sentences in which the symbol e occurs can be translated into sentences which do not contain e itself, or any symbol which is synonymous with e, but do contain symbols b, c, d........... In such a case it is said that e is a logical construction out of b, c, d........... The introduction of symbols which denote logical constructions is a device which enables us to state complicated propositions about the elements of these constructions in a relatively simple form.

Ayer explains that these logical constructions are not fictitious. While it is true that the English state, for example, is a logical construction out of individual people, and this table is a logical construction out of sense contents, it is not true that either the English State or this table are fictitious, in the sense in which hamlet or a mirage is fictitious. The assertion that tables are logical constructions out of sense contents is not a factual assertion at all, but it is a linguistic assertion, to the effect that the symbol 'table' is definable in terms of certain symbols which stand for sense contents, not explicitly, but in use. (But this does not mean that to say something about a table is ever to say the same thing about the relevant sense contents). The sentence 'I am now sitting in front of a table' can, in principle, be translated into a sentence which does not mention tables, but only sense-contents. But this does not mean that one can simply substitute a sense-content symbol for the symbol 'table' in the original sentence. If one does this, the new sentence, so for from being equivalent to the old, will be a mere piece of nonsense. To obtain a sentence which is equivalent to the sentence about the table, but refers to sense contents instead, the whole of the original sentence has to be altered.

Material things are logical construction out of sense contents. The problem of 'reduction' of material things to sense-contents, is the main philosophical part of the traditional problem of perception. According to O' Connor, as a matter of history the problem of perception have been important problems for nearly all those Philosophers who would consider themselves to be empiricists. And sense datum theories of perception have been central to the empiricist tradition.

According to Ayer, to think that 'what is the nature of a material thing' is a factual question, is just committing a mistake. Because it is a linguistic question, being a demand for a definition. And the propositions which are set forth in answer to it are linguistic propositions, they are about the relationship of symbols, and not about the properties of the things which the symbols denote. To speak about material thing is, a way of speaking about sense contents as each of us 'constructs' material things out of sense contents, and the relationship between the two sorts of symbols is revealed by showing what are the principles of this 'construction'. Or the answer to the question, 'what is the nature of a material thing?' can be given by indicating what are the relations that must hold between any two of one's sense contents for them to be elements of the same material thing. Ayer remarks, "Philosophical problems are not settled simply by our taking care that they should not arise. If the introduction of sense-data is permissible, then there exists a problem about the way in which they are related to physical objects. If this question can be raised, it is philosophically entitled to an answer."[12]

The solution of this 'Problem of perception services as a further illustration of the method of Philosophical analysis. Ayer begins his account with four preliminary definitions which are stipulative rather than analytical and are intended to provide a convenient terminology for the subsequent analysis. The relations defined are those of direct and indirect resemblance and of direct and indirect continuity. Two sense contents are said to directly resemble each other 'when there is either no difference, or only an infinitesimal difference, of quality between them' and to indirectly resemble each other 'when they are linked by a series of direct resemblances, but are not themselves directly resemblant. Likewise, two visual, or two tactual, sense-contents are said to be directly continuous 'when they belong to successive members of a series of actual, or possible, sense-fields, and there is no difference, or only an infinitesimal difference, between them, with respect to the position of each in its own sense-field' and to be indirectly continuous 'when they are related by an actual, or possible, series of such direct continuities.'

By way of explanation, he adds,

> "...to say of a sense experience, or sense field which is a part of a sense - experience, or a sense-content which is a part of a sense field that it is possible, as opposed to actual, is to say .... that it would occur if certain specifiable conditions were fulfilled. So when it is said that a material thing is constituted by both actual and possible sense - contents, all that is being asserted is that the sentences referring to sense contents, which are the translation of the sentences referring to any material thing, are both categorical and hypothetical. And thus the notion of a possible sense - content, or sense - experience, is as unobjectionable as the familiar notion of a hypothetical statement.

Having defined his terms, Ayer now takes the first and most cricuial step of his phenomenalistic analysis.

> "..................one may assert with regard to any two of one's visual sense-contents, or with regard to any two of one's tactual sense-contents, that they are elements of the same material thing if, and only if, they are related to one another by a relation of direct, or indirect, resemblance in certain respects, and by a relation of direct, or indirect, continuity."[13]

In connection with this he notes that since the two relations of direct-or-in direct resemblance and direct-or-indirect continuity are both symmetric and transitive, the definition ensures that 'no visual, or tactual, sense-content can be an element of more than one material thing.'

This is a consequence which he clearly regards as desirable.

Foster says that, "So far, the relation of being elements of the same material thing has only been defined for visual and tactual sense-contents taken separately. The definition divides visual sense-contents into same-thing groups and tactual sense-contents into same-thing groups, but it does not tell us what it is for two groups, drawn from different modalities, to belong to the same material thing.

> Ayer's next step supplies the answer, he says, "...........any two of one's visual and tactual groups belong to the same material thing when every element of the visual group which is of minimal visual depth forms part of the same sense-experience as an element of the tactual group which is of minimal tactual depth.

By the way of explanation, he adds,

> "We cannot here define visual or factual depth otherwise than ostensively. The depth of a visual or tactual sense-content is as much a sensible property of it as its length or breadth. But we may describe it by saying that one visual or tactual sense-content has a greater depth than another when it is farther from the observer's body, provided that we make it clear that this is not intended to be a definition.

It, can not be a definition, since, obviously, the concepts of physical distance and body cannot be primitive in the Phenomenalystic analysis. There is still, of course, no provision for the assignment of sense-contents from other sense-modalities to material things. But this can be done, Ayer thinks, 'by reference to their association with tactual sense-contents.'[14]

He says, "Thus, we assign sense-contents of taste to the same material things as the simultaneously occurring sense contents of touch, which are experienced by the palate, or the tongue. And in assigning an auditory or olfactory sense-content to a material thing, we remark that it is a member of a possible series of temporarily continuous sounds, or smells, of uniform quality but gradually increasing intensity, the series, namely, which one would ordinarily be said to experience in the course of moving towards the place from which the sound, or the smell, came, and we assign it to the same material things as the tactual sense-content which is experienced at the same time as the sound, or the smell, of maximum intensity in the series.

But Foster assumes that this procedure is not indented to be full-proof. For obviously, it would fail in certain cases, when one is moving towards some physical sound source of constantly diminishing intensity and where the diminishing of the intensity more than counterbalances the increasing proximity.

Ayer's final step is that' the provision of a rule for translating sentences which refer to the "real" qualities of material things.' The need for such a rule arises from the fact that the sensible appearance of a material object varies with the conditions of observation and this variation is not thought to involve any change in the object's intrinsic character. Thus the same coin, with presumably constant intrinsic shape, looks round when observed from certain viewpoints and elliptical when observed from others, and the same flower, with presumably constant intrinsic colour, looks white when observed at mid day but pink when observed at sunset.

Given such variation in sensible appearance, how is the notion of the 'real' (intrinsic) qualities of an object to be analysed in phenomenal terms? Ayer's answer is that "............to say of a certain quality that it is the real quality of a given material thing is to say that it characterizes those elements of the thing which are the most conveniently measured of all the elements which possess qualities of the kind in question. Thus, when I look at a coin and assert that it is really round in shape, I am not asserting that the shape of the sense-content, which is the element of the coin that I am actually observing, is round, still less that the shape of all the visual, or tactual, elements of the coin is round, what I am asserting is that roundness of shape characteries those elements of the coin which are experienced from the point of view from which measurements of shape are most conveniently carried out."[15]

In conclusion, Ayer notes that 'we define relations of quality, or position, between material thing, in terms of the relations of quality, or position, which obtain between such "Privileged" elements, i.e. elements which reveal the 'real' qualities of material things according to the specified criterion.

This then is, Ayer's 'analysis of the notion of a material thing'. The analysis is not intended to be an exhaustive elaboration of the phenomealist position. For, Ayer cannot suppose that he has provided, in any explicit form, a general procedure for translating physical statements into Phenomenal statements. In effect, all Ayer attempts to do is to specify some of the basic ways in which sense-experience can be organized in a Physically significant fashion (e.g. how a series of appropriately related sense-contents counts as the successive presentations of the same material object), in the hope that a translation-procedure, or specific procedures for specific types of physical statements, can be worked out on this basis. But he seems to think that, in its basic aspects, the physical organization of sense-experience can be phenomenally specified in very simple terms. And this is not so, as Ayer himself came to recognize in his later writings.

The most crucial part of the analysis is the initial step,

in which Ayer defines what it is for two sense-contents, which are either both visual or both tactual, to be elements of the same material thing. It is the most crucial part because it provides the initial bridge between the Phenomenal and the physical realms. The rest of the analysis has a chance of succeeding only if this bridge holds firm.

Now we look carefully at what the definition states, namely, that two visual, or tactual, sense contents are elements of the same material thing if, and only if, they directly or indirectly resemble each other in certain respects and are directly or indirectly continuous. But it is defective in at least two ways, each relating to the insufficiency of the (Phenomenal) definiens for the (Physical) definiendum.

The first defect is that it takes no account of hallucination. Hallucinatins are possible and even a Phenomenalist accepts that they actually occur. A phenomenalist says that a hallucination is an experience which is radically anomalous with respect to the overall theme in the experiences of the individual or the community. Now, if an experience is hallucinatory, its sense-contents are not, in Ayer's sense, elements of any material things. For, obviously a sense-content will only form an element of a material thing in the Phenomenalist's sense if there is some material thing which, the subject is (qua recipient of that sense content) perceiving. Two hallucinatory sense-contents (or two sense-contents one of which is hallucinatory) cannot be elements of the same material thing. But there is nothing to prevent their standing in relations of direct (or indirect) resemblance and direct (or indirect) continuity. But if two hallucinatory sense-contents stand in these relations, without being elements of any material thing, then they satisfy Ayer's definies without satisfying the definiendum.

The second defect is that, even within the domain of veridical experience, two sense-contents, which are elements of different material things may stand in the requisite relations. This problem, of course, stems from Ayer's use of the phrase 'in certain respects' to qualify the requirement of direct or indirect resemblance. But perhaps what Ayer means is that the resemblance must hold in all respects applicable to sense contents of the relevant type.

Ayer's analysis, then, is seriously flawed in its initial and most crucial step. And it is also flawed in its subsequent steps, as we shall see. In order to construct material objects with both visual and tactual properties, Ayer asserts that a same thing group of visual sense-contents and a same thing group of tactual sense-contents belong to the same material thing when every element of the former group which is of minimal visual depth forms part of the same sense-experience as an element of the latter group which is of minimal tactual depth. Here the difficulty is in even understanding what Ayer means by 'tactual depth'. His only explanation is that while visual and tactual depth are, as sensible qualities, only ostensively definable. Then can be said that a sense-content has greater senisible depth when it is farther from the observer's body. But in the case of tactual depth, this is not helpful. Presumably, to make sense of it at all, 'the body' should be taken as referring not to the whole body, but some main portion of it, probably thehead or trunk, since otherwise every tactual sense-content will turn out to be of minimal depth.

Again there is an objection. Here it is said that if Ayer is allowed this notion of tactual depth, his account of how visual and tactual groups are to be correlated is clearly erroneous. According to Foster, two groups may belong to the same material thing without satisfying the specified conditions. Foster gives a situation that, "I may first look at an object without touching it and then, closing my eyes, touch it without seeing it. In such a case the two groups would belong to the same material thing without any element in one being part of the same experience as any element in the other", though he is not sure whether this counts as a further objection to Ayer's thesis. For it is possible that Ayer only intends his specified conditions to be sufficient but not necessary, after all, he only says that two groups belong to the same material thing when, he does not say 'when and only when', these conditions obtain. So, Foster says that unless he intends the conditions to be both sufficient and necessary, this phase in his analysis of the notion of a material thing will be crucially incomplete.

Then, we see in the final step of his analysis, Ayer turns to the question of how we determine the 'real' qualities of a material thing, given that its sensible appearance varies with the conditions of observations. His answer is, that, with respect to each category of qualities (e.g. shape or colour), the member of this category which 'really' characterizes the material object is the one which the object manifests in those conditions in which qualities of that category are most conveniently measured. Thus, a coin is really circular, despite looking elliptical from certain (i.e, the oblique) viewpoints, because it looks circular from that (the frontal) viewpoint from which measurements of shape are most conveniently carried out. But again Ayer's position here is difficult to understand. In what sense is it more convenient to measure shape from one viewpoint unless we already know, independently of the convenience-criterion, that this is the viewpoint from which, uniquely, real and apparent shape coincide? Perhaps what Ayer has in mind is that from a frontal viewpoint, more shape-discriminations can be made, since the apparent shapes cover a larger portion of the visual field. This is in line with how the interprets his criterion in the case of colour, "........I assert that the real colour of the paper on which I am writing is white, even though it may not always appear to be white, because whiteness of colour characterised those visual elements of the paper which are experienced in the conditions in which the greatest discrimination of colours is possible."[16]

But, Foster says that it is hardly a matter of 'convenience of measurement' in any ordinary sense. He further says that "the real qualities are those which take their place in the best overall explanation of experience. Other factors, such as discrimination, are only relevant as corollaries. And, as far as I can see, convenience of measuremet, as ordinarily understood, has no relevance at all."

Thus we can see that Fostr does not find Ayer's analysis much satisfactory even from its own Phenomenalystic standpoint.

Connor says that the belief that our sensory information about the material world is direct and immediate is, in one sense, obviously justified in normal perception. As Ayer says, "The next step, continuing with our example, is to convert the sentence 'it now seems to me that I see a Cigarette Case,' into 'I am not seeing a seeming-cigarette case'. These seeming-objects are sense- data, and the conclusion may be more simply expresed by saying that it is always sense-data that are directly perceived.

But the Scientific Picture does raised serious dobuts about saying that normal sense perceiption is normal and immediate in an unqualified sense of the phrase. For to say that such events or processes are direct and immediate is surely to imply that there are no other hidden events and processes that are necessary intermediate stages between, say, opening my eyes and seeing what is before me. But the Scientific Picture shows that there are very complex and detailed intermediaries of this sort. So that it may be claimed that it is well established that in an accepted sense of the words our perception of the external world is rjar from direct and intermediate. But this consideration gives no ground for distinguishing between the visual field and the visual world in this respect. Sense-data are, in this sense, no more directly and immediately given than are the objects of the visual world.

But the scientific account of sense perception has further consequences. The first is that electrical processes in the nervous system are necessary, and in certain states, also sufficient conditions for the sensory experience. Our consciousness of a vivid dream or of the phenomena of a drug-induced hallucination requires no external stimulation of sense organs but only the internal activation of nervous mechanisms. No doubt such states present us with sensory fields which are both totally distinct from the objects of the external world and at the same time private to the observer.

But it may be said, they are both untypical and parasitic on our normal sensory transactions with the world of material objects. Without the normal states, we can hardly have the abnormal ones.

In ordinary sense-experience, nervous activity is necessary but not sufficient to produce a sense field. If such conditions are being listed that are individually necessary and jointly sufficient to produce a visual field, there must be included electromagnetic radiation of certain restricted wavelenghts reflected into the eye, a transparentmedium, an eye of normal efficiency, an intact optic nerve and so on. All of these are integrated into a causal process whose end product is the visual field. This end product is the final effect of the series of causes that are its necessary and sufficient conditions. If this conclusion is accepted, it is clear that visual sense data satisfy the two conditions of privacy and non-identity with the object that have traditonally been accorded to them.

But professor Mundle has an objection to this arguent. He says that it 'confuses the mechanism on which the prception is dependent with the objects that are perceived."[17]

Mr. Don Locke adds, "The theory is that stimulation of the retina, etc., produces a visual percepts in our minds, but quite obviously what these processes produce is not what we see but he perception itself. The end result of these causal processes is perception-what we perceive is the thing, whatever it is, that comes at the beginning, the thing that reflects the light waves on to our retina."[18]

According to waismann, ordinary empirical statements are to be analysed into 'elementary Propositions' whose whole meaning would consist in corresponding verificatory experiences.

To analyse a propositon means to consider how it is to be verified. Language touches reality with elementary propositions.........it is clear that assertions about bodies (tables, chairs) are not elementary propositions............what elementary propositions describe are: Phenomena (experience).

But how is such analysis to proceed? From the true statement that there is a table in my room, it would not follow that anyone is having a relevant experience, since there may not be anyone in the room. According to the view, known as Phenomenalism, a crucial role is played by hypothetical statements, such as, 'If someone were in the room, he would have such and such experiences.' But in what sense are such statements entailed by the statement under scruitny? Even if I am in the room, and endowed with normal eye sight, I may fail to see the table. 'You can't miss it' is notoriously unreliable.

There is also a difficulty about entailment in the other direction. From the fact that some one is having the experience of seeing something brown, it would not follow that there is a table in the room, and neither would it follow from one's having the experience of seeing table, for he might has these and other experiences in the course of a dream or hallucination. This sceptical view is encouraged by the empiricist reliance on 'experience', conceived as something that occurs in us, is 'imprinted by the senses,', etc. This problem has been recognized from the beginnings of empiricism, and in the case of logical empiricism it leads to the view that statements about tables and chairs are not 'conclusively verifiable'. Wittgenstein speaks of them as 'Hypotheses' which can not be definitively verified.'

A similar development takes place with regard to general statements, such as 'All men are mortal.' The 'all men' in this statement is not anlaysable into any finite conjunction of names, and the truth of the statement would not follow from any finite number of verificatory experiences. The same is true of scientific laws, such as' water expands below 4°C', whose meaning is not confined to any finite number of observations.

This discovery is serious for logical empiricism because it regards scientific statements as paradigms of meaningful discourse. Schlick presents a solution by denying that a scientific law is a statement, it is really, 'an introduction for the forming of statements.' A genuine statement must be 'conclusively verifiable', and this would be true only of the particular experiential statements which would be produced under that 'instruction'. He insists that a statement 'has a meaning only in so for as it can be verified, it only signifies what is verified and absolutely nothing beyond this' there cannot be a 'surplus of meaning' beyond that.

Again there are statements whose verification is impossible for technical reasons. Therefore, such statements are described as 'verifiable in principle'. But there are scientific statements or theories whose meaning seems to go for beyond their verificatory content, even 'in principle'. For example, the statement that the universe is expanding and we assume that it is based on the observation of a 'red shift' in the light emitted from remote galaxies. It seems clear that the statement is not merely about red shifts. Yet such a 'reduction' of meaning seems to be required by the verificationist analysis. In this connection verificationists enlist 'P.W. Bridgman's idea of 'operationism'. On this view, the meaning of statements about distant parts of the universe would indeed correspond to the relevant scientific 'operations', there would be no more to it than that. This means, as Bridgman Points out, that ordinary words might change their meaning when used in a scientific content. He claims that the meaning of 'length' 'has changed completely in character' in the context of astronomy.

A further difficulty arises about the analysis of statements about the past. The statement 'It rained yesterday' might be verified, in the ordinary sense, by present evidence including, perhaps, asking other people. But the statement obviously does not mean any of these presents things. Ayer offers a varity of analysis in attempting to meet the difficulty, including the bold claim that the tense of a statement is not part of its meaning, so that there would be no difference of meaning between 'George VI was crowned in 1937', 'George VI is being crowned in 1937' and 'George VI will be crowned in 1937'.

According to the positivists, the proper function of Philosophy is to analyse "the statements asserted by scientists", "study their kinds and relations and analyze terms as components of those statements and theories as ordered systems of those statements." The anlaysis of the linguistic expressions of science is what carnap calls the logic of science. This again consists of two branches. One of these studies the forms of the linguistic expressions of science, and is called logical syntax or formal logic. It does not enquire into the relations of expressions to objects, or the speakers or the audience. It simply analyses complex and compound sentences into simple ones, and the simple sentences into their component words, and discovers the laws governing the combinations of words, into significant sentences. It also investigates the logical relations of consistency and inconsistency, dependence and independence, among different sentences. Logical syntax or the formal analysis of the language of science thus enables us to realize the fundamental assertions of the different sciences, and their logical interrelations. The other branch of the logic of science is called semantics. It considers the relations of linguistic expressions to objects designated by them. Semantial analysis of the language of science discovers, for example, that a term may designate a certain particular object (e.g. the sun), or a certain property of things (e.g., iron), or a certain relation between things (e.g. fathership), or a certain physical function (e.g., temperature). It also reveals that two or more terms may be synonymous (e.g., 'homo sapience' of biology, 'person' of economics, and 'man' of ordinary use), and that one expression is reducible to another on the ground of identity of meaning.

The analysis of different kinds of statement's lead to the ultimate 'elementary propositions', variously described as 'experiential propositions', 'observation-statements' etc., whereby, as waismann puts it, 'language touches reality'. At this stage the speacker or hearer passes from linguistic activity to the occurrence of a suitable experience or sensation which is supposed to give meaning to the words. But here arises a problem that experience and sensation are personal and in some sense private. Carnap, in a book called 'Der logische aufbau der welt' (The Logical Construction of the World), makes an attempt to analyse every type of descriptive concept in terms of the Single undefined concept of remembered similarity, and the effect is to construe all empirical statements as descriptive of the actual or possible course of the subject's experience. The standpoint from which this book is written is called methodological solipsism, the word 'methodological' being put in to show that the solipsism is not to be taken seriously. But the aura of salipsism is not dispersed. For one's experience is private to him, then how can two persons ever succeed in communicating with each other? Schlick's solution of the difficulties of this problem brings about a serious division of opinion in the Vienna circle. This dispute becomes centered on the question of the character and status of what is called 'protocol statements', the basic reports of direct observations, by reference to which the truth of all other empirical statements is supposed to be tested. There is disagreement among the positivists on the exact, significance of a basic protocol. but they wish to select as protocol those statements which have been selected as pictures of atomic facts by the atomists.

Here the question arises that why these rather than others should be selected Schlick, Ayer and many other positivists answer substantially that sentences of this sort are to be accepted as protocols because direct reports of experience are of this type. Among protocols those which correctly record experience are to be accepted, the rest rejected 'This is red' is the right sort of sentence to be a protocol. Protocols are direct reports of the given and are justified with reference to the given. These reports can be inaccurate or be corrigible, but their direct justification by experience is agreed. Without such a basis, the claim of logical positivist or logical empiricist, to be an empiricist position may be abandoned.

But all positivists do not accept this position, notably carnap and Neurath reject it at this point, "Protocol statements are direct records of the given" Carnap says that, "the simplest statements in the protocol-language are protocol statements, i.e. statements needing no justification and serving as foundation for all the remaining statements of science "Carnap says that protocol statements are of the same kind as "joy now," "here now, blue", "there, red". But otto Neurath argues that such expressions cannot be fitted into the system of science, unless the reference of "now", and "hear", and the identity of the speaker, are known to others. According to Neurath, there are indeed, no statements having this status.

Carnap and Neurath maintain that these protocol statements must, like all other statements of fact, be inter-subjectively verifiable. They must refer to physical events, for it is assumed without argument that physical events are accessible to all alike. So statements which seem to report the individual's private experience have to be reconstrued as referring to the state of his body, or to his behaviour, in which his use of language in included. The general thesis is that the languge of physics is a universal language, and every universal in the sense that every empirical statements can be expressed in it. And it leads Neurath to insist so much upon the unity of science. He believes that, in spite of the differences in their professional vocabularies, they are all fundamental speaking the same language. They are all investigating the same Physical world. This is the old doctrine of meteralisin, in a modern guise.

Carnap and Neurath don't accept protocal statements as direct record of the given. It cannot be a tautology if it is to serve the purpose for which it is intended. It is not a statement of empirical science. Philosophers have no business to be making empirical statements. It seems then, that taken at face value it is metaphysics, nonsense. Wittgenstein calls it the attempt to talk about the relation of language to fact. This is not clarification of language.

The Physicalists say that, it makes no sense to speak of comparing statements with facts. Statements can be compared only with one another. Accordingly, they lead to adopt a coherence theory of truth, the criterion by which it is to be decided whether a statement is true is not its correspondence with fact but its consistency with other statements.

According to Ayer, the coherence theory of truth is quite untenable, but the thesis of Physicalism is open to serious objections. He says that, "............however strong the argument may be which go to show that when we seem to be speaking about the experiences of others we must be referring only to their behaviour, the conviction remains that we are not. On any view of Philosophy, this inner-outer problem is extremely difficult.

Ayer says that it is to be remarked that the process of analyzing a language is facilitated if it is possible to use an artificial system of symbols whose structure is known, such as Russell and Whitehead's so-called system of logistic. Russell, in the introduction which he wrote to Wittgenstein's Tractatus, attributes to Wittgenstein the view that it is impossible to speak about a language in the language itself. But Ayer does not find it necessary. And Carnap, be actually carrying out such an analysis, subsequently shows that a language can without self-contradiction be used in the analysis of itself.

The difficulty is to say that while the content of our experience is indeed incommunicable, their structure is not. Whatever may be the difference in the content of our private worlds, their structure is the same. This answer has some plausibility but it does not withstand analysis.

In a book called 'Logical Syntax of Language' Carnap makes a distinction between the material and formal modes of speech. A sentence is said to be in the material mode when it expresses a verbal statement which is made to look as if it is factual, translation into the formal mode makes the verbal character of the statement explicit. He gives the example that if one says 'a rose is a thing', he is not making a factual statement like 'croses have thorns' but he is expressing the syntactical statement that "rose" is a thing word. Similarly '5 is a number' is said to be more accurately rendered as "5" is a numeral, 'he lectured about Babylon' as 'the word' "Babylon" occurred in his lecture".

The material mode of speech looks like talk about things but in fact talk about words. If this doctrine is accepted, it can be said that even formerly Philosophers who apparently talk about facts, objects and the like are really talking about language, doing logical syntax, not taking metaphysics, even if they are sometimes not clear, or even positively mistaken, about what they are doing.

Carnap considers the material mode of speech a patent source of metaphysics, philosophers use the Pseudo-concepts of the material mode (things, quality, fact, & C.) as though they are genuine concepts. This metaphysical, nonsensical character can be brought out by attempting the translation into the formal mode which ought to be possible. Thus Wittgenstein's famous mystical 'There is also the inexpressible' is translated into 'there are also words which are not words'.

So, instead of clarifying the logical structure of the world by showing how all facts are complicated clusters of atomic, elementary or basic facts, and exhibiting the logical structure of these facts and clusters, here is a clarification of the structure of the language of science. Language is still conceived of as truth-functional in character, and the most abstract of physical theories must, therefore, be shown to be reducible to basic, Protocol statements, and to be validated by them.

By a syntactical statement carnap means one which is concerned with the form and order of symbols, as opposed to their meaning, but this does not hold even for his own examples. To say that '5' is a numeral, even if it is equivalent to saying that 5 is a number, which it is not, is not to say anything about the shape of the figure '5' but something about its use. To say that someone lectured about Babylan is obviously not to say merely, if at all, that he made the noise 'Babylon'. Thus, these statements are not syntactical but semantic. Urmson says that, "It is purely a matter of convention that we select sentences of this syntactical form as the basic protocol statements, and we accept those protocols which are accepted by the accredited scientists and reject those which are not. But Philosophy cannot just be logical syntax, nor can a language be characterized by a vocabulary understood as a list of marks on paper with formation and transformation rules."[19]

Carnap himself comes to recognize this. And he brings his logic to bear upon semantics. And which deals with this forbidden topic of the relation of words to things. Urmson says that "he was one of the few in the period of classical logical empiricism who honestly faced the need to maintain consistently that philosophy consisted solely of tautological transformations of analytical equivalences. But for his errors the need for some revision of the doctrine would not have been seen so quickly."

Now we may have a question that why to say that a statement is to be accepted because it records a fact is regarded as such a dangerous thing, and why it is regarded as metaphysical. Though it does not seem very similar to the more grandiose statements of speculative metaphysics. When Wittgenstein talks about a proposition picturing a fact he is certainly talking metaphysics, and intentionally. Again, if Wittgenstein's doctrine that a proposition is a picture of a fact is accepted, then it seems plain that one cannot talk about the relation of language to fact without violation of syntax, for one cannot produce a picture of the relation of a picture to what is pictured, the fact. This relation must show itself, and what is shown cannot be said.

It seems that later logical positivists partly think that all talk about facts must be as metaphysical as Wittgenstein's and partly accept the consequences of the 'picture' theory of language from Wittgenstein somewhat uncritically even when they abandon the theory of language itself.

But Philosophy has to be logical rather than empirical, and a logical inquiry is concerned, it seems, with statements and their relations to each other, not with the relation of language to fact. To some logical empiricists it seems more tolerable to abandon, or to treat as in the material mode of speech, such statements as apparently involved extra logical excursions than to allow any exception to the fundamental dichotomy 'logical-empirical'.

Urmson says that while abandoning the metaphysics of logical otomism, the logical empiricists retain substantially the same view of the scope and nature of analysis, but it is now conceived as revealing the logical structure of the language of science, of informative discourse, not of the facts with which science deals.

Now we can see, if a positivist is challenged for a reason for the activity of analysis, he claims that apart from the intrinsic interest of his results, two advantages are secured. First, an analysis of the language of science is likely to be of use to the scientist, especially in the frontier regions of progress. Secondly, if one does not understand language thoroughly, one is liable to misuse it, in particular, one is liable to fall into metaphysics.

Thus analysis becomes a prophylactic against linguistic abuses. It can be no small thing to understand the tool of all sciences and all skills, and understanding of a language is achieved by analysis.

References

1. J. O. Urmson, 'Philosophical Analysis', p. 115.
2. F. P. Ramsey, 'The Foundations of Mathematics', p. 263.
3. A. J. Ayer, 'The Meaning of Life And other Essays', p. 53.
4. A. J. Ayer, 'Language, Truth and Logic', p. 48.
5. Ibid, p. 49.
6. Ibid, p. 50
7. John Foster, 'Ayer', p. 46.
8. Ibid, p. 46-47.
9. J. O. Urmson, 'Philosophical Analysis', p. 119.
10. A. J. Ayer, 'Language, Truth and Logic', p. 68-9.
11. Ibid, p. 66
12. A. J. Ayer, 'The Problem of Knowledge', p. 98.
13. A. J. Ayer, 'Language, Truth and Logic', p. 66
14. Ibid, p. 67
15. Ibid, p. 67-8
16. Ibid, p. 68
17. 'Common-sense versus Mr. Hirst's Theory of Perception', Proceeding of the Aristotelian Society', 1959-60.
18. 'Perception and Our Knowledge of the External World', p. 116.
19. J. O. Urmson, 'Philosophical Analysis', p. 126.

5

The Problem of Perception of the Physical World

In the previous chapter we have seen how Ayer describes the nature of philosophical analysis. According to him, the statements about physical objects are somehow reducible to statements about sense-data. The problem of 'reduction' of material things to sense-contents, is the main philosophical part of the traditional problem of perception. Connor says, the problem of perception have been important problem for nearly all those philosophers who would consider themselves to be empiricists. In this present chapter, we shall take an account of the problem of perception of the physical world presented by Ayer.

Our knowledge of the physical world is one of the important topics covered by Ayer and we can see that this is the predominant concern of his epistemological writings. As an empiricist, Ayer believes that knowledge of the physical world is derived from sense-perception. Ayer often speaks of the skeptical problem about the physical world as the 'problem of perception'. According to Ayer, the problem of perception, as the skeptic poses it, is that of justifying our belief in the existence of the physical objects which it is commonly taken for granted that we perceive. In this, as in other cases, it is maintained that there is a gap, of a logically perplexing kind, between the evidence with which we start and the conclusions that we reach. If the conclusions are suspected it is because of the way in which they seem to go beyond the evidence on which they depend. The starting point of the argument is, as we have seen, that our access to the objects, whose existence is in question must be indirect.

Thus the question here is that why should we suppose that our access to physical objects is always indirect and that we can only know of their existence by inference from something else. It what sense could one be said to be only indirectly perceiving this sheet of paper when one sees it quite Clearly in front of him and feels its surface with his hands?

There are naive realists who believe that physical objects can be directly perceived, and their existence is thereby directly revealed. But the septic claims that our perception of a physical object is always indirect, since it is always mediated by the awareness of a non-physical item which represents it.

Ayer says that the view that our perception of physical objects is mediated in this way holds a very respectable place in the history of philosophy. Descartes maintains that physical objects perceived not directly but through the medium of what he calls ideas. Locke, under Descartes' influence, refers to the objects by which he thinks that perception is mediated, as simple ideas of sensation. Berkeley, following Locke, Speaks indifferently of our perceiving ideas and perceiving sensible qualities. Hume take the same position, but substitutes the world 'impression' for Berkeley's 'idea', reserving the world 'idea' for images or concepts. Kant speaks similarly of 'Vorstellungen', of which the favoured English rendering is 'representation'. J. S. Mill takes perception to consist in having sensations, and uses the word 'sensation'. In more recent times, philosophers like Moore and Russell characterize these objects as sense-data. Ayer believes that the word sense-datum is first used as a technical term in philosophy by Russell, and he defines sense-data as objects of acquaintance. Moore uses the term 'sense-content' as an alternative to 'sense-datum', and Ayer has also used it in 'Language, Truth and Logic', in a way corresponding to Russell's use of 'percept'. More recently still, the American philosophers, C.I.Lewis and Nelson Goodman use the term 'qualia' in a way that is reminiscent of Berkeley's reference to sensible qualities.

Ayer says that while there is a large measure of agreement in the ways, in which these various terms have been used, they are not in all cases exactly inter-changeable.

In his article 'Phenomenalism' Ayer describes that "the term sense-datum' is a means of referring to appearances without prejudging the questions what it is, if anything, that they are appearance of, and what it is, if anything, that they appear to."[1]

The ordinary man does, indeed, believe that he frequently sees and touches the 'moderate-sized specimens of dry goods' as Austin terms them. Austin justly remarks, it is a mistake 'to try to represent as some single kind of things the things which the ordinary man says that he "perceives".'[2]

But if the ordinary man thinks that he perceives physical objects without the mediation of other entities, it is a mistake of a different kind, a purely theoretical error. But then what grounds do we have for thinking that this is so?

And this creates the epistemological problem. The problem of justifying our belief in the existence of physical objects and our beliefs about their properties. For if the immediate objects of perceptual awareness are mental, how can we tell whether there are physical items which they represent? And even if there are such items, how can we tell what properties they possess? It seems that ultimately we have nothing but our knowledge of the mental objects to go on and that any belief about the physical world will have to be justified by inference from this.

The septic claims that the immediate objects of perceptual awareness are always private and mental. But on what basis does the sceptic make such claim? And Ayer notes, the basis which is most commonly employed is the so-called argument from illusion.

The starling point of this argument is that physical objects sometimes sensibly appear to us in ways, whish misrepresent, or at least differ from, their true character. For example, when partially immersed in water, a straight stick may look crooked, and, when viewed at an oblique angle, a round coin may look elliptical. It is then claimed that whenever a physical object is perceived, the immediate object of perceptual awareness is something which really possess the sensible qualities which the physical item appears to possess. Thus, when round coin looks elliptical, the immediate object of awareness is not the coin, which is round, but something which is actually elliptical. But apart from the physical abject perceived, there is no physical item which could form an immediate object of awareness in this way. So, where the sensible appearance of a physical object differs from its true character, the immediate object of awareness must be something non-physical, something momentary and mind dependent, in short, a sense datum. But from this, it does not follow that in every case of perception the immediate object of awareness is a sense datum. For one can say that in case where the perceptual existence is wholly veridical-where the physical object sensibly appears the way it really is -the immediate object of awareness is the physical item itself. To exclude this possibility Ayer presents the argument that.

From different angles the coin may appear a variety of different shapes, let it be assumed that one of them is the shape that it really is. There will be nothing to mark off this appearance from the others except a difference of aspect which may be extremely slight. There will in any case be no such difference between the way in which the coin is perceived in this instance and the way in which it is perceived in all the others as to render it at all plausible to say that they are generically distinct, that the object which is directly perceived in this instance is of a different kind altogether from that which is directly perceived in all the others... "In this way we are brought to the conclusion that, even granting that physical objects may sometimes be perceived as they really are, what is directly perceived is always something else."[3]

Thus we see that the immediate object of perceptual awareness is always a sense datum- a mental or mind-dependent entity internal to the awareness itself. This conclusion is known as the sense-datum theory.

But Ayer does not find this argument plainly conclusive. He further says,

"It makes perfectly good sense to talk of perceiving things which look in some way different from what they are, and there is at least no obvious reason why we should here feel bound to add that these thing are not perceived directly."

Why it is not said that the immediate object of awareness (i.e. what we directly perceive) is a straight stick which looks crooked or a round coin which looks elliptical? What reason is there for reifying the look as a mental object, which is detached from the physical item perceived and prevents any direct vision of it?

However, as Ayer sees, a further reason for accepting the sense-datum theory is provided by the possibility of complete hallucination. He says, "But it may also happen that one 'perceives' a physical object which is not there at all... an experience of this sort is like the experience of seeing a real physical object that hallucinations are possible. But in so for as the experiences are alike, their analysis should follow the same pattern. So if we are bound in one case to say that what is seen in a sense-datum, it is reasonable to hold that this is so in all."[4]

But the argument from hallucination does not need to claim that hallucinations, as experiences, are exactly like genuine perceptions. All it needs to claim is that, for any genuine perception, i.e. for any perceptual experience in which some real physical object is perceived, there could be a hallucination which is, as an experience, exactly like it. And this, surely, can be easily established. For, given any genuine visual perception, we can, envisage a situation in which the subject would have a visual hallucination which was, as an experience, exactly like it. For example-given any genuine visual perception, produced in the normal way by 'photic stimulation of the eyes, we can envisage a situation in which, with the subject blindfolded, a visual experience of exactly the same intrinsic kind is produced by electrically stimulating the optic nerves, though no physical item of the sort which such an experience would normally represent is present in the subject's environment.

And, by appropriately varying the details the same result can be obtained for every other sense realm. This is enough to establish that if sense-data are the immediate objects of awareness in the case of hallucination, they are also the immediate objects of awareness in the case of genuine perception. consequently, since each genuine perception could be experientially replicated by a hallucination, it is impossible to recognize sense-data as the immediate objects of hallucination without also recognizing them as the immediate object of perceptual awareness in every case.

To avoid this conclusion, a distinction is required between the subjective character of an experience and its intrinsic character. But such a position would be very hard to sustain, not only because the distinction between the subjective and the intrinsic character of an experience is dubious, but also because to exploit the distinction in the way proposed would involve giving a very peculiar and implausible account of the causation of experience.

Ayer, however, sees a quite different way in which the argument from hallucination can be resisted. He says, "It is only if we artificially combine the decision to say that the victim of a hallucination is seeing something with the ruling that what is seen must exist, that we secure the introduction of sense-data. But once again there seems to be no good reason why we should do this.[5]

But Foster does not agree with Ayer. He says, we can easily envisage a case in which someone has a visual hallucination but does not think that he sees any physical object at all. For example the subject 'knows' that his visual experiences are being artificially induced by the electrical stimulation of his optic nerves and, consequently, 'knows' that they are hallucinations. In such a case we cannot record his experiences in the way Ayer envisages-'he thinks he sees a bus'. The subject knows he is not seeing anything physical at all.

At this point, Ayer presents his other locution, where we say that someone sees some thing, without implying that there is something which he sees. But it does not work, because 'sees' continues to function grammatically as a transitive verb, with subject term and object term, but it no longer signifies a relation.

So, finding the argument from hallucination inadequate, Ayer takes the argument from illusion. But finds that it cannot establish the truth of the sense-datum theory or ever provides a reasonable basis for accepting it.

In 'The Foundations of Empirical knowledge' Ayer makes it more explicit that he is only advocating the adoption of a sense-datum language, not a sense-datum theory. He writes,

"For since in philosophizing about perception our main object is to analyse the relationship of our sense experiences to the propositions we put forward concerning material things, it is useful for us to have a terminology that enables us to refer to the contents of our experiences independently of the material things that they are taken to present. And this the sense-datum language provides."[6] .

The philosopher who says that he is seeing a sense-datum in a case where most people would say that they were seeing a material thing is not contradicting the fact received opinion of any question if fact...what he is doing is simply to recommend a new verbal usage. He is proposing to us that instead of speaking of seeing a straight stick which looks crooked, we should speak of seeing a sense-datum which really has the quality of being crooked and which belongs to a straight stick.

Foster says, "What Ayer intends to convey, I think, is that the nature of perceptual experience can be conceptualized in alternative ways one way being expressed by the terminology of naive realism, the other by the terminology of sense-data."[7]

The two sentences, 'It now seems to me that I see a cigarette case' and 'I am now seeing a seeming-cigarette case' do not express the same proposition, for the latter, unlike the former, involves a genuine ontology of seeming objects, i.e. sense-data. But, Ayer finds each of them a correct way of recording the content of one's experience. The only reason for preferring one option to the other is that it serves one's philosophical purposes better.

The reason of Ayer's this position seems to be that the question of what we directly perceive cannot be settled empirically. As he claims that the philosopher who employ the sense-datum terminology, 'He is not putting forward a new hypothesis which could be empirically verified or confuted."[8]

Ayer makes it explicit by arguing, 'I never see material things but only sense-data (see here means 'directly see) does not express a genuine proposition. He makes the remark that sense-data 'are not strictly needed for the formulation of the sceptics's problem'.[9]

He further says, 'A problem of this sort must arise once it is admitted that our ordinary judgement of perception claim more than is strictly contained in the experiences on which they are based.

Naive realism involves two claims-first, the physical objects can be directly perceived, second, that, through perception, we can acquire direct knowledge of physical facts, and sees these two claims as intimately connected. He thinks that it is by directly perceiving physical objects that we acquire direct knowledge of physical facts. But this connection does not hold, at least in any sense of 'knowledge' which would protect from the sceptical challenge.

According to Ayer, our perceptual access to the physical world may be direct, in the sense that, when a physical object is perceived, there is no intervening object of perceptual awareness, but this does not remove the epistemological problem, once it is recognized that our physical judgements, based on our perceptual experience, go beyond the evidence which these experiences supply.

Ayer says that naive 'realists' assumption that we directly perceive physical objects is not understood to entail that we always perceive them as they really are, but only that we do so, when the conditions are right. Now the question is that how then do we determine what perceptible properties a physical object really has? There should be an attempt to analyse the distinction between the real and the apparent.

But this is not a clear question since the word 'real' is used in many different ways, like 'That small speak in the sky is really a very large star', 'The penny looks elliptical from this angle but it is really round'. Austin points out that 'there are cases in which the distinction between the real and the apparent, which these examples illustrate, does not apply so smoothly.[10]

Ayer says that epistemologically, since the word 'real' descends from the Latin 'res', to be real is to be a thing, a usage which is preserved in our legal talk of real property. To make it clear, the distinction between the real and apparent should be drawn. But how it can be done? Ayer says that 'Evidently, since we are not able to inspect any physical objects in detachment from the various facets which they present to our perception, it must be drawn in terms of these facets, if it comes within the domain of perception at all."[11]

In fact, we denominate as the real colour of a physical object that colour which it looks, or would look to a normal observe under the conditions which we take as standard, as which are optimal, and make for the greatest possibility of discrimination. But the question gets complicated by our having to correlate the data of sight with the data of touch, and by the existence of further and indeed over-riding criteria in the operations of measurement.

Therefore, Ayer talks of a 'simpler more primitive system in which the properties which physical objects are judged really to have are straightforwardly selected from those that they appear to have."[12]

Though it may be thought here that if appearances are considered purely in themselves, one is as good as another, then we have no justification for discriminating between them as manifestations of reality. Russell says here, "It is evident, that there is no colour which pre-eminently appears to be the colour of the table or even of any one particular part of the table- it appears to be of different colours from different points of view, and there is no reason for regarding some of these as more really its colour than others."[13]

To avoid favouritism, Russell denies that the table has any one particular colour. But Ayer says, if neither the table nor any part of it has any one particular colour at a given time, it cannot be identical with what we see, unless our eyes are constantly deceiving us. Then Russell says, "The real table, if there is one, is not immediately known to us at all but must be an inference from what is immediately known."[14]

Ayer says that naive realist does not attempt to answer to the problem raised by this analysis. Ayer puts the questions that we think of the physical object as preserving its identity in the various guises in which it appears to us, but exactly how is this achieved? What is it that remains constant while its appearances varis? If the physical object is known to us only through it various appearances, in what way can we distinguish it from them? The naive realist ignores these questions because in treating the perception of physical objects as a primitive datum he has already gone beyond them.

Ayer says that naive realists are wrong in so far as they deny that our ordinary judgements of perception are suceptible of analysis, or deny that they embody inferences which can be made explicit.

Ayer takes the view of common sense that the physical object which we perceive continue to exist on their own in very much the form in which we normally perceive them. It is often suggested that science tells as otherwise that it leaves us with no good reason to believe that things as they are in themselves are at all similar, except perhaps in respect of structure, to anything that we perceive. Rullell identifies the common sense position with naive realism and says, "Naive realism leads to physics and physics, if true, shows that naive realism is false. Therefore, naive realism, if true, is false, therefore it is false."[15]

Russell gives the reason why physics is thought to falsify naive realism. He says, "That grass is green, that stones are hard, and that snow is cold. But physics assurses us that the greenness of the grass, the hardness of stones, and the coldness of snow, are not the greenness, hardness and coldness that we know in our own experience, but something very different. The observer, when he seems to himself to be observing a stone, is really, if physics is to be believed, observing the effects of the stone upon himself.[16]

Physical object is perceived, there is no intervening object of perceptual awareness, but this does not remove the epistemological problem, once it is recognized that our physical judgements, based on our perceptual experiences, go beyond the evidence which these experiences supply.

To avoid scepticism about the physical world Ayer adopts the reductionist strategy of the linguistic phenomenalist as we have seen in the previous chapter. According to it, the statements about physical objects can be translated into equivalent statements about sense-data, where the latter statements make no explicit reference to physical entities and are entirely devoid of any distinctively physical vocabulary. In its strong form it is called as 'analytical phenomenalism'.

Ayer, under the influence of his verification principle, accepts analytical phenomenalism in 'Language, Truth and Logic'. It is supposed to be an escape from scepticism. If physical statements can be translated into sensory statements, then, by consulting the translation manual, we can deduce physical conclusions from a record of our sensory evidence. Even to yield the simplest physical conclusion, the sensory evidence will presumably have to be fairly extensive. But as he attempts to elaborate this position by his 'analysis of the notion of a material thing' he does not get success in doing so. And later on he abandons phenomenalism in its analytical form. He realizes that, even from the standpoint of his strong verification principle, a strict translation of physical statements into sensory statements is unnecessary. Again he thinks that such translation is, in principle, impossible. A part of his this thinking is the apparently unlimited number of ways in which a physical state of affairs can maifest itself through sense-experience. Even if, the truth of a physical statement can be logically established on the basis of purely sensory evidence, there seem to be infinitely many different kinds of possible sensory evidence that can serve equally well for the same physical statement, and Ayer despairs of being able to find, within the confines of the phenomenal language, a finite way of covering the range. He says, '...if we try to describe what at any given moment would afford us direct evidence for the truth of a statement about a material thing by putting forward a disjunction of statements about sense-data... this disjunction will have to be infinite.[17]

Ayer takes this to be a consequence of the fact that physical statement cannot be conclusively verified, by undergoing a series of sense-experiences, someone can accumulate evidence in favour of some physical statement, but 'he can never reach a stage at which it ceases to be conceivable that further sense-experience will reverse the verdict of the previous evidence.'[18]

And from this he infers that 'no finite set of singular statements about sense-data can ever formally entail a statement about a material thing.

Though in a later article entitled 'Phenomenalism' he doubts about the premises of this argument. Again he thinks that perhaps, a finite series of sense-experiences can conclusively establish the truth of a statement, despite the possibility of further contrary evidence. But, Foster says, even if the premise is correct, it does not establish as much as Ayer supposes.

And at a point, Ayer rejects analytical phenomenalism on the grounds that the factualcontent of a physical statement cannot be finitely expressed in sensory terms.

In his later article, Ayer advances a further objection to analytical phenomenalism. He begins by nothing that, because physical objects, unlike sense-data, can exist unperceived, the analytical phenomenalist is obliged 'to hold that the statements about sense-data, into which, according to his programme, statements about physical objects are to be translated, are themselves predominantly hypothetical.'[19]

Some critics of analytical phenomenalism object to this

procedure on the grounds that it allows unperceived physical objects and events only a hypothetical existence. Ayer dismisses this objection as mere confusion, but he finds the procedure as problematic in another way. The problem concerns the vocablary used in formulating the antecedent clauses in these hypothetical statements-the clauses which specify the circumstances in which the relevant types of sense-data would occur. He explains it, "It is not enough for the phenomenalist to make such vague assertions as that what he means by saying that there is a table in the next room is that if he were there he would perceive it. For his being there is a matter of a physical body's being in a certain spatial relationship to other physical objects, and, on the assumption that to talk about physical objects is always to talk about sense-data, this situation must itself be described in purely sensory terms. But it is not at all easy how this could be done.[20]

Ayer makes the point with respect to a different example drawn from a famous passage in Berkeley's principles. Berkeley claimed that to say that the earth moves (although its motion is not actually perceived) is to say that, if we were placed in such and such circumstances, and such or such a position and distance, both from the earth and sun, we should perceive the former to move.'

Ultimately Ayer concludes that, for all these reasons, the programme of analytical phenomenalist 'cannot be carried through' and that 'sentences about physical objects are not formally translatable into statements about sense-data.'[21]

Foster writes that, "what is wrong with analytical phenomenalism is not its phenomenalism, but its strict analytic character. It fails not because physical statements describe a reality external to human minds, but because they describe the realm of human sense-experience in ways which the phenomenal language, with its explicit confinement to an ontology of sense-data, cannot exactly express.

After the end of Ayer's phenomenalistic phase, his thought develops in the direction of a form of realism, which he calls 'sophisticated realism' and which he differentiates from naive realism. And this development reaches its fruition in his 'The origins of Pragmatism', and its sequels, where a realist position is explicitly defended.

Now he sees that the world which emerges by this constructive process becomes ontologically independent on its sensory origins. The theory is developed to a point where the physical objects it postulates are thought of not just as representations of the sensory order, but as independently real, and, indeed, as causally responsible for the 'percepts' from which they have been constructed. Thus the physical theory, though epistemalogically derivative, becomes ontologically dominant.

Foster makes a comment by saying, "His characterization of the steps by which the realist physical theory evolves from its sensory origins, his philosophical writing of the highest calibre, in which analytical rigour and constructive artistry are perfectly blended.[22]

References

1. A. J. Ayer, 'Phenomenalism' taken from 'Readings in Introductory Philosophical Analysis', by John Hospers, p. 316.
2. J. L. Austin, 'Sense and Sensibilia', p. 8.
3. A. J. Ayer, 'The Problem of Knowledge', p. 89.
4. Ibid, p. 90.
5. Ibid, p. 90-1.
6. A.J. Ayer, 'The Foundations of Empirical Knowledge', p. 25-6.
7. John Foster, 'Ayer', p. 155.
8. A. J. Ayer, 'The Foundations of Empirical Knowledge', p. 251.
9. A. J. Ayer, 'The Problem of Knowledge', p. 112.
10. J. L. Austin, 'Sense and Sensibilia', p. 66.
11. A.J. Ayer, 'The Central Questions of Philosophy', p. 77.
12. Ibid.
13. Bertrand Russell, 'The Problem of Philosophy', p. 9.

14. Ibid, p. 11.
15. Bertrand Russell, 'An Inquiry into Meaning and Truth', p. 15.
16. Ibid.
17. A. J. Ayer, 'The Foundations of Empirical Knowledge', p. 241.
18. Ibid, p. 239.
19. A. J. Ayer, 'The Problem of Knowledge', p. 119.
20. Ibid, p. 123.
21. Ibid, p. 129.
22. John Foster, 'Ayer'.

6

A. J. Ayer's Distinction between A Priori and A Posteriori

The psychology of knowledge is after all, only one among the sciences, and, therefore, itself one of the subjects of epistemological analysis. The question "How do we know" presupposes the question "What do we mean".[1] Not the origin and psychological development of knowledge but its logical structure and empirical validation are the subject of a thus reformed epistemology.

As we have seen before that the analysis or, more broadly, the clarification of our concepts is the only legitimate business for philosophy, according to Ayer. In this order, he thinks about the basic concept of truth. He says that it is commonly supposed that the business of philosopher is to answer the question 'What is truth?' But when this famous question is considered, it becomes clear that it does not give rise to any genuine problem.

According to Ayer, all questions of the form, 'what is the nature of x' are requests for a definition of a symbol x in use, and it is to ask for the translation of this sentence into equivalent sentences which do not contain 'x' or any of its synonyms. Thus to ask 'what is truth' is to ask for such a translation of the sentence '(the proposition) P is true'.

Now, he says, if we analyse statements of truth (or

assertions, judgement, assumption, opinion or belief), we find that in all sentences of the form 'P is true' the phrase 'is true' is logically superfluous. When, for example, one says that the proposition 'Queen Anne is dead' is true, all that he says is that Queen Anne is dead. Similarly, when one says that the proposition 'Oxford is the capital of England' is false, we are just saying that Oxford is not the capital of England. The terms 'true' and 'false' are just marks of assertion or denial, there is no sense in asking us to analyse the concepts further.

Then, Ayer says, the question 'What makes a proposition true or false?' is a way of asking how propositions are validated. But first of all, we look at the distinction, which is made between two kinds of knowledge- a priori knowledge and a posteriori knowledge.

In much of the modern western tradition, the term a priori is considered to mean propositional knowledge that can be had without, or "prior to" experience. A priori knowledge is knowledge gained or justified by reason alone, without the direct or indirect influence of experience. (here, experience usually means observation of the world through sense-perception). It is usually contrasted with a posteriori knowledge, which requires experience. Mathematics and logic are generally considered a priori disciplines. Statements such as "2+2=4" for example, are considered to be "a priori", because they are thought to come out of reflection alone.

A posteriori knowledge is propositional knowledge obtained by experience. It is contrasted with a priori knowledge, or knowledge that is gained through the apprehension of innate ideas, "intuition", "pure reason", or other non-experiential sources. A posteriori knowledge is a sort of knowledge, the attainment or justification of which requires reference to experience. This is also called empirical knowledge. The natural and social sciences are usually considered a posteriori disciplines. Statement like "The sky is usually mostly blue", for instance, might be considered "a posteriori" knowledge.

Philosophers in different times, have used the term in

many different ways. According to Socrates, knowledge is concerned with the general and typical, not with the particular and accidental.

Plato believes that the source of knowledge lies in reason and not in sense-perception. Experience, however, plays an indispensable role in knowledge, our a priori ideas are aroused and suggested by experience.

Aristotle uses the term in a slightly different manner. When he writes of "A priori" knowledge, he means to say knowledge of the causes of things.

The use of the term gains foothold through rationalist thinkers like Rene Descartes and Gotfried Leibniz, who argue that knowledge is gained through reason, not experience. Descartes considers the knowledge of the self, or Cogito Ergo Sum, to be a priori, because he thinks that one need not refer to past experience to consider one's own existence.

Modern use of the terms begins with Immanuel Kant who adds the distinction between analytic and synthetic truths to the distinction between a priori and a posteriori knowledge. He argues that propositions known a priori are necessarily true, while propositions known a posteriori are contingent, because a priori knowledge has always been true, according to Kant. A posteriori propositions depend on external conditions, which may change in time, making the proposition false.

Saul Kripke argues in "Naming and Necessity' against Kant, that a prioricity is an epistemological property, and should not be conflated with the separate, metaphysical matter of necessity. In support of this argument he offers several pleas to intuition - "Hesperus is Phosphorus' is necessary if true, but known a posteriori, while on the other hand, "That bar is one meter long" is contingent (it could have Shrunk etc.) but known a Priori.

The discussions of a priori and a posteriori knowledge almost always concern propositional knowledge, or, roughly, "knowledge that". Now one of the fundamental questions in epistemology is, whether there is any non-trivial a priori knowledge. Generally speaking, rationalists believe that there is, while empiricists believe that all knowledge is ultimately derived from some kind of external experience.

The vast bulk of the empirical knowledge that ordinary people possess is gained via a mixture of direct experience and the testimony of others about what they have experienced. More complicated and organized methods of gaining empirical knowledge are the methods of science-which results in perhaps the best examples of rigorously codified, scientific empirical knowledge, namely, physics.

The view of philosophy, adopted by logical positivists is a form of empiricism. So they find is necessary to deal with the objection brought against empiricism, that it is impossible on empiricist principles to account for their knowledge of necessary truths. For, as Hume shows, the fact that a law has been substantiated in n-1 cases affords no logical guarantee that it will be substantiated in the nth case also, no matter how large n is taken to be. This means that no general proposition referring to a matter of fact can ever be shown to be necessarily and universally true. It can at best be a probable hypothesis. This applies to all propositions which have a factual content.

But the empiricist face difficulty with the truths of formal logic and mathematics, for they appear to everyone to be necessary and certain. The empiricists must deal with those truths in one of two ways- either say that they are not necessary truths, and then account for the universal conviction that they are, or say that they have no factual content, and then explain how a proposition without factual content can be true and useful and surprising.

If neither of these courses proves satisfactory, it will give way to rationalism, to accepting that thought is an independent source of knowledge more trustworthy than experience and thereby upset the main argument of empiricism. And, this is obvious that empiricists would not like to accept this alternative.

It is usually accepted that the fields of knowledge most often suggested as having a priori status are logic and mathematics, which deal primarily with abstract, formal objects. But extreme empiricists such as John Stuart Mill rejects the notion of a priori truths entirely, claiming that all truths come out of experience, and so are a posteriori. Now we see that Mill takes the first alternative that the truths of logic and mathematics are not necessary or certain. He denies that mathematical propositions are 'necessary truths' in the strict, logical sense of that phrase As 'real' propositions, he argues, they must be generalizations from experience-subject to correction, therefore, in the light of subsequent experience.

In thus disputing the claim of mathematical propositions to be necessary truths, Mill receives an explanation from one of his contemporaries. William Whewell, who is an upholder of the doctrine of necessary truths. Whewell writes, "Necessary truths are those in which we not only learn that the proposition is true, but see that it must be true, in which the negation of the truth is not only false but impossible, in which we cannot even by an effort of the imagination, or in a supposition, conceive the reverse of that which is asserted."[2]

Here Mill replies that Whewell is confusing logical and psychological necessity. Mill maintains that the propositions of logic and mathematics are inductive generalizations based on an extremely large number of instances. The falsity of a proposition comes to be 'inconceivable' he argues, as a result of the association of ideas, since all our experience impresses upon our mind that two and two make four, we reach a point at which we cannot conceive that they should make five. But many propositions which men once could not 'conceive' to be false have, in the end, been universally rejected, inconceivability is not, therefore, a prove of necessity.

But Mill's explanation is not satisfactory. Ayer does not find this solution acceptable. We all know that Kant has already established that, although there can be no doubt that all our knowledge begins with experience, it does not follow that it all arises out of experience.[3]

Now Ayer says that when it is said that logical and mathematical truths are known independently of experience, it does not mean that they are innate. Ayer maintains that they are independent of experience in the sense that they do not owe their validity to empirical verification. They can be discovered through an inductive process , but once we apprehend them, we see that they are necessarily true, that they hold good for every conceivable instance. And this distinguishes them from empirical generalizations for we know that a proposition whose validity depends upon experience can not be seen to be necessarily and universally true. Ayer says that in rejecting Mill's theory he is obliged to be somewhat dogmatic. He tries to show that of the two ways of dealing with logic and mathematics which are open to the empiricist, the one which Mill adopts is not the one which is correct.

Ayer says, "But even the claim that a priori propositions are certain is not without its difficulties. For surely it is possible to doubt them."[4] He explains that people do mistake in mathematics and in logic, they miscalculate, they draw invalid inferences, they construct abstract systems which turn out to be self-contradictory. But they don't doubt the validity of any a priori statement. They doubt the procedure which they try to carry out.

In this order, he examines some cases in which these logical and mathematical truths might seem to be confuted. For example- it might easily happen that a person has five pairs of objects and when he counts them, he finds that they only amount to nine. But no one will say that the mathematical proposition "2x5=10" has been confuted. One will say that the person is wrong in supposing that there were five pairs to start with, or that one object had been taken away while he was counting, or that two of them had coalesced, or that he had counted wrongly. Ayer says, "One would adopt as an explanation whatever empirical hypothesis fitted in best with the accredited facts. The one explanation which would in no circumstances be adopted is that ten is not always the product of two and five."

Ayer takes an another example, if what appears to be a Euclidean triangle is found by measurement not to have angles totalling 180 degrees, we do not say that we have met with an instance which invalidates mathematical laws. We say that we have measured wrongly or that the triangle is not Euclidean. Ayer says, "And this is our procedure in every case in which a mathematical truth might appear to be confuted. We always preserve its validity by adopting some other explanation of the occurrence.

For formal logic, Ayer takes an example relating to the so-called law of excluded middle, which states that a proposition must be either true of false. One might suppose that a proposition of the form 'x has stopped doing y' would in certain cases constitute an exception to this law. For instance, if my friend has never written to me, it seems fair to say that it is neither true nor false that he has stopped writing to me. But one would not take it as an invalidation of the law of excluded middle. One would point out that the proposition 'My friend has stopped writing to me' is not a simple proposition, but the conjunction of the two propositions, 'My friend wrote to me in the past' and 'My friend does not write to me now', and, furthermore, that the proposition 'My friend has not stopped writing to me' is not, as it appears to be, contradictory to 'My friend has stopped writing to me', but only contrary to it. For it means 'My friend wrote to me in the past, and he still writes to me'. Ayer says that thus we preserve the law of the excluded middle by showing that the negating of a sentence does not always yield the contradictory of the proposition originally expressed.

And Ayer says that whatever instance we take, the principles of logic and mathematics are true universally simply because we never allow them to be anything else. And the reason for this is that we cannot abandon them without contradicting ourselves. Ayer says that this indicates that Mill is wrong in supposing that a situation can rise which will overthrow a mathematical truth.

Now Ayer says that the truths of logic and mathematics are analytic propositions or tautologies. Here he is aware of the fact that he is making an extremely controversial statement. But before we go in the depth of this establishment, we see the most familiar definition of an analytic proposition or judgement that is given by Kant.

Kant distinguishes between analytic (that is true by definition) and synthetic (that is factual) sentences and between a priori (logically independent of experience) and a posteriori (empirical) validity. But here it should be noted that Kant does not create the analytic. Synthetic distinction. According to professor Bernard the distinction between analytic and synthetic is firstly presupposed by Descartes, while Fisher and Lewis relate it to John Locke. Again we find it in Hume's distinction between relations of ideas and matters of fact. But Kant's importance is to attempt a rigorous treatment of this distinction.

Kant says that in a judgement, "either the predicate B belongs to the subject A, as something which is (covertly) contained in this concept A, or B lies outside the concept A, although it does indeed stand in connection with it. In the one case I entitle the judgement analytic, in the other synthetic."[5]

Analytic judgements, Kant explains, add nothing to the concept of the subject, but merely break it up into those constituent concepts that have all along been thought in it, although confusedly. Synthetic judgements, on the other hand, add to the concept of a subject a predicate... which has not been in any wise thought in it, and which no analysis could possibly extract from it. Kant gives an example of an analytic judgement that 'all bodies are extended' on the ground that the required predicate can be extracted from the concept of 'body'. As an example of a synthetic judgement he gives 'all bodies are heavy', and '7+5=12' on the grounds that the concept of twelve is by no means already thought of in merely thinking of the union of seven and five.

But this distinction of Kant has been criticized on various grounds. First of all, it is confined only to subject- predicate form excluding relational or existential prepositions. Secondly, the phrase subject contains the notion of predicate is purely metaphorical.

Caired objects Kant's distinction of analytic and synthetic

that it has mark only in psychological state of knowledge. Every knowledge is synthetic during the making but analytic when completed. A particular judgement may be synthetic for one and analytic for others. Caired says that both are required and we cannot talk of them in isolation.

Korner, in order to defend Kant, presents Kant's distinction in more logical form as- 'A judgement is analytic if its denial is self-contradictory and if not, it is synthetic.' This definition is applicable even to relational and existential judgements. But many philosophers object to the authenticity of law of thoughts and they don't accept that analytic judgements can be defined in terms of law of contradiction alone.

Garden J. Britton, in his book 'Kant's Theory of Science' proposes a new definition of analytic proposition and distinguishes it from synthetic one. He says, "A proposition is analytic if, and only if, it is true in all possible world, on the other hand if a proposition is true only is some possible world then it is synthetic. A bachelor is unmarried is analytic while B is an unmarried man is synthetic.

Rudoly Carnap also makes this distinction. He maintains that truth of any proposition is dependent upon linguistic and extra linguistic facts. He says that some propositions are bereft of factual content and therefore they only possess linguistic content. It is for this reason they can be termed as a priori and analytic. But contrary to this those propositions which only possess factual content and are deprived of linguistic one are called basic propositions. Basic propositions are mere nomenclature of sensedatum. So Carnap makes a clear cut distinction between a priori and basic propositions. Following Leibnitz and Wittgenstein, Carnap defines an analytic truth as a sentence which holds in every state description (in heibnitz' terminology, in all possible worlds). To know that a sentence holds in every state description we do not need any experience, these are 'truths of reason', independent of all empirical facts.

Sibjiban Bhattacharya shows that the concept of the a priori is often identified with a number of related concepts.

In this manner, we find some pairs of terms- for example we can see this list-

a priori	-	a posteriori
analytic	-	Synthetic
universal	-	Particular
necessary	-	Contingent
Formal	-	material

He says that the philosophers have a tendency to identify the first members of all these pairs (and also the second members). According to the philosophers 'A priori' has the same meaning as 'analytic', 'universal', necessary' and 'formal', and 'a posteriori' the same meaning as 'Synthetic', Particular', 'contingent' and 'material'.[6]

Now, he distinguishes between two senses of the term 'a priori'–

(a) The term 'a priori' is generally used as an adjective of 'knowledge, judgement, proposition etc. A judgement is a priori if, and only if, it is known independently of experience. This may be called the 'epistemological' sense of the term 'a priori'.

(b) A proposition is a priori if and only if its truth is independent of empirical facts. This may be called the 'logical' sense of the term 'a priori.

Now the definition of a priori, in the epistemological sense, involves the term 'independent of experience'. A knowledge may be said to be a priori, i.e., independent of experience, if, and only if, it is acquired before we have experience. This is suggested by Plato's theory that knowledge is recollection. This may be called the temporal sense of the term 'a priori'. But philosophers do not take this definition seriously as it presupposes the existence of knowledge which precedes experience in time an assumption which is hard to justify.

Then, Bhattacharya says, there is a causal definition of a priori, that is-

A knowledge is a priori if, and only if, it is not produced by sensibility (either alone or in conjunction with some other faculty). But there are some necessary conditions of this definition as-

(*a*) Here the existence of different faculties has to be assumed.
(*b*) The same knowledge can never be produced by two different faculties.
(*c*) One faculty cannot produce two different types of knowledge.

But this definition also is not satisfactory.

After that we see the logical sense of the term 'a priori'. It is said that "A proposition is a priori if, and only if, its truth is independent of empirical facts." All tautologies and logically true propositions involving quantification, identity are a priori in this sense.

Now, we come back to Ayer who says that the a priori truths of logic and mathematics are analytic propositions or tautologies. But he is aware of the fact that he is making an extremely controversial statement. It goes perhaps without saying that most rationalists have believed that a priori knowledge went beyond tautology. Plato and Aristotle, Augustine and St. Thomas, Descartes and Spinoza, Hegel and Bradley, Royce and Mc Taggart, were confident that by the use of reason they could travel from point to point in the conceptual framework of the world, moving along lines of logical necessity to truths that were genuinely new.

It is apparently Kant who first realizes to the full the difficulty of this conviction and treats this issue by showing the possibility of synthetic a priori knowledge. Now we see how it can be possible. The two dichotomies (a) a priori and a posteriori, and, (b) Analytic - Synthetic, give rise to four possible forms of judgement—

Analytic a priori judgement

Synthetic a priori judgement

Analytic a posteriori judgement and

Synthetic a posteriori judgement

No judgements would be considered analytic a posteriori judgements. An a posteriori judgement is dependent on experience, and hence gives us information, which an analytic judgement being uninformative, does not. Synthetic a posteriori judgements are simply informative judgements about concepts derived from experienced objects which may be proved false by future experience. None of these judgements constitutes certain knowledge in the older rationalist sense, since they rest upon experience. On the other hand, the triviality of analytic a priori judgements, although they are certain, insures that they cannot give us knowledge, or add to what we already know.

Knowledge, for Kant, consists primarily of synthetic a priori judgements, which are informative because they are synthetic, yet certain because they are a priori and cannot be contradicted by experience. The concept of synthetic a priori judgement is really revolutionary in spirit as it reconciles empiricism with rationalism. In order to have knowledge judgement must have universality, necessity and novelty.

According to Kant, Synthetic a priori judgements are found in mathematics and natural science. For example- '7+5=12' is a synthetic a priori judgement. It is universal and necessary and the subject 7+5 contains nothing over and above the uniting of two numbers into one. Similarly geometric propositions are synthetic a priori. Again, Kant says, pure physics contains synthetic a priori judgements as 'everything that happens or event has a cause'. Being universal and necessary it is a priori while the predicate (cause) is not contained either in parts or in whole in the subject (event) so synthetic.

H.W. Cassirer says that Kant has conceived synthetic a priori judgement in purely logical terms and not in psychological operations, so we must presume that the relation between a priori judgement and empirical ones is likewise to be though of as logical in character.

But Carnap denies the very possibility of synthetic a priori propositions. Carnap identifies the analytic with the a priori, because, according to him, there is only one way of knowing a priori propositions, viz, by logic, and logic cannot gie us any new knowledge. Kant can hold that these are synthetic a priori judgements, simply because he holds that we have a priori intuition (which is sensuous according to Kant).

Friedrich Waismann says that it is not at all clear what meaning can be given to the phrase 'synthetic a priori judgement.' He says, "To maintain that a particular proposition is a synthetic a priori judgement, one has to demonstrate in a precise way that it cannot be deduced from mere conventions as to the use of language. Such an inquiry would be opposite to a formalized language, where all the rules can be laid down in a precise and unambiguous way. But even in our everyday life, it is difficult to 'demonstrate' that an expression like 'red and green exclude each other' is not a grammatical rule. Therefore there is an irremovable lack of clarity inherent in the formulation of this question. Again, Waismann says, "We neither deny nor affirm the existence of synthetic a priori judgements...We are altering the angle from which the question is generally regarded, namely by comparing the cases generally adduced as examples of the existence of synthetic a priori judgements with other examples which lead us step by step to cases which are quite clearly conventions as to the use of language.' And he says, "by considerations of this kind we unsettle certain prejudices and help the other person to look at things with a less partial eye. And when he begins to undertake grammatical investigations of this kind, his need to speak of synthetic a priori judgements will soon disappear."[7]

Windelband describes synthetic a priori as a crossbreed of analytic a priori and synthetic a posteriori.[8]

Now, we see how Ayer reacts on Kant's synthetic a priori

judgements. Ayer seriously challenges Kant's concept of synthetic a priori. He says that Kant's thesis is based upon a slight confusion between two criteria, which are logical and psychological. It says that a judgement like '7+5=12' may be synthetic if judged by psychological criterion (since the concept of 12 is not contained in 7+5), but when judged from logical criterion '7+5=12' is an analytic judgement (since the denial of '7+5=12' is self-contradictory). And according to Ayer, the logical criterion is more important than psychological one and judged by that criterion there is no possibility of synthetic a priori. Ayer says, "...it is clear that it is this logical proposition, and not any psychological proposition, that Kant is really anxious to establish. His use of the psychological criterion leads him to think that he has established it, when he has not."[9]

Kant's synthetic a priori is rejected because it seems to rest on a distinction that is both drawn in psychological terms and is inapplicable to a large range of our judgements. And, if this distinction is drawn more precisely, we can see, as schlick says, "that there are no other a priori judgements than the analytic, or rather, as we prefer to say today, that only tautological propositions are a priori."[10]

Now, we find such distinction in two chief forms. The first one is presented by Ayer. To avoid Kant's confusion, Ayer defines these propositions by saying that, "A proposition is analytic when its validity depends solely on the definitions of the symbols it contains, and synthetic when its validity is determined by the facts of experience."[11]

Ayer explains it through examples. He says the proposition, "There are ants which have established a system of slavery" it a synthetic proposition. Because one has to resort to actual observation of the behaviour of ants. On the other hand, the proposition, 'Either some ants are parasitic or none are' is an analytic proposition. If one knows what is the function of the worlds 'either', 'or', and 'not' then one can see that any proposition of the form 'either P is true or P is not true' is valid, independently of experience.

Ayer says that analytic propositions provide no

information about any matter of fact. These analytic propositions are entirely devoid of factual content. That is why no experience can confute them.

Now Brand Blanshard shows the application of the definition presented by Ayer. We ask whether 'red is a colour' is analytic. We ask for the definition of 'red' and find that any attempt at logical definition must begin "red is a colour which..." and thus it is obvious that the validity of 'red is a colour' does follow from its definition and the statement is analytic. Though it is clear that red so possesses colour that any definition of it must stress the connection, but what sort of connection this is? The mere fact that the connection follows from the definition shows nothing. By failing to recognize that the characters within a definition may be connected in extremely different ways, it assimilates judgements whose elements are necessarily connected to those whose elements are connected arbitrarily.

But if it is so, if all statements are to count as analytic whose validity follows from the definition of their terms, the cases that have commonly been thought the clearest instances of the synthetic a priori will be brought into the analytic camp by mere stipulation.

After that we look at Ayer's criterion of the synthetic. A proposition is synthetic, Ayer says, 'when its validity is determined by the facts of experience." But the problem remains here. The contention of rationalist philosophers is that there are synthetic judgements that are a priori, that is, not determined by the facts of experience, but presented to intelligence as necessary. If synthetic judgements are defined as empirical, these philosophers are of course all mistaken. But this is not so. They have merely been ruled mistaken by so defining terms that they could not be right.

Thus we see that the distinction presented by Ayer does not give us the needed clarity. Now, we see the second form of distinction, which is also presented by the positivists. it says, "a proposition is analytic when its validity follows from applying to it the law of contradiction, that is, when to deny it would be to contradict oneself, when its contradictory, would be, or would entail, self-contradiction." But again this criterion is so wide that it includes a great variety of judgements of the most different types. If the test of the analytic is to be the self-contradictoriness of the denial, these will be equally analytic. And that deprives the classification of any genuine interest.

Thus, we find, neither Kant's basis of distinction, then, nor either of the two new once offered by the positivists is satisfactory. Kant was confused as to what his basis is, and, the positivists gloss over vital distinctions. The problem, therefore, remains.

Now, let us see how Ayer explains that in saying that analytic propositions are devoid of factual content, it has not been suggesting that they are senseless in the way that metaphysical utterances are senseless. Though, Ayer says, there is a sense in which they may be said to add nothing to our knowledge. For they tell us only what we may be said to know already. Ayer, explains that if I know that may Queens are a relic of tree-worship and I discover that may Queens still exist in England, I can employ the tautology, 'If p employees q, and p is true, q is true' to show that there still exists a relic of tree-worship in England. But it does not provide any new knowledge, in the sense in which empirical evidence that the election of May Queens had been forbidden by law would provide new knowledge-

Ayer, further says, though they give us no information about any empirical situation, they do enlighten us by illustrating the way in which we use certain symbols. Thus, in saying that 'if all Bretons are Frenchmen, and all Frenchmen are Europeans, then all Bretons are Europeans' no matter of fact is being described. Here, only the convention is being indicated which governs the usage of the words 'if' and 'all'.

But, again he says that there is a sense in which analytic can give us new knowledge. They call attention to linguistic usages and reveal unsuspected implications in our assertions and beliefs. Ayer says that philosophical truths are analytic by a priori reasoning. A philosopher can legitimately hope to establish the truths which are already implicit in our concepts- truths which he can make explicit by conceptual analysis and clarification.

Ayer says that if one had to set forth all the information one possessed, with regard to matters of fact, one would not write down any analytic propositions. But one would make use of analytic propositions in compiling one's encyclopedia, and besides enabling one to make one's list of information complete, the formulation of analytic propositions would enable one to make sure that the synthetic propositions of which the list is composed, formed a self-consistent system.

Now Ayer talks about the analytic character of the truths of logic and mathematics. He says, the analytic character of the truths of formal logic is obscured in the traditional logic through its being insufficiently formalized. For in speaking always of judgements, instead of propositions, and introducing irrelevant psychological questions, giving the impression that traditional logic is concerned with the workings of thought. What it was actually concerned with was the formal relationship of classes, as is shown by the fact that all its principles of inference are subsumed in the Boolean class-calculus, which is subsumed in its turn in the propositional calculus of Russell and whitehead. Their system makes it clear that formal logic is not concerned with the properties of men's minds, much less with the properties of material objects, but simply with the possibility of combining propositions by means of logical particles into analytic propositions, and with studying the formal relationship of these analytic propositions, in virtue of which one is deducible from another. Their procedure is to exhibit the propositions of formal logic as a deductive system, based on five primitive propositions, subsequently reduced in number to one. The system of Russell and whitehead itself is probably only one among many possible logics, each of which is composed of tautologies as interesting to the logician as the arbitrarily selected Aristotelian 'laws of thought'.

Ayer shows that a point not sufficiently brought out by Russell is that every logical proposition is valid in its own right. It's validity does not depend on its being incorporated in a system, and deduced from certain propositions which are taken as self-evident. Ayer says, "The construction of systems of logic is useful as a means of discovery and certifying analytic propositions, but it is not in principle essential even for this purpose. For it is possible to conceive of a symbolism in which every analytic proposition could be seen to be analytic in virtue of its form alone."[12]

Ayer explains that the validity of an analytic proposition does not depend on its being deducible from other analytic propositions. And this is the justification for disregarding the question whether the propositions of mathematics are reducible to propositions of formal logic, in the way that Russell supposes. It is not possible to reduce mathematical notions purely logical nations. Mathematics may form a special class of analytic propositions containing special terms, but is analytic all the same.

After that Ayer talks about the propositions of geometry. One might pardonably suppose the propositions of geometry to be synthetic. For it is natural for us to think, as Kant thought, that geometry is the study of the properties of physical space, and consequently that its propositions have factual content. But now, Ayer says, we know that this view is plausible enough in Kant's day, when Euclid's is the only known geometry, the subsequent invention of non-Euclidean geometries show it to be mistaken. We can see now that the axioms of a geometry are simply definitions, and that the theorems of a geometry are simply definitions, and that the theorems of a geometry are simply the logical consequences of these definitions. A geometry is not in itself about physical space, but a geometry can be used to reason about physical space. Whether a geometry can be applied to the actual physical world or not, is an empirical question which falls outside the scope of the geometry itself. Ayer says, "All that the geometry itself tells us is that if anything can be brought under the definitions, it will also satisfy the theorems. It is therefore a Purely logical system, and its propositions are purely analytic propositions."[13]

Again, it might be objected that the use made of

diagramms in geometrical treatises shows that geometrical reasoning is not purely abstract and logical, but depends on our intuition of the properties of figures. But it is not right. Geometry is a purely logical system, its propositions are purely analytic, its diagramms are not essential to completely rigorous geometry. And the fact that most of us need the help of actual diagrammatic examples to be made aware of the consequences of geometric applications shows merely that our intellects are unequal to the task of carrying out very abstract processes of reasoning without the assistance of intuition.

Thus the propositions of pure geometry are analytic and this leads us to reject Kant's hypothesis that geometry deals with the form of intuition of our outer-senses. Similarly, the propositions of arithmetic are analytic leads us to reject Kantian hypothesis that arithmetic is concerned with our pure intuition of time, the form of our inner-sense.

Ayer says that these analytical propositions are necessary and certain. They can not be confuted in experience because they do not make any assertion about the empirical world. They simply record our determination to use words in a certain fashion, If we try to deny them, it will be self contradictory. As Wittgenstein Puts it, "Our justification for holding that the world could not conceivably disobey the laws of logic is simply that we could not say of an unlogical world how it would look."[14]

It is clear, our knowledge that no observation can ever confute the proposition '7+5 = 12' depends simply on the fact that the symbolic expression '7+5' is synonymous with '12'. An another example is—All oculist is an eye-doctor without the help of any logical laws, since it denotes that subject and predicate are synonymous, so analytic. And the same explanation holds good for every a priori truth. However Quine tries to condemn synonymity criteria of analytic judgments.

Now, Ayer shows, how these tautologies sometimes can be surprising. Poincare says, "If all the assertions which mathematics puts forward can be derived from one another by formal logic, mathematics cannot amount to anything more than an immense tautology." But, here, the question is, that, can we really allow that these theorems which fill so many books serve no other purpose than to say in a roundabout fashion "A = A?" Poincare's own theory is that the sense of invention and discovery in mathematics belongs to it in virtue of mathematical induction, the principle that what is true for the number I, and true for n+I, when it is true for n, is true for all numbers. And he claims that this is a synthetic a priori principle. Ayer says it is, in fact, a priori, but it is not synthetic. Ayer says, " If poincare were right about mathematical induction; he would not have Provided a satisfactory explanation of the paradox that a mere body of tautologies can bc so interesting and so surprising."[15] Again, Ayer says that discoveries can be made, not only in arithmetic, but also in geometry and formal logic, where no use is made of mathematical induction.

Ayer finds this explanation very simple. He says that the power of logic and mathematics to surprise as depends, like their usefulness, on the limitations of our reason. A being whose intellect is infinitely powerful will take no interest in logic and mathematics. For he will see at a glance everything that his definitions implied. But our intellects are not of this order, even so simple a tautology as 91 × 79 = 7189 is beyond the scope of our immediate apprehension and requires as to resort to calculation, which is simply a process of tautological transformation. The multiplication tables are rules for carrying out this process in arithmatic, and the laws of logic are rules for the tautological transformation of sentences expressed in logical symbolism or in ordinary language. And, then, Ayer says, "Clearly the risk of error in logical reasoning is proportionate to the length and the complexity of the process of calculation. And in the same way, the more complex an analytic proposition is, the more chance it has of interesting and surprising us.

The rules of deduction belong to the internal regulative mechanism of a consistent language. Logical rules guide us in the transition from premises to conclusions. The appearance of genuine novelty in deductive inference is only psychological, because it is due to our incapacity to comprehend in one flash of insight the implications of more complicated sets of premises.[16]

Thus Ayer shows that the propositions which we know to be valid independently of all experience, are so only in virtue of their lack of factual content After showing that validity of a priori propositions is determined, Ayer puts forward the criterion used to determine the validity of empirical propositions. All propositions are either a priori or empirical. And it is clear that the criterion by which the validity of an a priori or analytic proposition is determined is not sufficient to determine the validity of an empirical or synthetic proposition. Because the validity of an empirical proposition is not purely formal. An empirical proposition is said to be false, not because it is formally defective, but because it fails to satisfy some material criterion.

But what this criterion is, it is still to be discovered. All a priori propositions are validated in the same way but this does not hold good of empirical propositions also. Many philosophers talk about 'ostensive' propositions, those recording immediate experience, are not mere hypotheses, but are absolutely certain. For they are supposed to be purely demonstrative in character, and so incapable of being refuted by any subsequent experience.

But Ayer does not admit that any synthetic proposition can be purely ostensive. For one cannot in language point to an object without describing it. In describing a situation, one is not merely 'registering' a sense-content, one is classifying it in some way or other, and this means going beyond what is immediately given. So, consequently, no synthetic proposition can be absolutely certain. Only tautologies are certain.

Empirical propositions are hypotheses, which may be conformed or discredited in actual sense-experience. Ayer says that when one speaks of hypotheses being verified in experience, it is never just a single hypothesis which an observation conforms or discredits, but always a system of hypotheses. If a scientific law is found to be invalid by experience, we can say that conditions were not what they seemed to be or we had dismissed some relevant factor, or that we were hallucinating. A proposition which we maintain in the face of all experience is not a hypothesis, but a definition. Thus, many of our 'laws of nature' are merely disguised definitions in incontestable, confused by the fact that our definitions are not immutable. If experience says that all A's have property B, we tend to take possession of this and ultimately refuse to call anything A unless it has B And in that case 'All A's have B', originally a synthetic generalization, comes to express a plain tautology. The famous 'All men are mortal' is a case in point.

Ayer says that we formulate hypotheses, in science for instance, to enable us to make accurate predictions. We assume that a system of hypotheses which has broken down once is likely to break down again. And we alter our hypotheses to increase the probability of them anticipating experience. It is therefore necessary to make clear what is meant by 'probability'.

Roughly speaking, increased probability means increased confidence, and confidence is what we place on rational belief. There is no absolute standard of rationality. We trust, says Ayer, contemporary Science because they have been successful in practice. In future, it is possible that we adopt different methods, and view the present ideas as irrational.

Thus according to Ayer, every synthetic proposition is a rule for the anticipation of future experience, distinguished from other synthetic propositions in that it is relevant to different situations. And to say that a proposition is true a priori is to say that it is a tautology which does not contain any information about any matter of fact. Ayer says, any genuine proposition must be either tautologous (analytic) or empirically verifiable.

Here it is relevant to know that the radical empiricism of Quine propounds the doctrine that apart from experience there cannot be any genuine and legitimate source of knowledge for necessary truth. Quine in his article "Two

Dogmas of Empiricism' refers to empiricist dogmatist notion when statements are analyzed into linguistic and non linguistic components. Quine accepts a holistic view of language that truth is neither matter nor form but the whole language of them. There can be no rationale for making a distinction between a priori and a posteriori as distinction is only matter of degree and not of kind. The 'Holism' and 'indeterminacy of meaning' as put forth by him leads to startling results that there is no proposition which is not subject to correction and is not doubtful and indeterminate, so there cannot be any a priori and analytical knowledge which can claim to have apodeictic certainty.

Quine refutes different versons of analytic - Synthetic judgments by saying - we cannot define analytic - synthetic on the grounds of self contradiction. Since the notion is as vague as the analytic - synthetic themselves. Next is, analytic judgment can not be true witness of meaning alone cause then it will become an intermediate between a word and its reference which is absurd. Again, it is also not possible to define an analytic proposition as symantical rules because symantical rules themselves presuppose the concept of analytic.

P.F. Strawson answers Quine by writing a paper "In defence of Dogma". For Strawson an expression is meaningful so far as it has definiteness and if the use of an expression is clear and precise and its meaning is definite then we can always say whether it is synthetic or analytic. There may be a case of indecision but a border line case does not refute a distinction.

Again Quine maintains that analytic, self-contradiction, symantical and definite are member of the same family. Thus anyone of them cannot be defined in terms of other usage. But Strawson does not accept it, since truth and fact belong to the same category, yet truth can be defined by facts.

But Quine inspite of propounding the doctrine of indeterminacy of meaning later on accepts that the meaning of logical connectives are definite, well defined, clear and distinct. The logical principles like De Morgan Theorm is true by virtue of its meaning of logical connectives. It is on the basis of this solid foundation it can be stated safely that these logical principles are analytical in nature.

Brand Blanshard says that according to positivists, knowledge of the actual world comes exclusively from perception. But if necessary propositions say nothing about fact, what do they Say? Here comes the essence of the present day empiricist's contention. Positivists say that—

(*a*) necessary statements are reports of linguistic usage,
(*b*) they represent conventions,
(*c*) they are analytic, and
(*d*) they say nothing about fact.

According to positivists, necessary statements like 'All bachelors are unmarried', 'a material thing cannot be in two places at once' are all reports of linguistic usage. By saying that 'all bachelors are unmarried' no insight into the connection of two attributes in nature is being declared, for being a bachelor and being unmarried are the same thing. If we apply one of them to a person, we can never think of denying the other.

It follows that necessary statements reflect conventions. They simply record our determination to use words in a certain fashion. The laws of logic are themselves rules of language, and like other such rules, are conventions.

According to positivists, necessary statements are analytic. They merely explicate what we mean, and therefore give us nothing new. Here he means nothing logically new, not psychologically new.

Besides being linguistic, conventional and analytic, necessary propositions are held to be non-factual, that is, they say nothing about nature, nothing about the realm of existent things and events. 'They are entirely devoid of factual content. And, this is for this reason that no experience can confute them." We know that if there are seven plus five, there must be twelve, for by the two terms we mean the same. No observations of things or events could affect this identity of meaning.

Blanshard says that this account of a priori knowledge is ingenious, plausible, and extremely important. It is important because, if true, it effectively discredits the main instrument of speculative philosophy and theology, and also many of what were supposed to be their self-evident conclusions. Blanshard says, "We have seen that the main instrument of metaphysicians from Plato to MC Taggart has been reason, conceived as revealing the nature of things. In the positivist conception of reason, the necessity of an insight is no guarantee that it applies to nature or reveals anything outside the confines of meaning."[17]

Again, many of the questions raised by philosophers have received answers that, once understood, were supposed to be seen as self - evident and necessary. 'what is matter?' as answered by Berkeley, 'what is mind?' as answered by Bosanguet, 'What is causality?' as answered by MC Taggart, 'what is justice, or piety, or Courage?' as answered by Plato - they were supposed to tell us not only what words mean, but what things are - And we see that if positivism is right about necessity, this is a mistaken pretension.

The positivist view of a priori knowledge, unlike some other positivist theories, has been taken over by the majority of analytic philosophers. It has been established conclusively. Now Blanshard attempts to inquire it. In this order he starts with the first of the positivist's contentions about necessary propositions that they are in some sense statements about language "They call attention to linguistic usages, of which we might otherwise not be conscious...' such statements are scattered through the literature of logical empiricism, but they are ambiguous. Those just repeated certainly sound like statements about how words are in fact used. Necessary Propositions "Simply record our determination to use words in a certain fashion", is it the fact or the resolution that is here recorded? Blanshard takes the first view that necessary statements are records of actual usage. "Blue is a colour' tells us that people do not use the first word in situations where they would refuse to use the second. Thus necessary propositions 'report facts of actual linguistic usage.' It means they do say something about fact and it is inconsistent with the central teachings of positivism that necessary propositions say nothing about fact.

Again positivists say that all necessary propositions are analytic. But it is clear that statements about how words are used by myself or others are not analytic in any sense of the term, they are one and all synthetic - when a person talks about the calour red, he is not talking about the usages of any particular language like English, French, German or set of languages, he is not talking about usage at all, but about something that could be equally well referred to in any number of languages, namely the colour red and its characteristics. The word 'red' and the colour red are utterly different things.

A sentence must be in some particular language, such as English or Hittile, and it is perfectly plain that necessary propositions such as "red is a colour" are not statements about English or Hittite sentences. How were the positivists to hold at once that necessary statements had to do with the use of language and also that they had a universality independent of any particular language? Here carnap explains that pure syntax does not deal with this or that language, it concerns itself. "With the possible forms of sentences, without regard either to the designs of the words of which the sentences are composed, or to whether any of the sentences exist on paper somewhere in the world."[18]

Carnap says that for syntactical study, "the meaning of the words is quite inessential to the purpose, and need not be known." But it can not be accepted. It is idle to deal with words except through their meanings. Indeed words without meanings are not strictly words at all. Ayer writes in 1936, "I think, that our view must be that what are called a priori propositions do not describe how words are actually used, but merely prescribe how words are to be used. They make no statement whose truth can be accepted or denied. They merely lay down a rule which can be followed or disobeyed."[19]

The positivists agree that a priori statements are necessary and rules of usage have no necessity whatever, But, Blanshard says, to hold at once that such propositions are necessary and also that they are arbitrary prescriptions about usage is thus self contradictory. It may be replied that the necessity and the freedom fall in different steps, but this is untrue. There is no possible manipulation of words that will affect it in the least.

If a priori statements are really prescriptions about usage, then not only will they not be necessary, they will not even be true or false. Positivism at times accept this consequence Ayer writes, "just as it is a mistake to identify a priori propositions with empirical propositions about language, so I now think that it is a mistake to say that they are themselves linguistic rules. For apart from the fact that they can properly be said to be true, which linguistic rules can not, they are distinguished also by being necessary, whereas linguistic rules are arbitrary. At the same time, if they are necessary it is only because the relevant linguistic rules are presupposed."[20]

After that Blanshard turns to the second of the positivist thesis that a priori statements are conventions. The transition is not a sharp one, since the conventions are alleged to be themselves linguistic. Now the point is not whether they are verbal but whether they are arbitrary. Schlick says, "The rules of language are in principle arbitrary."[21]

Ayer says, "It is perfectly conceivable that we should have employed different linguistic conventions from those we actually do employ."[22]

But it is self contradictory. To say that a proposition is necessary is to say that the state of things it asserts could not be otherwise, and hence that there are no possible alternatives to it. To say that it is conventional is to say that there are possible alternatives to it. Hence to hold that it is both necessary and conventional is to held both that there are, and that there are not, alternatives to it. Thus they are maintaining that 7+5 need not make twelve, that red need not to be a colour. For the ordinary mind, such statements seem absurd. But if necessary statements are really arbitrary conventions, it is open to us to choose their opposites as our conventions, and then all the above statements may hold.

There is no rational ground for preferring any convention of thought or conduct to any other.

When a priori statements are called conventional, the discussion about the character of logical laws takes place inevitably. And it can be said that if the laws of logic are conventions merely, in the sense that alternative laws which deny them have an equal claim to validity, then there is not such a thing as a reliable proposition, either a priori or empirical, in the range of what was once called knowledge. But professor Williams puts the point that, "although we can invent artificial systems of logistic ad infinitum, whatever postulates, definitions, formative rules we lay down, with whatever language or metalanguage we operate, their consequences are what they are, irrespective of convention and convenience, by the one inescapable sort of necessity."[23]

To say that logic is conventional, is to say that laws of logic, including the law of contradiction, have alternatives. But this statement can not be empirical because no statements of logic are empirical. But cannot be an analytic statement, for an analytic statement is defined as one whose contradictory is self-contradictory and this rules the present statement out. Thus the statement that logic is conventional is neither empirical nor analytic, and hence on their premises no statement at all. So, no one, not even the positivist, has succeeded in living up to the theory that logic is convention merely.

According to positivists being linguistic and conventional, a priori statements are analytic also, that is, to be mere tautologies. But for the seeker after knowledge a tautology is a vain repetition, it gives truths of a kinds but certainly not of the kind he most want. Whether a priori knowledge does in fact give only tautology is a difficult and technical question. Dr. Ewing Says, "The question is one of the most important in the whole of philosophy. If there are no synthetic a priori judgements..... thought can never give us new truth but only the same truth as we has before but expressed in different words, all deductive inferences and self-evident proposition will be a matter of arbitrary verbal convention, there will be no philosophy beyond the ordering and clarification of propositions known, if known at all, in some other way, mathematics will be merely a game with symbols, there will be no relation of entailment or necessary connection in the objective world but merely a set of brute facts any of which might perfectly well exist without the others existing also."[24]

Kant shows the possibility of synthetic a priori knowledge but synthetic a priori knowledge means to concede that in advance of all experience of the connection one is asserting, one can gain fresh knowledge of the nature of things simply by sitting down and thinking. But the empiricists are not ready to accept such a faculty, and they scrutinize Kant's account with sceptical and hostile eye. But neither Kant, nor Ayer gets success in solving this problem and the problem remains there.

Now, Blanshard takes the fourth contention about a priori knowledge, made by positivists, that is, a priori statement and reasoning are proposals regarding usage, namely that they say nothing about the actual world. When I say that two straight lines cannot enclose a space, or that the same surface can not be black and non-black, I am not saying anything about the objects mentioned, but only illustrating my usage. Positivists tell us that in asserting such entailment as 'if a proceeds b, and b proceeds c, then a proceeds c' we "say nothing". Now the question is that 'what it is that is true if nothing is said?" If nothing said, nothing is true, if something is true then something must have been said.

But it does not look satisfactory: When Bradley says that reality is consistent, he means something about the world. He is not merely making a declaration about his linguistic practice.

Dr. Ewing maintains that the statement "You cannot take a shilling from a purse which contains only six pence" is a necessary statement that also says something about reality.

But there is a reply that if you cannot take a shilling from a purse containg only six pence, that is a logical impossibility, which state nothing about fact, since no fact could turn up that would falsify it.[25]

But, Blanshard says, this is odd reasoning. How a priori statements can be true at all if they are not true of the actual world. When one says that whatever is red is extended, he is supposed to be talking about all possible red things, including all the red things that have existed, do exist or will exist. To hold that one is saying nothing about the existent at all is very odd.

Though, says Blanshard, we can see that there are some a priori propositions, which are universal, the terms they connect are as - suches, but all that exists is particular, and hence such statements cannot be true of it. "What is red is extended" means "if anything is red, then it is extended" and this neither says nor implies that there is, has been, or will be, any red thing in the world.

Blanshard says that it is true that a priori statements deal with as-suches, but these as-suches may exist and be given. Indeed the attempt to draw a line between the universal and the existent is fundamentally wrong-headed, for unless universals were present in individual cases, it would be meaningless to call them cases at all. But if necessary propositions may thus be meant and seen to hold of individual cases, they may clearly be true of the existent.

John Foster writes, "Ayer regards analytic truths as devoid of factual content, this seems to have the unpalatable consequence that philosophers can only avoid nonsense at the cost of vacuity.

Blanshard says that suppose, positivist is right in saying that while a priori proposition are not true of the actual world, they are somehow true nevertheless. Of what realm or region are they true? If they are statements about what we actually mean by our words, they are obviously statements of fact. If, again they are statements about pure concepts and their linkages, about an order of Platonic ideas, subsistent but not existent, they introduce a kind of non sensible entity that the positivist wants above all things to avoid. Nor do they apply to possibilities alone as opposed to the actual. But is a priori statements are true neither or the existent nor of the subsistent, neither of the actual, nor the merely possible, of what realm or region are they true? Some positivists deny that these assertions are propositions at all, and hold them to be arbitrary rules of syntax. But there is no thinkable alternative to this particular type of convention.

Foster raises some problems against Ayer's theory of analytic proposition. In Ayer's terminology, a proposition is said to be a tautology if, and only if, its is 'analytic', and it is said to be analytic if, and only if, 'its validity depends solely on the definitions of the symbols it contains." But Ayer's wording here is a bit loose, since strictly it is sentences, not propositions, which contain symbols. But, Foster says, presumably Ayer means that an analytic proposition is one which is expressed by an analytic sentence and that an analytic sentence is one whose meaning ensures that it expresses a truth.

Again foster says, "As we have seen part of what Ayer wants to achieve by his criterion is a restriction on the a priori methods of philosophy. The elimination of metaphysics involves, amongst other things, denying the existence of any intellectual faculty by which philosophers could acquire a priori knowledge of the nature of reality. Thus it is only by vindicating his claim that all a priori truths are analytic that Ayer can hope to restrict philosophy to what he regards as its sole legitimate business, that of conceptual clarification and analysis.

When we try to find out that how the problems of analytic-synthetic arose at all, some of the problems can be traced back to Plato and Socrates, who made the distinction between knowledge and opinion. According to them, there are propositions which are eternal truths, and some others which, even if they are true for some time, may become false. But the position has completely changed now. Metaphysical propositions have long ceased to count as eternal truths or even as truths, propositions of pure physics, regarded by Kant as necessary, seem to have lost their former status. Even logic and pure mathematics, providing examples of eternal truths down the ages, seem to have suffered at the hands of modern logicians.

Thus instead of regarding analytic truths a truths 'which we will not surrender at all' and 'which are destined to be maintained independently of our observations of the world'.[26] Many logicians now tend to regard them as truths 'which we seem to be least ready to give up'. The distinction between analytic and synthetic is thus reduced to difference in degree and the only problem is to explain the comparative obstinacy with which we hold to the analytic truths.[27]

This is a view held not merely by individual logicians like Quine and Morton white thefall of logic and mathematics seems to have been general and due to two entirely different factors. First, the development of alternative systems of mathematics and logic show that a proposition which is analytic in one system need not be so in another. This leads to the view that there are no analytic propositions as such, but only analytic proposition relative to a system. But if logic and mathematics are conceived as arbitrary systems, they cannot be a source of knowledge. They are, at best, games in which some people find interest. The laws of logic and mathematical propositions are not really proposition at all. They are stipulations or rules, and cannot be characterized as true or false. Hence they cannot afford examples of analytic truths. And the second factor, responsible for the degradation of mathematics (and also of logic), is the discovery of serious defects in the foundations of mathematics. It is now proposed that laws of logic and mathematics may be nothing but empirical generalizations. 'The negative results obtained by the mathematical method confirm the assertion of materialistic philosophy that mathematics is in the last resort a natural science, that its notions and methods are rooted in experience and that attempts at establishing the foundation of mathematics without taking into account its originating in natural sciences are bound to fail.'[28]

Thus, it can be said that there is no longer a naive belief in the infallibility of logic and mathematics. The philosophical problem of a priori- a posteriori now is not merely a problem of giving exact definitions of the terms, but also of proving that there can be any such things as a priori truths at all.

The mere assertion that analytic truths are logical truths is not sufficient we shall also have to prove that logic can give us knowledge of truths, and of truths which are different in kind from empirical truths.

References

1. Feigl. H., 'Logical Empiricism', "Twentieth Century Philosophy", Ed. Dagobert D. Runes, p. 387.
2. Whewell, W., 'History of Scientific Ideas',
3. A. J. Ayer, 'Language, Truth and Logic', p. 69.
4. A. J. Ayer, 'Basic Propositions', in Philosophical Analysis.
5. Kant, I., 'The Critique of Pure Reason' trans. N. K. Smith, p. 48.
6. S. Battacharya, 'Doubt, Belief and Knowledge', p. 135.
7. F. Waismann, 'Synthetic A Priori Judgements', Reprinted from 'Principles of Linguistic Philosophy', p. 57-68.
8. Wilhelm Windelband, 'A History of Philosophy', Ist Ed., Vol. II.
9. A. J. Ayer, 'Language, Truth and Logic', p. 73.
10. M. Schlick, in 'Reading in Philosophical Analysis', Ed. H. Feigl and W. Sellars, 280.
11. A. J. Ayer, 'Language, Truth and Logic', p. 73.
12. Ibid, p. 77.
13. Ibid, p. 78.
14. L. Wittgenstein, 'Tractatus-Logico-Philosophicus', 3-031.
15. A. J. Ayer, 'Language, Truth and Logic', p. 82.
16. H. Feigl, 'Logical Empiricism', 'Twentieth Century Philosophy', Ed. Dagobert D. Runes.
17. B. Blanshard, 'A Priori Knowledge' Reprinted from 'Reason and Analysis'.
18. R. Carnap, 'The Logical Syntax of Language', 7.
19. Analysis, Vol. 4, 20.
20. A. J. Ayer, 'Language, Truth and Logic', Preface 1946 Ed.

21. Feigl and Sellars, 'Reading in Philosophical Analysis' 165.
22. A. J. Ayer, 'Language, Truth and Logic', p. 84.
23. Analysis Vol. 5, (September 1938), 93.
24. Ewing, 'A Short Commentary on Kant's Critique of Pure Reason', 20-21.
25. Ewing, "The Linguistic Theory of A Priori Propositions" Proceedings of the Aristotelian Society, Vol 40, 207.
26. W. V. Quine, 'Truth by Convention'.
27. W. V. Quine, 'The Methods of Logic'.
28. A. Mostowski, 'The present state of Investigation on the Foundation of Mathematics'.

7

The Problem of Personal Identity and the Knowledge of Other Minds

In this chapter we shall discuss the problem of personal identity and the knowledge of other minds. Both problems are related to the concept of person. First we take the problem of personal identity.

The problem of personal identity is not just a problem for philosophers, it has always been a practical problem for self-conscious people. It is a problem we all face, either explicitly or implicitly, every self-conscious minute of our lives. In everything that we do, we adopt some conception of our identity, whether we are called upon to articulate it or not. For example- one walks into a classroom with certain conceptions of his own abilities and intelligence, his status among other students and a certain vanity about his looks, his grades etc. But is it really what can be called personal identity? It is just concerned with status and role among other people?

But before we describe what personal identity is, it is important for us to know what a person is? And to answer this question, we look back to the traditional mind-body problem. We can see that the separation of mind and body, or at least, soul and body is as old as Christian theology, but it was not considered a serious problem untill Descartes. There is no such separation in ancient times. When Aristotle writes about "the soul", he means nothing other than "the form of the body". He says, "We have, then, given a general definition of what the soul is: it is substance expressed as form. It is this which makes a body what it is..."[1]

Descartes is really the first to develop a systematic theory about the nature and interrelationship of mind and body. He interprets the human as being both a mind (res cogitans) and a body (res extensa). For him, both body and mind are substances of different sorts, body is a thing extended in space and unthinking, mind is a thinking thing un-extended in space, and both are so ultimately united in the human being that mental events can affect bodily events and vice versa.

Some philosophers attempt to resolve the mind-body problem either by absorbing the body into the mind or by absorbing the mind into the body. The former are absolute idealists like Berkeley who claims that minds and the perceptions of those minds are the only things that exist. The latter are materialists like Rudolph Carnap and Otto Neurath, who maintain that whatever exists is physical. Both of these positions are monistic in contrast to Descartes' dualism.

Actually these philosophers, aware of the perplexing problems associated with dualism, reject dualism in favour of monism which affirms one substance either mind or body, but not both.

The twentieth century philosopher, Gilbert Ryle lines up with those monists who affirm the body. He says that Descartes made a serious logical mistake in his claim that the human is a body and a mind. Ryle favors the claim that the human is merely a body. "Although he allow us to say that minds and mental processes "exist", they exist only as things we talk about. They do not exist as entities that act and react with other things as bodies do."[2]

Even if we don't want to talk of substances at all, there is still the problem of explaining how our minds effect our bodies and how our bodies effect our minds. Now, we have a question, "Are there ways of conceiving of ourselves without falling into the Cartesian trap of talking about minds and bodies?"

And we see that a few possibilities can be suggested here. The first, perhaps is advanced by Ludwig Wittgenstein in his Philosophical Investigations. He wants to deny the very idea that human beings are a curious combination of two very different substances or kinds of entities or events. Rather, there are just people, not minds plus bodies.

P.F. Strawson defends this Wittgensteinian view. He present the concept of a person by saying that, "The concept of a person is logically prior to that of an individual consciousness. The concept of a person is not to be analyzed as that of an animated body or of an embodied anima. This is not to say that the concept of a pure individual consciousness might not have a logically secondary existence, if one thinks, or finds, it desirable. We speak of a dead person a body- and in the same secondary way we might at least think of a disembodied person, retaining the logical benefit of individuality from having been a person."[3]

Strawson attacks the idea that each of us is first of all a mind who 'has' a body. He says that each of us is first of all a person, and the concept of "having a body" is no less essential than the concept of "having a mind," We are essentially, according to strawson, "thinking things", only if by that we mean "thinking persons". Descartes Worries about how the two parts of a person can come together, strawson says that they should never have been separated in the first place.

Similarly, we see that Marleau Ponty rejects the traditional way of dividing up mind and body and suggests a very different conception of persons. He says, "...the body is not a self-enclosed mechanism on which the soul could act from the outside... In this case it would be better to say that bodily functioning is integrated with a level which is higher than that of life and that the body has truly become a human body."[4]

Ponty defends a thesis which is so strikingly similar to that defended by Wittgenstein and Strawson. He says, one cannot treat a person as an uneasy conglomerate of mental parts and body parts, but must begin with the whole person. The body itself is not only alive but, in an important sense, conscious. It is itself aware. Again he says that my body and myself are essentially one, and to try to separate them, as Descartes had done is to make the relationship between "me and my body" into an unnecessary mystery.

Again, we see that William James rejects the traditional Cartesian dualism. James, like Wittgenstein and Strawson, attacks the idea of separate "mental" events or "consciousness" and insists that "there is no such thing." But he is not denying that we are conscious. He is rather saying that we have to think of these as "functions" of the overall person, not as independent and possibly separable entities.

In this order, its will be good to know that, there is another theory which rejects daulism very strongly by saying that there are not two things at all, as there appear to be, but only one. Mind and body or, more accurately, mental events and certain bodily events are identical. This is called 'identical theory'. Jerome Shaffer writes, "It is the theory that thoughts, feelings, wishes and the rest of so-called mental phenomena are identical with, one and the same thing as, states and processes of the body... "Identical" in the sense that the actual events picked out by mentalistic terms are one and the same events are those picked out by physicalistic terms."[5]

Shaffer disagrees with the identity theory, but both his presentation and his criticism of it are central to the ongoing debate today. This theory is presently one of the hottest controversies in American philosophy.

So, while describing the mind-body problem, we see how different philosophers have presented the concepts of a person. After that we come back to the problem of personal identity. There are a number of questions which are to be answered, like, 'who am I', 'Is there something that can truly be called 'myself' without reference to anyone else?", 'How should we identify ourselves?' 'How do we?' 'Whether personal identity is a matter of personal choice or whether certain facts, factors or other people define our identity for us?'

It is not enough to say that a person is the sum total of facts about him or her. Surely some such 'facts' are simply irrelevant, and some facts are more essential then others. What is it about one without which one would not be the same? Presumably one would still be the same even if he never polishes his car. But what if he has a sex change operation? Or what if he completely loses his memory, all recollection of his family and friends?Or what if he physically disappears altogether, remaining only a whispy consciousness, a spirit or a ghost without a body? Would it then make sense to say that one is still the same? Thus we see that personal-identity is a question of essential properties.

Here it is important to know that traditionally there are two criterions through which personal-identity can be examined. First is the 'Mentalistic Theory' which is based on the criterion of memory. Second is the 'criterion of bodily identity.'

This problem has long troubled European philosophers. In the middle ages, Christian philosophers argue forcefully that all of this, except for one's individual religious attitudes and the soul, is irrelevant. One's identity is or should be simply a soul seeking salvation before God.

In the modern age, so many philosophers deal with this problem of personal identity. An important and still influential tradition in philosophy, from Descartes and Locke to Hume and Kant, focuses on self-consciousness as the sole key to personal identity.

Now we see how philosophers deal with this problem. We start with Descartes. He says, "But what then am I?" A thing which thinks. It is a thing which doubts, understands, affirms, denies, wills, refuses, which also imagines and feels." According to him, it is not his body that provides him with an identity or with the self from which he begins his philosophy. The particular aspects of the body cannot be essential to one's identity either. The self-identity is in mind, in thinking, doubting etc. Descartes says that, "...it is certain that this I (that is to say, my soul by which I am what I am) is entirely and absolutely distinct from my body, and can exist without it..."[6]

Thus according to him, personal identity depends wholly on self-consciousness, and that human identity is therefore different from the identity of anything else in the world.

Now we see Hume's argument where he talks about the identity or sameness of objects, and argues that human identity is ultimately no different. He says, "We now proceed to explain the nature of personal identity, which has become so great a question in philosophy, especially of late years in England, where all the abstruser sciences are study'd with a peculiar ordour and application... The identity, which we ascribe to the mind of man, is only a fictitious one, and of a like kind with that which we ascribe to vegetables and animals bodies. It cannot, therefore, have a different origin, but must proceed from a like operation to the imagination upon his objects."[7]

Hume questions here that on what basis do we create the 'fiction' of identity? And then he thinks over the elements which create it. First, there is spatis-termoral continuity of the thing. Again, in addition to spatio-termporal continuity, resemblance is also used as a criterion for identity. But Hume says that there are so many situations to think about. For example- if someone suddenly vanishes "into thin air", or casually replaces the lower two-thirds of his or her body with another, then what will be one's reaction? According to Hume, if something changes only a "small part" at a time, we call it the same, but if a person has a total change of appearance and personality right before our eyes, then what can we think? Can this radically changed person be the same? Or it is a different person?

These considerations lead philosophers to reject bodily continuity and resemblance as criteria for personal identity and turn instead to purely mental criteria. We can see Locke's argument. He says that, "In the state of living creatures, their identity depends not on a mass of the same particles, but on something else. For in them the variation of great particles of matter alters not the identity, an oak growing from a plant to a great tree, and then lopped, is still the same oak, and a colt grown up to a horse, sometimes fat, sometimes lean, is all the while the same horse, though, in both these cases, there may be a manifest change of the parts, so that truly they are not either of them the same masses of matter, though they be truly one of them the same oak, and the other the same horse... the identity of the same man consists, viz, in nothing but a participation of the same continued life, by constantly fleeting particles of matter, in succession vitally united to the same organized body."[8]

After that Locke distinguishes between the soul, which might be found in any number of different individuals, the "man", who is to be identified in the same way as animals or things, by its external characteristics, and the "person" which is what we mean by "personal" self identity. He says that, "If the identity of soul alone makes the same man, and there be nothing in the nature of matter why the same individual spirit may not be united to different bodies, it will be possible that those men, living in distant ages, and of different tempers, may have been the same man, which way of speaking must be from a very strange use of the word man, applied to an idea out of which body and shape are excluded... To find wherein personal identity consists, we must consider what person stands for:- which, I think, is a thinking intelligent being, that has reason and reflection, and can consider itself as itself, the same thinking thing, in different times and places, which it does only by that consciousness which is inseparable from thinking, and, as it seems to me, essential to it, it being impossible for anyone to perceive without perceiving that he does perceive.'...Since consciousness always accompanies thinking, and it is that which makes everyone to be what he calls self, and thereby distinguishes himself from all other thinking things, in this alone consists personal identity, i.e. the sameness of a rational being, and as far as this consciousness can be extended backwards to any past action or thought, so far reaches the identity of that person, it is the same self now it was then, and it is by the same self with this present one that now reflects on it, that that action was done."[9]

Thus the main thesis of Locke's argument is, that, personal self-identity is based upon self-consciousness, in particular, upon memories about one's former experiences. He argues that man is different from animals, whose identity is based on the continuity of the body. The identity of "man" as a biological organism is the same as the identity of animals, but the identity of a "person" that is, "personal" identity, depends on self- consciousness. Locke rejects the idea of the soul being the seat of self-identity, for the soul alone provides none of the characteristics that allow for the identity of either man (as the same organism) or of people (as the same persons).

It can be said that this way of equating personal self-identity with self-consciousness has been the main theory of modern thought. The ancient philosophers, for example, Aristotle does not believe this. For him, self-identity is essentially bodily identity without any particular reference to self-consciousness.

But Hume Criticizes this modern thesis. He turns his skeptical eye to the concept of the self-. According to him, the self is not only a "fiction" but a philosophical illusion based on those other fictions of metaphysics, substance and causation. He rejects the notion of substantive ego on the ground that no such entity is observable. He says, "When I enter intimately into what I call myself, I always stumble on some particular perception or other, of heat or cold, light or shade, love or hatred, pain or pleasure. I never catch myself, at any time, without a perception, and never can observe anything but the perception."[10]

And this leads him to assert that a self is 'nothing but a bundle or collection of different perceptions.' But here the question arises that in pronouncing concerning the identity of a person, do we observe some real bonds among his perceptions, or do we only feel one among the ideas we form of them. According to Hume, self-identity is nothing really belonging to these different perceptions and uniting them together. He says that, "The mind is a kind of theatre, where several perceptions successively make their appearance, pass, re-pass, glide away, and mingle in an infinite variety of postures and situations. There is properly no simplicity in it at one time, nor identity in different, whatever natural propension we may have to imagine that simplicity and identity."

Hume finds that memory must be regarded not as producing, but rather as discovering personal identity. Whereas self-consciousness has to be defined in terms of memory, self-identity can not be, for he says, the number of my perceptions which I can remember at any time always falls for short of the number of those which have actually occurred in my history, and those which I can not remember are no less constitutive of my self than those which I can.'

Ayer says that, "But having, on this ground, rejected the claim of memory to be the unifying principle of the self, Hume was obliged to confess that he did not know what was the connection between perceptions in virtue of which they formed a single self."[11]

Thus, we see that Hume believes that, "The whole of this doctrine leads us to a conclusion, which is of great importance in the present affair, viz. that all the nice and subtile questions concerning personal identity can never possibly be decided and are to be regarded rather as grammatical than as philosophical difficulties."[12]

Solomon says, "But Hume's argument that "I never can catch myself..." suffers from a self-contradiction. He can't even deny that there is a self without in some sense pointing to himself in order to do it."[13]

Now we see that Kant does not miss this point. He says that Hume's error is in confusing the supposed experience of self-consciousness with the transcendental rules with which these various experiences are tied. Kant accepts that Descartes and Locke are both correct in equating self- identity and self-consciousness, but Kant does not accept Descartes' view that the self is therefore a "thing" that we find in experience.

Kant gives this curious idea of the self as a rule a

formidable name, "the transcendental unity of apperception." The self for Kant is, indeed, essential to self-consciousness, but it is not "in" self-consciousness. It can be said that it is "behind" self-consciousness, that is, it is the activity of bringing our various experiences together in accordance with the basic rules of our experience.

The self, Kant says, is the thread that ties together our various experiences. It is not in the bundle of our experiences, but, as the "transcendental" thread that holds them all together, is as real as any experience.

Thus Kant turns Hume's argument towards the opposite conclusion. Kant accepts that I never find a self "in" my experiences, but I can always find myself in that "I" which has the experience. The self is the activity of applying the rules by which we organize our experience.

The self, we can say, defines us through our various changes, and identifies us from year to year, day to day and mood to mood. But the function of the self is also to serve as a way of identifying ourselves in distinction from other people and other things. Thus we can see that the question of self-identity now divides into two questions- (1) what is essential to being a self? and (2) what is essential to being a particular self?

Descartes concept of the self as a thinking thing is not sufficient to tell as what makes one person different from another, and he finds it necessary to supplement his concept of self with an account of how a person is composed of a self and a body in some special way. Similarly, Locke distinguishes between personal identity and identity as a man and tells us that both are necessary for us to understand how one particular person is different from another particular person.

Kant's conception of self, the transcendental self, only answers the first question. There is nothing in the notion of transcendental self that allow us to distinguish between different people and tell them apart. Accordingly, he identifies another "self" that he calls the "empirical self", which includes all of those particular things about us that make us different people. Differences in our bodies, our looks, our size, our strength are such differences. So to are our different personalities, our different thoughts and memories.

Thus it is the empirical self that identifies us as individual persons. It is the transcendental self that makes us human. But the distinction between Kant's transcendental and empirical selves is not the same as Locke's distinction between "person" and "man", most of the characteristics of both of Locke's distinction can be part of what Kant calls the empirical self.

These have been the traditional answers to the philosophical problem of personal self-identity. What is it that makes one "the same person" from moment to moment and year to year? the spacio-temporal continuity of the body seems to be a part of the owner. But philosophers since (and before) Descartes have seen quite clearly that this is never enough, that it is also self-consciousness that provides the key to personal-identity. But even this has not solved the problem.

Contemporary philosophers, enamored by the growth of science, often talk as if our ultimate personal-identity is or should be what we know. The self is considered nothing other than the locus of knowledge, other things, as our looks, athletic abilities, enjoyments and actions-might be amusing or curious distractions but not the essence of personal identity. The problem of personal identity, both in each individual case and as a general problem, is the problem of deciding which of the many possible characteristics should be chosen as our own standards for personal identity.

Ayer says that it is customary for the authors of epistemological treatise to assume that our empirical knowledge must have a basis of certainty, and that there must therefore be objects whose existence is logically indubitable. And they consider it their business, not merely to describe the objects immediately 'given' to us, but also to prove logically the existence of objects which are not so 'given'.

According to positivists, there are no objects whose

existence is indubitable. For since existence is not a predicate, assertions that an object exists are always synthetic propositions, and we have already seen that no synthetic proposition is logically sacrosanct. Our empirical knowledge can not have a basis of logical certainty.

Ayer says that in the case of the problem of 'perception', to avoid metaphysics, he adopts a phenomenalist standpoint. And he finds that the same treatment should be applied to the traditional 'problems' of our knowledge of our own existence, and of the existence of the other people.

Ayer says that the problem concerning the possibility of bridging the gulf between mind and matter are fictitious problems arising out of the senseless metaphysical conception of mind and matter, or mind and material things, as 'substances'. And then he says that being freed from metaphysics, we see that there can be no a priori objections to the existence either of causal or of epistemological' connections between mind and material things.

Ayer considers the question whether it is or is not logically possible for a sense-content to occur in the sense history of more than a single self. And then he proceeds to give an analysis on the notion of a self.

He says that if a self is not to be treated as a metaphysical entity, it must be held to be a logical construction out of the sense-experiences. And to ask about the nature of the self, is to ask what it the relationship that must obtain between sense-experiences for them to belong to the sense-history of the same self. The answer is that for any two sense-experiences to belong to the sense-history of the same self, it is necessary and sufficient that they should contain organic sense-contents which are elements of the same body. But the relation of belonging to the sense-history of the same self is symmetrical and transitive, it fallows necessarily that the series of sense-experiences which constitute the sense-histories of different selves cannot have any members in common. Thus it is logically impossible for a sense-experience to belong to the sense-history of more than a single-self. But if all sense-experience are subjective, then all sense-contents are subjective.

For it is necessary by definition for a sense- content to be contained in a single sense-experience.

Ayer says, to many people, the account of self may appear paradoxical. For many people regard the self as a substance. Many of them suggest that it is revealed in self-consciousness, but, Ayer says, this is not the case. The possibility of self-consciousness in no way involves the existence of a substantive ego. And then it is not revealed anywhere, the existence of such an entity is completely unverifiable.

Ayer says that the postulation of mental substances is not needed to explain self-consciousness. The part which these substances are supposed to play has simply not been written for them.

It can be said that if something is felt, surely there must be something to feel it, call it a mind, or a soul, or a self, or what you will. As Bradley criticizes one of Mill's disciples by saying that, "Mr. Bain Collects that the mind is a collection. Has he ever thought who collects Mr. Bain?"[14]

Ayer find this argument plausible but fallacious. He says that, "I am able not only to be aware of my present feelings, but also to be aware that I am aware of them, and perhaps even aware that I am aware that I am aware of them..."[15]

Some philosophers feel the need to supply this series with an upper term. They, notably Kant, postulate a self which is always a subject and never in its turn an object of consciousness. Kant calls it 'transcendental' self. Its labours make our experiences possible, but because it is not a possible object to experience it is not itself, in space or time.

But Ayer believes that there can be no empirical evidence for the existence of any such entity. Kant's attempt to put the transcendental ego outside the world is a failure. This ego becomes, as William James says, 'simply nothing'.[16]

Ayer says that the assumption of its existence is no less metaphysical than Locke's discredited assumption of the existence of a material substratum. It is clearly no more significant to assert that an 'unobservable somewhat' underlies the 'self' than it is to assert that an 'unobservable somewhat' underlies material things. Ayer raises some questions, like how are these substances related to the experiences, which they are supposed to own or to the bodies which they are supposed to occupy? What criteria are there for their identity? Would it make any noticeable difference to me if I kept my memories and my physical continuity, but woke every morning with a different soul? How do I know that this does not actually happen? Without any answer to such questions, Ayer says, we have no concept to evaluate. An entity which is neither observable nor fulfills any explanatory function, can have no interest for us, says Ayer.

Here Ayer, or we can say that the positivists agree with Hume. For Hume, a self is 'nothing but a bundle or collection of different perceptions.' And because of this, Ayer says that the rationalist authors find it impossible for a consistent empiricist to give a satisfactory account of the self.

To solve this problem, Ayer presents his view about personal identity. He raises the question that, "what makes a person the person that he is?" And the answer is, that certain properties are after allessential, the property of having some Human characteristics, perhaps also the property of occupying some position or other in space and time. It can be said here that since various descriptions apply to the same thing, or person, there must be something that holds them together. But what is it that makes a set of descriptions, which are logically independent of one another, into descriptions of the same person.' How do we succeed in recognizing people? What makes it possible to say that the man whom we can now see is the same man as we saw a week ago? Ayer says that there have to be such criteria if our talk of persons is to have any meaning at all.

And here, Ayer talks about the general criteria of personal identity, that is, physical identity. When we say that the man whom we can now see is the same man as we saw a week ago, it is because he looks the same, that there is a fairly close resemblance between the appearance of this man and the appearance, as we remember it, of the man we saw last week. And this recollection is possible because the appearances are similar. Ayer says, "The fact that people's physical characteristics tend to be distinctive,' and the many constant features commonly persist throughout what is only a gradual process of change, makes this, as we have noted, a practical method of identification."[17]

Thus Ayer defines personal identity in terms of bodily identity and bodily identity here is defined in terms of the resemblance and continuity of sense-contents. Ayer says that, "My present experiences and those that accounted before the interval of unconsciousness belong to the same series because they are alike compresent with percepts which are associated with the same body."[18]

Ayer does not hold, as Hume did, that the self is an aggregate of sense-experiences, or that the sense experiences which constitute a particular self are in any sense parts of it. Ayer says that, "What we hold is that the self is reducible to sense-experiences, in the sense that to say anything about the self is always to say something about sense-experiences, and our definition of personal identity is intended to show how this reduction could be made."[19]

Ayer does not accept the realist analysis of our sensations in terms of subject, act and object, for none of these is in the least capable of being verified. Ayer does not deny that a given sense-content can legitimately be said to be experienced by a particular subject, but this relation of being experienced by a particular subject is to be anlaysed in terms of the relationship of sense-contents to one-another, and not in terms of a substantival ego and its mysterious acts. Accordingly a sense-content is not defined as the object, but as a part of a sense-experience. And from this it follows that the existence of a sense-content always entails the existence of a sense-experience.

Ayer says that those who look forward to life after death do not expect an empirical but a metaphysical existence, and Ayer says, this is one which has no logical connection whatever with the self.

Though in a sense, the identity of a person is founded on the identity of his body, but here is a question that is this the only sense in which we can meaningfully speak of a person's being the same individual? Many philosophers accept that the procedure of deriving the identity of persons from the identity of their bodies is the only one that can be significantly applied, so long, as the words are being used in any ordinary sense. They find it meaningless to speak of a person's inhabiting different bodies at the same or different times, or of there being more than one person in the same body, or of the separation of person's from their bodies.

Ayer says that if this view is shown to be correct, then it is needed to-re-examine the question of phenomenalism. According to the phenomenalist, the identity of any physical body is subject to analysis in terms of sense-data. It turns on the possibility of there being a series of successive sense-fields in which corresponding positions are occupied by similar sense-data. One might hope to reformulate the essential condition of spacio-temporal continuity. But sense data are means of expressing how things seem to people. And the problem here is that if sense data have to be defined in terms of persons, and the identity of persons is itself derived from the identity of their bodies, then the analysis of physical identity in terms of relations between sense-data appears to create a vicious circle. The only way of escape is to deny that sense-data have to be defined in terms of persons. A phenomenalist takes the concept of sensedatum as basic, everything else, including the concept of a person, is to be analysed in terms of it, and it is not to be expected that sense-datum should itself be analysable in terms of anything else. But it must at least be sown to be intelligible. And while it is useful in the analysis of perception, it is not at all clear that it remains intelligible when its customary attachments are removed, just as in the case of a hallucination. There may be sense data which are not the appearances of any physical object, so, there may be actual sense-data which do not enter into the experience of any sentient being. And if there are sense-data of this kind, nobody will know of their existence. Therefore, Ayer does not find this conception of unowned sense-data significant.

Again there are some problems with bodily identity.

According to Ayer, there are some essential properties that make a person the person that he is, like having some human characteristics, having some position or other in space and time. The possession of such properties is necessary to one's being a person at all, but they do not serve to differentiate one person from another. Again, the properties which do so, i.e. which do individuate, properties such as that of being at a certain place at a certain time, or having such and such physical traits, or being the author of such and such a work, which are in fact uniquely characteristic of the person in question, Ayer says, they are not essential. Any one of them can be denied to their owner without self -contradiction.

Ayer says that to identify a person is, then to say, not what, but who he is. In this order, we look at some of the descriptions that he satisfies, and preferably those that he satisfies uniguely. But if he alone satisfies them, it is a matter of empirical fact, not of logical necessity. Logically they might apply to others as well, or they might not apply to that person.

Ayer discusses the next case- we say that the man whom we can now see is the same man as we saw a week ago, it is because he looks the same, the appearances are similar. But again, Ayer says that as a criterion, it is, however, neither necessary nor sufficient. People can look very different, indeed at different periods of their lives, and different people can look very much alike. Ayer thinks of a situation that if the movements of a man, during a certain period, can be traced and spatio-temporal continuity can be found, then it can be said reasonably that this is the same man. But again, this criterion of spatio-temporal continuity is not, indeed, sufficient by itself. If the bodily appearances of this man are changed at any point to a very considerable extent, it can easily be said that this is not the same man. One must allow for the possibility that a man, like any other object, alters his identity, that he is, as it were, replaced by something else.

Now we see there is a view which Ayer does not consider- that people are differentiated from one another, not by the possession of any special properties, but by being different spiritual substances, or souls. Ayer does not find it intelligible because there is no criterion to decide the existence of such spiritual substance. There come so many questions as, whether the same soul inhabits different bodies, simultaneously or successively? Does it every happen that two souls get into a single body? Can there be any exchange of souls from one living body to another? Ayer says, "there might, indeed, be phenomena which would lead us to consider the possibilities of co-consciousness or reincarnation. We might be induced to admit exceptions to the rule of one body, one person. But then it is the phenomena in question that would supply us with out new criteria of personal identity."[20]

But, Ayer says, the reference to soul is intended to account for a person's being the person that he is, not merely to record the fact that one has some how been identified.

Ayer, further says that it does not seem necessary that two different people should always be descriptively distinguishable. People can differ otherwise than through their properties. But it only means that they differ in substance. Ayer says that, "Philosophers have fallen here into the mistake of supposing that because referential expressions are not used to describe properties, they must be used to describe something else, and substances are then brought in to fill the gap."[21] Since this argument applies not only to people, but to any individual thing, it doesn't establish the existence of the soul. Though, Ayer says, if the proof were valid, that one was at least a substance would be an important contributory step.

Ayer thinks about an another alternative to the criterion of bodily identity, which is relation between experiences. This is the Humean view that the self is 'a bundle of perceptions', and many empiricists hold it, in one form or another. But such relations between experiences are hard to discover- they must again be factual. On this view, each experience is a distinct occurrence, there can therefore be no logical connection between them. Thus it is logically conceivable that there should be experiences which are not the experience of any person, experiences which are not owned by anything at all. Ayer does not find it meaningful.

He says that it is indeed true that our distinct perceptions are distinct existences, in the sense that they are logically independent, one can describe the character of any one of them in a way that does not entail anything about the character of the others. But from this it does not follow that they are not factually connected. What unites them in the main is that either they are experienced together, or if they occur at different times, they are separated by a system of experience which, is felt to be continuous.

But this answer to Hume does not go all the way. Because it is not in fact the case that all one's experiences do form a sensibly continuous series. There are gaps in consciousness. Ayer says, he has no doubt that he is the same person as went to sleep so many hours before, (it is sufficient to break the continuity), but what it is that unites his present experiences with those that he had then? Ayer says, "It is, indeed, through memory that I discover my self-identity over this period of time, but it cannot be memory that produces it."[22]

Though he accepts the criterion of memory but gives the preference to bodily identity. He says that we commonly speak of a man surviving memory loss or personality change, but it is self-contradictory to speak of a man as surviving his body. But again Ayer says, there are problems. For example- if a person's identity depends upon the identity of his body, it must be logically impossible that he should exist in a disembodied state. But the notion of survival is not self- contradictory or meaningless. Many people believe in it. Ayer says that the hypothesis of survival must be taken as implying the re-animation of the body. But it does not fulfill the condition of spatio-temporal continuity, so the dissolution of the body destroys the person. If it is so, then we can say that the concept of personal identity does not depend upon the identity of one's body.

Now the question is that what should be the criteria in such a situation? Let us see on example- If one day, one finds himself in a disembodied state and unable to make his presence known to others, then what he can do? The answer is that it is necessary that one should remember the experiences that one had before one's death. Similarly, Ayer says, in the case of reincarnation, the continuity of memory should be there to give any sense to it.

In the case of reincarnation and in the case of one's existing in a disembodied state, the continuity of memory may be necessary, but will not be sufficient. The fact that the claims of memory are not in themselves sufficient to bridge a gap in sensible continuity does not mean that they carry no weight at all.

A further objection is that to remember an experience entails claiming it as an experience of one's own, from which it seems to follow that personal identity cannot be founded on this type of memory since it is already presupposed by it. But Ayer says that, "...in using the first person, one need not be raising the question whether any criteria of personal identity are satisfied, otherwise, it would always be sensible to ask of any experience whether it was one's own."[23]

In general the two criteria of memory and bodily identity work together. If the results to which they lead conflict only occasionally, one's memory is adjusted to be at fault. Ayer says, "we shall, however, see that if they were 'radically divergent, there might be circumstances in which the criterion of memory could be allowed to prevail, not perhaps to the extent of our being able to dispense altogether with the physical criterion, but at least to the point where we could allow the possibility of there being something other than a one to one relation between different series of experiences and the bodies to which they are attached."[24]

Ayer describes that even if the existence of an experience entails the existence of a person, an analysis of personal identity in terms of experiences could be informative. And, similarly, the existence of sense-data, which are indeed to be counted as perceptions, in Hume's sense, may be made to depend upon the existence of physical objects, or of other sense-data, but no sense-datum can exist entirely on its own.

This alone does not exclude the possibility of giving a phenomenalist account of the self.

Thus Ayer concludes that there are not any other criteria of personal identity than those that depend upon the identity of the body. No relation could be discovered by which the constituents of Hume's bundles could be adequately held together. Some continuity of memory is necessary, but not sufficient. It needs to be backed by some other relation that holds between experiences when they are constituents of the same consciousness. Ayer says, "The alternative is to regard it as a necessary proposition that a person's existence is tied to the existence of his body. But I am not convinced that this proposition is necessary though I believe that this is true."[25]

Solomon tries to show, through examples that these criterions, which are bodily identity and the continuity of memory, are not sufficient to decide personal identity. He presents two examples—

(a) Jones has an emergency brain operation. His own brain is removed and replaced by the brain of Brown (who is recently deceased) "Jones" still looks like Jones, still carries the same driver's license, and lives in the same house, but all of his memories and personality traits are those of Brown. Is he still Jones? Or is he Brown in Jones body? Now suppose one had been (or is) Brown, could he claim to be still alive in Jones body? We get no answer to these questions.

(b) Smith undergoes a personality split. He splits, head to toe, each haly of him forming an exact duplicate of the original, same memories and personality, same habits, knowledge, likes and dislikes, skills etc. Which of the two is smith? Does it make any sense to say that both are? Can it be said that the other smith is merely someone else?

And we see that we do not get satisfactory answers to these two puzzles.

There is an example presented by Locke in his 'An Essay Concerning Human Understanding', which is - The soul of a prince, carrying with it the consciousness of the prince's past life, enter and inform the body of a cobbler, as soon as deserted by his own soul, every one sees he would be the same person with the prince, accountable only for the prince's actions, but who would say it was the same man? The soul with all its princely thought about it, would not make another man, but he would be the same cobbler to everyone besides himself.

None of the two criteria can remove these difficulties. The supporters of these criterions try to answer these questions from their own viewpoint. But no criteria alone is sufficient to satisfy us. Solomon says that these examples "show us that our traditional conceptions of personnel identity are not as adequate as they might be."[26]

Sidney Shoemaker writes, "Underlying the theories about persons and personal identity that I have been criticizing is the idea that the criteria for the truth of statements about persons, and therefore the criteria that reveal the nature of persons and personal identity, must be criteria that we use in making these statements in the first person."[27] 'I have a toothache' is not inferred from anything (not even from criterial evidence), yet this statement is made with certainty and it seems unquestionable that we are justified in making them.

He says that psychological facts are logically independent of bodily and behvioural facts, and that personal identity is logically distinct from bodily identity. If one has to a make present tense psychological statements about oneself, one does not have to observe facts about one's body or behaviour (except some psychological states as being in love, anger etc.)

And while making a past-tense statement about oneself on the basis of memory, one does not have to observe facts that are evidence for the truth of statements about the identity of one's body. But if there are facts that one must observe in order to make such statements, and if these facts are the criteria for the truth of the statements, then the criteria are not physical (bodily or behavioral) criteria. Shoemaker says, "And if this is so, the relationship between physical and psychological facts, and between bodily identity and personal identity, can only be contingent relationships."[28]

And, he further says that the non criterial knowledge that a person has of his own identity, or of his own past history, can be shared with, or, communicated to other persons. If a person reports that he remembers doing a certain thing, other persons can accept his reporting this as evidence that he, the very person who reports this, did do the thing in question. Thus it can not be said that bodily identity is the sole criterion of personal identity.

One of the most powerful schools of contemporary thought, however, has been dedicated to the idea that personal identity, in every case, is a matter of individual choice. This school is existentialism. According to Jean Paul Sartre, there are no set standards for personal-identity, either for individuals, or for people in general. There is, he argues, no such thing as "human-nature", and what we are, and what it means to be a human being-are always matters of decision Sartre says, "If, however, it is true that existence is prior to essence, man is responsible for what he is... when we say that man chooses himself, we do mean that everyone of us must choose himself, but by that we also mean that in choosing for himself, he chooses for all men."[29]

But, Solomon says that this existentialist doctrine of choice complicates the problem of personal-identity instead of making it any easier. According to the existentialist, this is made even more complex by the fact that a person choose which facts are to be considered as essential. Are the facts alone ever sufficient to determine our identity? Sartre denies it. In Judging a person's identity, there must be considered more than the facts that are true of him or her. Their projection into the future, their ambitions, plans, intentions, hopes and fantasies must also be considered. But this way of viewing the person makes the question of personal identity impossibly complex, in fact, irresolvable.

Sartre talks about bad faith, which means, refusing to

accept the facts about oneself. Bad faith points to the most important single fact about personal identity - there is not any. In somewhat paradoxical terminology, Sartre tells us, "One is what one is not, and one is not what one is." In other words, whatever the facts about one, he is always something more than those facts. As long as a person is alive, he or she is identified by intentions, plans, dreams and hopes as much as what is already true by virtue of facts.

We can see that this and some other western conceptions are typically concerned with striving and ambition, status and planning for the future, "making something of yourself". Hermann Hesse refers to Buddhist concepts of the self which presents a very different picture of unqualified acceptance of things as they are, rather than struggling to change them, which involves a rejection of such notions as 'status' and 'making something of yourself. Buddhists, on the one hand, deny that there is a self and reject the views of self-identity. They say, "give-up your self-identity", "give up your self". On the other hand, this too is a conception of self-identity. They talk about "Buddha-nature".

"The concept of an 'ego-personality' is something that has been imagined by a discriminating mind which first grasped it and then became attached to it, but which must abandon it. On the contrary, Buddha nature is something indescribable that must first be discovered. In one sense, it resembles an "ego-personality" but it is not the "ego" in the sense of "I am" or "mine".

Attachment to an ego-personality leads people into delusions, but faith in their Buddha-nature leads them to enlightment."[30]

This Buddhist conception may be an ideal secular aspiration, however, for example, in contemporary China, and it is the goal of a large variety of ancient and contemporary forms of meditation.

We have seen that how so many philosophers, in different ages, deal with the problem of personal identity. How do they define the self, person and personal identity and what criterions they present to decide personal identity.

Now we shall take the next problem which is about the knowledge of other minds. It is also related to the concept of person.

According to the skeptics, the existence of consciousness in beings other than myself is a typical insoluble problem. There is no imaginable imaginable way of deciding it. And when some philosophers answer that - the behaviour of all human beings, and also the behaviour of all animals down to insects and worms, is, in the most important respects, so similar to my own behaviour that I must infer the existence of consciousness 'within' them, the sceptic refuses to accept it.

The problem is that 'how can I know that other people really have thoughts and feelings, when I can only observe their bodily movements and the sounds they utter.

Descartes, as is well known, maintains the view that only human beings are endowed with 'consciousness' and that we must look upon animals as mere automata, behaving exactly 'as if' they were 'conscious' creatures, but in reality being condemned to a 'soulless' existence. One man easily and justly point out that Descartes' argument might be extended to our human fellow beings. How can I ever be sure that my human brothers and sisters are more than mechanical automata and possess a consciousness similar to my own?)

Ayer says that Berkeley credits himself with having a notion of other spirits. These spirits are somehow attached to other bodies, but since these bodies are composed of Berkeley's own ideas, it is not at all clear that any provision is made for the accompanying spirits also to perceive ideas.

We see that the positivists combine a thoroughgoing phenomenalism with the admission that all sense-experiences, and the sense-contents which form part of them, are private to a single self. But here an objection is likely to be raised. It can be said that anyone who maintains both that all empirical knowledge resolves itself on analysis into knowledge of the relationship of sense- contents, and also that the whole of a man's sense history is private to himself, is logically obliged to be a solipsist, that is, to hold that no other people besides himself exist, or at any rate that there is no good reason to suppose that any other people beside himself exist.

The problem of our knowledge of other mind has provided a happy hunting ground for the sceptic, says Ayer.

In the new philosophy this problem of knowledge is transformed into one about meaning. What does it mean to say that another person has such and such a feeling? According to the new philosophy, it can mean no more than what is observable.

Sceptic says that in the case of other minds, our claims to knowledge or justified belief must be abandoned. In place of these claims, we are to acknowledge that we have no way of discovering what states and episodes occur in the minds of others and that we do not even have adequate grounds for believing that they have minds at all.

As to other persons, it may be argued that the sense experience of another person cannot possibly form part of his own experience, and, if people are nothing but logical constructions out of their sense-experiences, he can not have the slightest ground for believing in the existence of any other people. While such a solipsistic doctrine cannot be shown to be self-contradictory, it is known to be false.

Ayer says that if the personality of others cannot possibly by observed, then there is no reason to believe in the existence of anyone else. Ayer and many other philosophers hold that a sense-content cannot belong to the sense-history of more than a single self.

Ayer says that he must regard other people as metaphysical objects, for it is assumed that their experiences are completely inaccessible to his observation.

But further he says, "just as I must define material things and my own self in terms of their empirical manifestations, so I must define other people in terms of their empirical manifestations - that is in terms of the behaviour of their bodies and ultimately in terms of sense - contents."[31]

And he finds a good reason to believe in the existence of other people as he has to believe in the existence of material things. He says, "For in each case my hypothesis is verified by the occurrence in my sense-history of the appropriate series of sense - contents.[32]

He makes it clear that one should not think that this reduction of other people's experiences to one's own in any way involves a denial of their reality. He says, "If I know that an object behaves in every way as a conscious being must, by definition, behave, then I know that it is really conscious."[33]

Ayer says that if one is to avoid metaphysics, one must define the existence of other men in terms of the actual and hypothetical occurrence of certain sense-contents, and then the fact that the requisite sense-contents do occur in his sense-history gives him a good reason for believing that there are other conscious beings besides himself.

Ayter that, Ayer tries to show that in the sense in which we severally claim to have experiences we can also attribute them to others. But here again is the philosophical question how this is possible? The source of the difficulty is that one is postulating the existence of something that one can not conceivably observe. Here, Ayer says, it is necessary to distinguish between statements which are unverifiable by anyone and those that are unverifiable by some particular person. Ayer says that, "We saw in the case of statements about the past, that the fact that they were made by persons who could not observe the events to which they referred did not entail that these events were altogether unobservable. Might not the same apply to statements about 'other minds'?[35]

Here, it can be argued that one's inability to observe a past event is due to the accident of one's position in time, but it is not an accident that one is not someone else. It is not even logically possible that one should be identical with another person. Ayer says, "Thus, if my inability to observe what goes on in the mind of another is due to our being separated persons, there is no possible adjustments of my situation by which it could be overcome."[36]

Nevertheless, Ayer says, there is a way in which the parallel still holds. The meaning of a statement which refers to a person's experience is not affected by the fact that it is made by someone other than the person himself, anymore than the meaning of a statement which refers to an event occurring at a certain position in time is affected by the fact that it is made in a subsequent time. In either instance, the statement may be formulated in such a way as to convey information about the circumstances in which it is expressed, but this information is not part of what it states.

John Foster says that he can, to some extent, discern the thoughts and feelings of other people, not, admittedly through any special telepathic powers of the sort attributed to the mind-reader, but simply by observing how they behave and what they say. He presents an example—if I see someone at a bus stop put out his arm as a bus approaches, I conclude, other things being equal, that he wants the driver to stop, and I become quite confident that I have correctly interpreted his arm-movement if I subsequently see him get on the bus and buy a ticket. Foster says that in this case he reaches his conclusion about the mental condition of the other person by inference from something he perceives in the physical realm-from his bodily condition, his physical circumstances, his behaviour, his utterances. Foster says, "Nevertheless, if I am asked to justify the conclusion, it is to the physical evidence that I am obliged to appeal. And if the conclusion cannot be legitimately inferred from such evidence, perhaps in the light of other things I know, then it seems that my confidence in its correctness is misplaced."[37]

Philosophers present different solutions to the problem of our knowledge of other minds. Here, we shall see three main doctrines presented by different contemporary philosophers. These are –

1. The Behaviourist Theory.
2. The Criteriological Theory.
3. Argument from Analogy.

Some philosophers, in order to solve the problem of other minds adopt the behaviomistic theory. Gilbert Ryle, the ordinary language philosopher, syas that mind is the pattern of our behaviour, and not 'behind' behaviour at all. Ryle denies that a person's life is "a double series of events taking place in two different kinds of stuff."[38]

He says that the whole mind-body problem assumes that mind and body, mental processes and physical processes exist in the same sort of way. But it is not so. He talks about 'category mistake' which is mistaking one type of thing for another. For example – what color is the number 3? Makes a category mistake and it gives rise to the "impossible" "Ghost in the machine" notion of a person as a body united with mind.

Ryle says that physical processes are primary and every mental process can and must be explained in terms of witnessable physical processes. All our talk about the mind is translatable into talk about behaviour. For example, when we say that 'Socrates had a keen mind' the meaning we are conveying is that Socrates did certain witnessable things very well, such as, he asked penetrating questionjs, he debated well at his trial, he could sort out and solve puzzling problems, and so forth. We are not entitled, says Ryle, to claim that he possessed an immaterial entity, inside his body that can be called "Keen".

"Although he allows us to say that minds and mental processes "exist", they exist only as things we talk about. They do not exist as entities that act and react with other things as bodies do."[39]

According to Ryle, the function of the word "intelligence" is to describe human behaviour, not to name an entity.

The objection, here, can be made that we cannot tell by bare inspection of an act that it is intelligent, it might be a mere fluke. Ryle says that we have to "look beyond" the isolated act in order to determine whether it displays 'intelligence'. This 'look beyond' does not consist in trying to penetrate to a secret, mental phenomena, which is, indeed, by hypothesis, quite inaccessible to us.

But there are some shortenings in this theory. It needed to be shown that such things as identity, willing, understanding, desiring, exercising, even thinking, may in concrete instances consist in nothing more then the fact that the person of whom they are predicated is behaving or is disposed to behave in such and such a fashion. There is a great deal of mental activity that remains to be accounted for. Most importantly it has not been shown that perceiving can be analyzed in behavioural terms.

The next solution to this problem is the criteriological theory. Some philosophers maintain that although one can not in any sense observe the existence of other people, one can infer their existence with a high degree of probability from one's own experiences.

According to them, there must be logically adequate criteria for the knowledge of other minds. Wittgenstein says that, "An inner process requires outward criteria."[40]

Their argument is that my observation of a body whose behaviour resembles the behaviour of my own body entitles me to think it probable that that body is related to a self which I can not observe, in the same way as my body is related to my own observable self. Thus they attempt to answer the logical question, what good reason one has for believing in the existence of other people.

These philosophers give an example - If I say that I am in pain, I am referring to a feeling of which I alone am conscious, if my statement is true it may be that I also show certain outward signs of pain, but I do not imply that this is so, it is not part of what my statement means, and even if it so, it is not all that it means. But if I say of someone else that he is in pain, all that my statement is supposed to mean is that he displays signs of pain, that his body is in such and such a state, or that he behaves, or is disposed to behave, in such and such ways. For this is all I can conceivably observe.

An objection, Ayer says, to this thesis is that it entails that the statements, which I make about my feelings cannot have the same meaning for any other person as they have for me. So, if someone asks me about my pain, then my reply that I am, is not an answer to this question. For my reports are of a certain feelings while his question is about my physical condition. And if he does not believe me, he is not strictly contradicting me, because our meanings are different. Ayer says, "In so far as there is a regular connection between such conscious states and the physical manifestations by which they are defined for others, this discrepancy might not be practically important. But the connection is not perfect, and the fact that it might not obtain is itself sufficient for our argument."[34]

Ayer says that when we talk about our own mental states, we are referring to experiences of which we can be directly aware, but when we talk about the mental states of others, we are referring to their physical condition or behaviour.

Ayer finds this theory inconsistent. For a philosopher who maintains it does not merely wish to argue that the statements which he makes about his own feelings have a different meaning for him from that which they can have for anyone else. Ayer says that If a philosopher talks about the fortresses of others, he can be doing no more than describing their battlements. He can never imagine that other people are in the same situation as himself.

It is said that physical behaviour cannot be a sufficient criteria for the knowledge of the mental states of others. There can be only contingent relationship between them.

Some contemporary philosophers do not accept that we shall have to start from our mental states in order to have knowledge of the mental states of others. Strawson says that one can have no P-concept, unless he knows how it can be ascribed to others. So he cannot start with his mental states. Wittgenstein, in Philosophical investigations, says that one could not intelligibly ascribe sensations to oneself unless one had been taught to ascribe them to others.

Thus we see that these two theories do not succeed in achieving their aim. Now we see what the argument from analogy says. Ayer accepts it. He explains it by saying that on the basis of my own experience I form a general hypothesis to the effect that certain physical phenomena are accompanied by certain feelings. When I observe that some other person is in the appropriate physical state, I am thereby enabled to infer that he is having these feelings, which are similar to those that in similar circumstances I have myself.

Some philosophers object to this argument that its conclusion is unverifiable, but Ayer faces this difficulty. He says that the objection that one is generalizing from a single instance can perhaps be countered by maintaining that it is not a matter of extending to all other persons a conclusion which has been found to hold for only one, but rather of proceeding from the fact that certain properties have been found to be conjoined in various contexts to the conclusion that they remain conjoined in further contexts.

Ayer gives an example to explain this – when I have an injected tooth I feel considerable pain and that I tend to express this feeling in certain characteristic ways. Ayer says that these connections hold independently of other circumstances such as my residence, my hair style, the state of the whether etc. but it is not independent of the sate of my nervous system. So when I observe that same other person is similarly afflicted and that he acts in a similar way, I may infer that a similar feeling is also present, unless there is something in the circumstances that would make the connection fail. If he is anaesthetized, for instance, I might conclude that he did not feel pain, that, although he behaved as if he felt it, he was only pretending.

Now Ayer puts the question that, "having found that in various circumstances, the possession of certain properties is united with the possession of a certain feeling, does this union continue to obtain when the circumstances are still further varied? So, the basis of the argument is broadened by absorbing the difference of persons into the difference of the situations in which the psycho-physical connections are supposed to hold.

Though now the argument gets strength, but it may still be objected. For the variety of conditions in which these psycho-physical hypotheses can be examined is extremely limited. There are so many properties that can not be avoided or acquired. Again, one can easily behave like anyone else. He displays every Sign of consciousness when one would expect him to. But this is not disputed. The question here is that do I have the right to infer the existence of something 'behind' this behaviour?

Ayer says that 'I distinguish my own states of consciousness from their physical expressions and I wish to do the same for others. But then the possibility that they differ from me, or from one another, just in this respect, has a claim to be considered seriously.

Ayer Says that "I should need to vary my own attributes as much as possible, in order to increase the range over which my psycho-physical hypotheses were known to hold, and I should have to examine other people to see how far the analogy could be made to extend."[41]

But the skeptic can say that if this is the best evidence, he has no reason to be convinced, it does not even measure up to the standards of scientific proof. Ayer says that one has only a limited experience of the connection of 'inner' states with their outer manifestations. He says that, "As we have several times remarked, it is by insisting of an impossible standard of perfection that the septic makes himself secure."[42]

Ayer says that, "knowing that we ourselves have inner thoughts and feelings we can attribute them to others by analogy."

Foster says that since all the evidence for the correlation has to be drawn from one's own case, it might seem that such an inference is clearly illegitimate. But Ayer does not accept it. He says that, "this is a normal type of inductive argument, and I cannot see that it is in any degree invalidated by the fact that, however far one is able to extend the positive analogy, it always remains within the compass of one's own experience."43

Professor Putnam says, "our acceptance of the proposition that others have mental states is both analogous and disanalogous to the acceptance of ordinary empirical theories on the basis of explanatory induction."[44]

Foster makes his comment that 'for the evidence, though supporting the conclusion, may still be too weak to justify belief. This is something which has to be separately evaluated, and, Foster says, Ayer tries to do this later.

And we see further that as the argument from analogy remains open to the objections, consequently Ayer adopts the 'behaviouristic' interpretation of propositions about other people's experiences.

He says, "I believe that it is to be found in some combination of the admittedly shopworn argument from analogy with the theory that the ascription of conscious states to other supplies the best explanation for their overt behaviour.

Thus we see that the philosophical problem of 'our knowledge of other people' is not the insoluble, and, indeed, fictitious problem of establishing by argument the existence of entities which are altogether unobservable, but is simply the problem of indicating the way in which a certain type of hypothesis is empirically verified.

And Ayer says about sceptic that, "If he is able to persuade himself that he has been cast into a world in which only he is conscious, there is no way in which he can be refuted... he can believe that every thing is and will continue to be as if other people had minds, though in reality they do not."[45]

In this chapter, we have discussed two problems. A personal identity is a mask and a role that we wear in every social encounter. It is the way we think of ourselves and the standards by which we judge ourselves in every moment of reflection and self-evaluation. The question as "who am I" "How does one decide?" we can't ever avoid asking, but at the same time, we can never succeed in answering. It gets more complicated yet.

In the mind-body problem we realize today that the customary approaches neither of monism nor of dualism lead anywhere. Logical analysis merely examines possibilities and makes explicit the basic assumptions or programs of research. "The thesis of physicalism, in the sense of the unity of the language of science amounts to the same view as that which was previously called "logical (or methodological) behaviourism."[46]

References

1. Aristotle, 'De Anima' here taken from 'Introducing Philosophy : Problems and Perspectives' by Robert C. Solomon, p. 338.
2. "The Difficulties with Naturalism" taken from 'An Introduction to Modern Philosophy: Examining The Human Condition' by Alburey Castell and Donald M. Borchert, p. 47.
3. P.F. Strawson, "Persons", in Minnesata studies in the philosophy of science", vol. 2.
4. Maurice Marleau-Ponty, 'The Structure of Behaviour'.
5. Jerome Shaffer, 'The Philosophy of Mind'.
6. Rene Descartes, "Meditation VI" in Meditations on First Philosophy.
7. David Hume, 'A Treatise of Human Nature'.
8. John Locke, 'An Essay Concerning Human Understanding'.
9. Ibid.
10. David Hume, 'A Treatise of Human Nature', Book I, Part II, Section VI.
11. A. J. Ayer, 'Language, Truth and Logic', p. 135.
12. David Hume, 'A Treatise of Human Nature'.
13. Robert C. Solomon, 'Introducing Philosophy, Problems And Perspectives', p. 277.
14. F. H. Bradley, 'Ethical Studies', p. 39.
15. A. J. Ayer, 'The Central questions of Philosophy', p. 119.
16. William James, 'The Principles of Psychology', Vol. I, p. 365.
17. A. J. Ayer, 'The Problem of Knowledge', p. 188-89.
18. A. J. Ayer, 'The Central Questions of Philosophy', p. 116.
19. A. J. Ayer, 'Language, Truth and Logic', p. 136.
20. A. J. Ayer, 'The Problem of Knowledge', p. 185.
21. Ibid, p. 187.
22. A. J. Ayer, 'The Central questions of Philosophy', p. 115
23. A. J. Ayer, 'The Problem of Knowledge', p. 196.
24. A. J. Ayer, 'The Central questions of Philosophy', p. 116.

25. A. J. Ayer, 'The Problem of Knowledge', p. 199.
26. Robert C. Solomon, 'Introducing Philosophy: Problems and Perspectives', p. 280-81.
27. Sidney Shoemaker, 'Self-Knowledge and Self-identity', p. 211.
28. Ibid, p. 213.
29. Jean-Paul Sartre, 'Existentialism as Humanism'.
30. The Teaching of Buddha.
31. A. J. Ayer, 'Language, Truth and Logic', p. 139.
32. Ibid, p. 139.
33. Ibid, p. 140.
34. A. J. Ayer, 'The Problem of Knowledge', p. 215.
35. A. J. Ayer, 'One's Knowledge of Other minds', Theoria, Vol. XIX. Reprinted in Philosophical Essays.
36. John Watling, 'Ayer on other minds', Theoria, Vol. XX.
37. John Foster, 'Ayer', p. 128.
38. Gilbert Ryle, 'The Concept of Mind', p. 167.
39. Gilbert Ryle, 'Am I a Body and a Mind', in 'An Introduction to Modern Philosophy', Examining the Human Condition, by Castell and Borchert, p. 47.
40. Wittgenstein, 'Philosophical Investigations', Sec. 580.
41. A. J. Ayer, 'The Problem of Knowledge', p. 221.
42. Ibid, p. 222.
43. A. J. Ayer, 'One's Knowledge of other Minds', Philosophical Essays, p. 214.
44. Hilary Putnam, 'Other Minds', p. 82.
45. A. J. Ayer, 'The Central questions of Philosophy', p. 135
46. 'Twentieth Century Philosophy', Ed. by Dagobert D. Runes.

8

A.J. Ayer's Analysis of The Judgements of Ethics and Theology

In the beginning of the twentieth century, we can see ethics is predominantly metaphysical. The most important writers on moral philosophy explicitly link their discussions of morals with views about the nature of the universe as a whole, and man's place in the universe. A system of ethics is what such philosophers aim to set out, and this mean a total explanation of the way things are, which contain as part of itself an explanation of the demands and the requirements of ethical behaviour.

In Ethical studies, Bradley shows the problems of ethics, that is, of the nature of the end for end for man, and of the supreme good. Then he states the solution that the good is self-realization, and that this is the end or the purpose of the moral man's life.

In 1903 G. E. Moore's Principia Ethica is first published, in which he tries to distinguish clearly two kinds of question, that are, 'what kind of things ought to exist for their own sake' and 'what kind of actions ought we to perform?' Moore takes to be the main purpose of his book, is to distinguish thoes ethical judgments which are susceptible of proof by reference to evidence from those which are not.

After the publication of principia Ethica, the climate, in England, is on the whole unfavourable to metaphysical speculation in ethics. His whole method of writing seems to demand that in future, philosophy must be written carefully, and attention must be paid to the actual literal meaning of what is said. And a group of writers named Carritt, Prichard, Ross, and Joseph, and in Cambridge, C.D. Broad, like Moore, renounce all claim to deduce on ethical theory from any wide explanatory theory of the nature of reality at large.

Thus, the Chang in the traditional attitude can be seen clearly. In this order there come the logical positivists who have great respect for science and mathematics and complete distaste for metaphysics. But before we see their views about ethics and theology, first we try to understand what kind of knowledge should ethics be?

The two-thousand year old plan to establish ethics on cognitive basis results from a misunderstanding of knowledge, from the erroneous conception that knowledge contains a normative part. From the time of Plato to that of Kant mathematics is conceived as a system of laws of reason that central the physical world, from such a synthetic a priori there was only a short step to the conception that reason can dictate to us moral directives which have an objective validity, such as, is assumed for the laws of mathematics. If it turns out that mathematics does not supply laws of the physical world but merely formulates empty relations that hold for all possible worlds, there is no longer any space left for a cognitive ethics. Knowledge cannot provide the form of ethics because it cannot provide directives.

Thus, if ethics is considered as a form of knowledge, it cannot supply moral directives. Knowledge divides into synthetic and analytic statements, the synthetic statements inform us about matters of facts, the analytic statements are empty. Now the question is that to which of the two categories does ethics belong?

If it is synthetic, it should inform us about matters of fact. This is a descriptive ethics which informs us about the ethical habits of various peoples and social class, such an ethics is a part of sociology, but it is not of a normative nature.

If ethics is analytic knowledge, however, it will be empty and can not tell us what to do, either. If ethical statements are analytic, they are not moral directives. Thus, the modern analysis of knowledge makes a cognitive ethics impossible.[1]

Now we see what is the attitude of logical positivism towards ethics? As we have seen before that one of the main objectives of logical positivists is to provide a way of demarcating the meaningful statements of Science and ordinary life from the pseudo-statements of metaphysics. According to them, 'a statement is meaningful, means, something, only, if there is a way in which it could be verified (or 'tested'). A sentence has literal meaning if, and only if, the proposition it expresses is either analytic or empirically verifiable.

Now an important question is that how are ethical statements to be accommodated under verificationist criteria'. Should they be accommodated at all? Carnap, at one stage, declares, 'we assign them to the realm of metaphysics,' Bu while it may be thought that metaphysical discourse can safely be set aside as unnecessary for the conduct of human life, this can hardly be so in the case of moral discourse. The question here is, can the latter be regarded perhaps, as a kind of empirical discourse?

The statements of value, whether moral or aesthetic, are important kind of statements which the acceptance of the verification principle makes it difficult to treat as statements of fact. With regard to statements of value, the verification principle excludes the metaphysical view that they are descriptive of a realm of values, which somehow exists on its own independently of the natural world. But this leaves several other alternatives open.

Thus, we see, Schlick, in his book called "Fragen der Ethik" treats ethical statements as empirical. He upholds a form of utilitarianism according to which the validity of moral judgments depend on certain facts about human happiness and the means by which it is to be attained.

Schlick says, "If there are ethical questions which have meaning, and are, therefore, capable of being answered, then ethics is a science."[2]

He maintains that all of these conditions are fulfilled in the case of ethics. Every Science is, as such, purely theoretical, it seeks to understand, hence the questions of ethics, too, are purely theoretical problems. Ethics is a Science, it is a system of knowledge, and nothing else, its only goal is the truth.

Ethical questions concern the 'good'. Schlick claims that words such as 'good' are used to express desires, and these belong to the Science of psychology. The 'proper task of ethics' is to examine the causal process, social and psychological, which will explain why people have the desires they have. But it does not have the task of producing the good. Its task cannot be to produce morality, or to establish it, or call it to life.

Schlick further says that in modern philosophy since Kant, the idea repeatedly appears that ethics is a normative Science is something completely different from the factual Sciences.

It does not trouble itself with what is actually valued, but asks, 'what is valuable? What should be valued? And here, obviously the question is quite different.

But according to Schlick, this manner of opposing normative and factual Sciences is fundamentally false. Even as a normative Science, a Science can do no more than explain, it can never set up or establish a norm. The origin of norms always lies outside and before Science and knowledge. If the philosopher answers the question 'what is good' by an exhibition of norms, this means only that he tells us what 'good' actually means, he can never tell us what 'good' must or should mean?

Again Schlick says that the question regarding the validity of a valuation amounts to asking for a higher acknowledged norm under which the value falls, and this is a question of fact.

Now, it can be asked that cannot something be described as morally good or desirable even if people do not desire it? According to Schlick, it makes no sense. He says, "If, I assert that a thing is desirable simply in- itself, I cannot say what I mean by this statement, it is not verifiable and is therefore, meaningless."

Kant lays so much emphasis on the conflict between desire and duty, which is such a familiar aspect of moral life, but Shlick does not accept this aspect of morality. He rejects Kant's account of moral discourse, accusing him of being out of step with the ordinary meaning of 'I ought'. Yet, Shlick accepts, it makes good sense for a person to say, for example, that he ought to do x because he promised, even though it is contrary to his desire.

Since modern ethics often speaks of this absolute justification as the fundamental problem of ethics, it must be said that the formulation of the question from which it proceeds is simply meaningless. For example, J. S. Mill believes himself able to deduce what is in-itself desirable from what actually is desired. And he faces criticism for that. The question whether something is desirable for its own sake is no question at all, but mere empty words. On the other hand, the question of what actually is desired for its own sake is of course quite sensible, and ethics is actually concerned only with answering this question.

After it, Schlick continues by saying that such norms as are recognized as the ultimate norms, or highest values, must be derived from human nature and life as fact. Its norms cannot demand or command anything that is in a real opposition to those final norms recognized by life. An apparent difference can, of course, occur, for language and thought are very imperfect in daily life. The ultimate valuations are facts existing in human consciousness, and even if ethics were a normative Science it would not cease because of this to be a Science of facts. Ethics has to do entirely with the actual.

Now, we see how Ayer deals with the statements of ethics and theologies. Ayer's starting point here is the problem that the verification principle seems to preclude the literal significance of a certain class of ordinary assertions. According to this principle, no statement can be said to have meaning which is not either analytic or empirically verifiable. The propositions of logic and mathematics, and all definitions of symbols, fall into the first category, the propositionsof Science and of ordinary life, in so far as these simply state matters of fact, fall into the second category. There are no other categories. It can be seen at once that this creates a problem for ethics as ethical propositions do not come under either of the possible headings. These statements are not analytic, they do not, in Ayer's words, 'simply record our determination to use symbols in a certain fashion'. Again, they are not capable of verification by ordinary sense experience. It can not be said that one literally sees or hears the goodness of an action or motive.

Ayer says, "There is still one objection to be met before we can claim to have justified our view that all synthetic propositions are empirical hypotheses. This objection is based on the common supposition that our speculative knowledge is of two distinct kinds that which relates to questions of empirical facts, and that which relates to questions of value. It will be said that "statements of value" are genuine synthetic propositions, but that they cannot with any show of justice be represented as hypotheses, which are used to predict the course of our sensations, and accordingly that the existence of ethics and aesthetics as branches of speculative knowledge presents an insuperable objection to our radical empiricist thesis."[4]

Ayer divides ethical propositions into four main classes. There are propositions, which express definitions of ethical terms, there are propositions which describe moral experience, there are exhortations to virtue, and finally there are actual ethical judgments, that such and such a thing is good or is bad. He says that, it is easy to see that only the first of our four classes can be said to constitute ethical philosophy. Descriptions of moral experience are matters for psychology or anthropology; and the two remaining classes turn out really to be one. So, we can see Ayer is perfectly explicit about the task of moral philosophy.

Actually, this function of moral philosophy is demanded by his theory of the function of philosophy in general. In the preface to the first edition of 'Language' Truth and Logic' having explained that any proposition which fails to pass the test of empirical verifiability is literally senseless, Ayer says 'it will be found that much of what ordinarily passes for philosophy is metaphysics (i.e. senseless) according to this criterion and, in particular, that it cannot be significantly asserted, that there is a non-empirical world of values.........' And he adds that the philosopher's function is 'to clarify the propositions of Science by exhibiting their logical relationships and by defining the symbols which occur in them.'

The moral philosopher, then, has first to show that the propositions of morals are not scientific, that is, that they do not state empirical facts, and has then to analyse the terms which they do contain.

Ayer sets out to deal with this problem. He says, "It is our business to give an account of 'judgments of value' which is both satisfactory in- itself and consistent with our general empiricist principles."

John Foster raises this problem by putting an example, if it is said that 'Hitter was wicked' or 'Hitter's actions were morally wrong' then the question is- how are the propositions expressed to be classified in Ayer's system? Clearly they are not analytic (true solely in virtue of their meaning), to deny these propositions may reveal historical ignorance or moral insensitivity, but it is not, even implicitly, self-contradictory. On the other hand, the propositions do not seem to be purely empirical. So, it seems that, if Ayer's verification principle is correct, these ethical sentences do not express genuine propositions at all, that they are devoid of literal significance. And this is a difficult conclusion to accept.

First, Ayer talks about the content of ethics. What really falls within the sphere of ethical Philosophy? He says, that the systems of ethics is very far from a homogeneous whole, not only is it apt to contain pieces of metaphysics, but its content is of different kinds.

He says that a strictly philosophical treatise on ethics make no ethical pronouncements, but give an analysis of ethical terms. He says that ethical philosophers often discuss the possibility of reducing all ethical terms to one or two fundamental terms. But he thinks, this is not here a matter of concern to discover which term is to be taken as fundamental, whether, for example, 'good' can be defined in terms of 'right' or 'right' in terms of 'good', or both in terms of 'value'. What is to be inquired here is whether statements of ethical value can be translated into statements of empirical fact.

Ayer first considers the suggestion that, while ethical propositions cannot be directly verified by appeal to sense-experience, yet they can be translated without loss into propositions which can be so verified. If this suggestion is accepted, value judgments can be saved, since they can fit ultimately, though not immediately, into the second class of meaningful statements.

For this Ayer considers the alternatives which are naturalism and absolutism. Ayer thinks over two versions of naturalism, which are subjectivism and ulilitarisnism. Naturalism claims that statements containing ethical terms can be translated into statements containing no ethical or evaluative terms into statements wholly formulated in the empirical vocabulary employed in descriptions of the physical world and the human mind. Ayer recognizes that such a position is convenient from the standpoint of the verification principle, since it reveals ethical judgments to be empirical hypotheses, and ethical principles to be tautologies. But he rejects this thesis because it does not match-up to the actual meaning of our ethical assertions. He says, "we reject the subjectivist view that to call an action right, or a thing good, is to say that it is generally approved of, because it is not self-contradictory to assert that some actions which are generally approved of are not right, or that some things which are generally approved of are not good. And we reject the alternative subjectivist view that a man who asserts that a certain action is right, or that a certain thing is good, is saying that he himself approves of it, on the ground that a man who confessed that he sometimes approved of what was bad or wrong would not be contradicting himself. A similar argument is fatal to utilitarianism. It is not acceptable that to call an action right is to say that it would cause the greatest happiness because sometimes it is wrong."

Again he takes some other words like 'hooray' and 'damn'. They cannot be defined, because they do not stand for characteristics of things. In uttering them, one does not state facts about things but expresses his feelings. The names of feelings can of course be defined, and in using them, one makes factual statements.

But in spite of the close similarity in the actual form of their rejection of naturalism, even their purposes in rejecting it are wholly different. Moore's main concern is to state what are the things which are good in themselves. His interest in the language of ethics is simply preliminary to this. While Ayer, or logical positivists conceive the business of ethics to be the analysis of the language of morals.

Thus, subjectivism and utilitarianism are rejected not as proposals of a new ethical system, but as ways of analysing ethical notions. And therefore, Ayer thinks that no translation of ethical terms into empirical terms is possible. But it is important to know that it is only normative ethical symbols, and not descriptive ethical symbols that logical positivists hold to be indefinable in factual terms.

Ayer says that ethical terms are emotive or at any rate non-descriptive. Ayer is careful to distinguish normative uses of ethical terms form descriptive uses. If one says that 'something is good' and means nothing more than that it is enjoined by a certain code. In this case 'good' is being used descriptively, and in this use it can be defined. But if one uses 'good' properly, then he is merely expressing his feelings. In this case 'good' cannot be defined, because it does not stand for any concept which could be analysed. Therefore, in the sense in which definition is equivalent to analysis, 'good' is indefinable, necessarily.

The most obvious feature of this theory is its firm rejection of naturalism, Ayer, like Moorè, bases his rejection of naturalism on logical grounds. Moore's formula for its rejection it as follows, it can always intelligently be asked "is D good' and it shows that D is not really being treated as equivalent to good. Ayer puts it in the way, it can always be denied without contradiction that D was good and here also D is not being treated as equivalent to good.

John Foster says that Ayer is correct is doing so. No doubt it is fatal to naturalistic utilitarianism, which defines 'right' as 'maximizing happiness'. But Ayer's only error is that he seems to think that it is fatal to utilitarianism altogether. While, a utilitarian may merely claim that the maximization of happiness is what makes a right action right, without claiming that 'right' and 'maximizing happiness' are synonymous. Foster says this is something which Ayer seems to have overlooked.

Since normative ethical concepts are irreducible to empirical concepts, it seems that the way is clear for the 'absolutist' view of ethics. Ayer describes absolutism as, "the view that statements of value are not controlled by observation, as ordinary empirical propositions are, but only by a mysterious "intellectual intuition."[5]

But this theory makes statements of value unverifiable. For it is notorious that what seems intuitively certain to one person may seem doubtful, or ever false, to another. And a mere appeal to intuition is worthless as a test of a proposition's validity.

But foster thinks Ayer's description of 'absolutism' is misleading. Foster says that a utilitarian absolutist will claim that 'stealing is always wrong' can only be tested empirically, by discovering whether stealing always fails to maximize happiness. But an absolutist of other moral persuasion may claim that this sentence express an a priori truth which is morally self-evident.

It is thus clear that an 'absolutist' theory of ethics does not go with the main argument of logical positivists that a synthetic proposition is significant only if it is empirically verifiable.

There is a claim made by moralists that they 'know' their moral judgments are correct. This is of purely psychological interest, is not verifiable and has not the tendency to prove the validity of any moral judgment. So, on the absolutist theory, there is no relevant empirical test and here ethical statements are held to be unverifiable.

So logical positivists reach to a difficult position. Now the correct treatment of ethical statements is afforded by a third theory which is compatible with their radical empiricism. Ayer begins by admitting that fundamental ethical concepts are unanalysable, as there is no criterion of validity. And they are not real concepts at all. They are mere pseudo concepts. The predicates used in value judgments are not proper predicates, they do not stand for qualities of things which can be picked out by the senses. They are not descriptive of anything and they cannot be either true or false.

Later he admits that this view 'is in an obvious sense incorrect', since in ordinary English 'it is by no means improper' to speak of ethical statements as statements of description, or to describe these as true or false. Ayer says, "when one considers how these ethical statements are actually used, it may be found that they function....... very differently from other statements.' After all 'if someone still wishes to say they are statements of fact, only it is a queer sort of fact, he is welcome to do so'.[6] So here again is a wish to deny that ethical facts are facts, because they do not conform to a preferred model.[7]

He explains his view by saying, "if I say to someone, "you acted wrongly in stealing that money", I am not stating anything more than if I had simply said, "you stole that money." In adding that this action is wrong I am not making any further statement about it, I am simply evincing my moral disapproval of it. It is as if I had said, "you stole that money" in a peculiar tone or horror, or written it with the addition of some special exclamation marks. The tone, or the exclamation marks, adds nothing to the literal meaning of the sentence. It merely serves to show that the expression of it is attended by certain feelings in the speaker. If, I now generalize my previous statement and say, "Stealing money is wrong", I produce a sentence which has no factual meaning that is, express no proposition which can be either true of false. It is as if I had written "stealing money!!" where the shape and thickness of the exclamation marks show, by a suitable convention, that a special sort of moral disapproval is the feeling which is being expressed. It is clear that there is nothing said here which can be true or false.

A little later Ayer introduces an additional factor. He adds that, "It is worth mentioning that ethical terms do not serve only to express feeling. They are calculated also to arouse feeling, and so to stimulate action. Indeed some of them are used in such a way as to give the sentences in which they occur the effect of commands."[8]

He explains it with an example, like the term 'duty' as it occurs in 'it is your duty to tell the truth', may be regarded bot's as the expression of a certain sort of feeling about truthfulness and as the expression of a command 'tell the truth'. What distinguishes the phrases 'you ought to' and 'it is good to' from 'it is your duty to' is simply a dimination of emphasis that can reduce a command such as 'tell the truth' to a less categorical command and then to a mere suggestion. "In fact, we may define the meaning of the various ethical words in terms of the different feelings they are ordinarily taken to express and the different responses they are calculated to provoke."[9]

An ethical imperative like the Golden Rule simply means, "would that everybody behaved toward his fellowmen as he excepts them to behave towards him." This sentence having its accent in the emotive appeal, cannot possibly be deduced from a knowledge of facts only, it is neither true nor false. It is rather an invitation (suggestion, request exhortation, or command) to make the contained factual sentence true.[10]

Thus Ayer shows it impossible to find a criterion for determining the validity of ethical judgments. Not because they have an 'absolute' value mysteriously independent of sense-experience, but because they have no objective validity whatsoever. According to the verification principle, a pure value judgment does not qualify as a meaningful statement at all. If a sentence makes no statement at all, there is obviously no sense in asking whether what it says is true or false. Pure expressions of feeling do not come under the category of truth or falsehood. They are unverifiable because they do not express genuine propositions.

It follows further, on Ayer's view that it is impossible for two people to contradict each other on points of morals (or indeed of aesthetics either, for all value judgments are analysed in the same way). Nor can I contradict myself if I say first that something is right and then that it is wrong. By using the words 'right' and 'wrong', just my ethical feelings are being expressed.

Ayer accepts that his theory of ethics may fairly be said to be radically subjectivist but he finds his theory different in a very important respect from the orthodox subjectivist theory. The orthodox subjectivist holds that ethical propositions are about the speaker's feelings. If this is so, ethical judgments can be true or false depending on whether the speaker has the relevant feelings. Furthermore, they can be significantly contradicted. While on Ayer's theory they cannot be contradicted. Ayer differentiates between the expression of feeling and the assertion of feeling. He presents an example that he can say "I am bored" by tone or gesture without speaking at all, or may be lying about his feelings. Therefore, ethical statements are excitants of feeling which do not necessarily involve any assertions. And this is the distinction between Ayer's theory and the ordinary subjectivist theory.

The main objection to the ordinary subjectivist theory, which Ayer's theory escapes, is, that the validity of ethical judgment is not determined by the nature of their author's feelings. But there is a celebrated argument against subjectivist theories which Ayer's theory does not escape. Moore points out that if ethical statements are simply statements about the speaker's feelings, it will be impossible to argue about questions of value.[11]

But we do dispute about questions of value, so Moore

concludes that the particular form of subjectivism which he is discussing is false.

But we can see Ayer holds that it is impossible to dispute about questions of value, and that no one really ever does so. He says this may seem paradoxical, but when someone disagrees with us about moral value, we do not attempt to show that he has wrong ethical feelings. We attempt to show that he is mistaken about the facts of the case, or we employ general arguments about which actions produce what effect.

Ayer, further says, since there are really no specifically moral statements, strictly speaking there is no moral disagreement. Ayer says, "another man may disagree with me about the wrongness of stealing, in the sense that he may not have the same feelings about stealing as I have, and he may quarrel with me on account of my moral sentiments. But he can not, strictly speaking, contradict me. For in saying that certain type of actions is right or wrong, I am not making any factual statement, not even statement about my own state of mind. I am merely expressing certain moral sentiments."[12]

The quarrel feels like real disagreement, perhaps. But given the real nature of the conflict, which is revealed by philosophy, Ayer claims that there is no point in asking which of the parties is in the right.

Ayer explains that if our opponent has had different moral conditioning from ourselves, so that, even when he acknowledge all the facts he still disagrees, we say that it is impossible to argue with him because he has a distorted moral sense. Our judgment that it is so is itself a moral judgment, and so outside the scope of argument. We finally resort to mere abuse. We praise or condemn in the light of our own feelings.

If anyone doubts this, he can try to construct an argument on a question of value which does not reduce itself to an argument about logic or empirical fact. Ayer is confident that one will not succeed in producing single example. All that one may legitimately inquire is, what are the moral habits of a given person or group, and what causes them to have these? And this is a job for the social sciences.

Ayer talks about casuistry, which is investigation of how a moral code causes effects. But Ayer says that casuistry is not a Science, it is the analytical investigation of a given moral system, it is an exercise in formal logic.

According to Ayer, various ethical theories have an essential defect that they treat propositions which refer to the causes and attributes of our ethical feelings as if they are definitions of ethical concepts. While ethical concepts are pseudo concepts and consequently indefinable.

Ayer proceeds by saying that these conclusions about ethics apply equally to aesthetics. Words like 'beautiful' and 'hideous' are employed as ethical words are employed, not to make statements of fact, but simply to express certain feelings and evoke a certain response. So, Ayer concludes that there is nothing in aesthetics or ethics to justify the view that embodies a unique knowledge.

Providing data for our psychological and sociological generalizations is the only way in which these moral and aesthetic experiences serve to increase our knowledge. They cannot be used to establish the existence of a transcendent god.

Ayer says that this mention of God brings us to the question of the possibility of religious knowledge. But now the philosophers admit that the existence of a (non-animist) god cannot be proved. The existence of god cannot be deduced because the conclusion of a deductive argument is contained in its premises and the premises are uncertain. We cannot prove god a priori, because such judgments are tautologies from which nothing further can be found. The existence of regularity in nature does not prove "God exists", it just means "there is regularity in nature".

According to Ayer, 'God exists' is a metaphysical utterance which cannot be either true or false. It does not possess any literal significance. We can see that unlike atheists (who say god does not exist) or agnostics (who say god might exist), logical positivists hold that all utterances about the nature of God are nonsensical. Logical positivists offer the theist the same comfort as they give to the moralist. When the theist claims that in asserting the existence of a transcendent god, he is expressing a genuine proposition then logical positivists are entitled to disagree with him.

Again, Ayer says, in cases, where deities are identified with natural objects, assertions concerning them may be allowed to be significant. For example, a man tells that the occurrence of thunder is alone both necessary and sufficient to establish the truth of the proposition that Jehovah is angry. One may conclude that the sentence 'Jehovah is angry' is equivalent to 'it is thundering'. But sophisticated religions foster the illusion that god is real by giving the concept a noun.

Ayer talks about on another issue. He says it is common to find belief in an after-life. but to say that there is something imperceptible inside a man, which is his soul or his real self, and that it goes on living after he is dead, is to make a metaphysical assertion which has no more factual content than the assertion that there is a transcendent god.

Ayer says that there is no logical ground for antagonism between religion and natural Science. It is acknowledged that one of the ultimate sources of religious feeling lies in the inability of men to determine their own destiny. There cannot be any transcendent truths of religion. The sentence which the theist uses to express such 'truths' are not literally significant. In fact the views of logical positivists accord with theists, to whom God is a mystery which transcends human understanding, and therefore, cannot significantly be described.

If a mystic admits that the object of his vision is something which cannot be described, then he must also admit that he is bound to talk nonsense when he describes it. Religious experience is psychologically interesting, but does not imply that an act of intuition can reveal truth about matter of fact unless it is a verifiable proposition.

"A corollary of this v w is that it is not especially the business of the philosopher to make value judgements, to tell people how they ought to live. He is free to make value judgements, like anybody else, but he is not professionally entitled to a special hearing. It is not his particular province."[13] Ayer writes in the editorial foreword to Novelsmith's book that, "There is a distinction, which is not always sufficiently marked, between the activity of a moralist, who sets out to elaborate a moral code, or to encourage its observance, and that of a moral philosopher, whose concern is not primarily to make moral judgements but to analyse their nature.

So, the positivists are not concerned with questions such as what people actually adopt as their ends. They find it clear that scientifically verifiable statements cannot include any ethical propositions, or evaluations of any kind.

As we have seen, Schlick regards moral statements as factual and verifiable, while Carnap and Ayer try to dispose of them in other ways. C. L. Stevenson tries to analyse them into factual and non-factual components. According to the first of Stevenson's 'working models' the statement 'this is wrong' means 'I disapprove of this, do so as well'. (He deals similarly with the words 'ought' and 'good'.) The first part of this, he points out, is amenable to verification, while the second, being an imperative is not.[14]

A difficulty with which Stevenson wrestles is about applying this account to someone who is asking himself whether "x" is wrong. This is not a factual psychological question, about whether he does in fact approve of "x", the question for him will be whether he ought to approve of it.

Another difficulty is that of making sense of the imperative 'do so as well'. A person can be requested to do something only if he can choose to do it, but this is not the case with approval. If suitable reasons can be given, he may came to see that "x" is wrong, but he cannot do so at will, in response to an imperative.

The connection with reasons is, however, denied by Stevenson. He admits that 'a man's Willingness to say that "x" is good, and hence to express his approval, depends partly on his beliefs', but points out that 'his reasons do not 'entail' his expression and approval'.

Now this is true enough, indeed, it is not clear in what sense an expression can be 'entailed'. But it remains the case that on the basis of suitable reasons one may come to see (recognize, know it to be a fact) that "x" is wrong and ought not to be done. If such facts do not conform to the reductionist programme of logical empiricism, then it may be the programme that should be questioned, rather than the status of moral facts.

Logical positivists reject the claims of the intuitionists to be able to apprehend certain non-scientific properties of things. According to positivists, ethical and evaluative language is not informative at all, it is not concerned with the properties of objects, whether scientific or metaphysical. Evaluative language is concerned to do something else, namely, to express.

"Philosophers seemed pleased to have found this out that they were content to use the word 'emotive' to cover a large number of quite different things which language could do."[15]

John Foster writes that this emotivist analysis of ethical terms is certainly ingenious. But it is also, very implausible. To claim that when I say 'stealing is wrong' I do not even purport to say how things objectively are that I merely express my disapproval of stealing and/or issue a command against it just seems to misrepresent the actual meaning of the sentence. There are no objective moral facts and consequently, there is nothing to make ethical sentences true of false. But one can hardly reach this result. Because, it is true that ethical concepts are inherently objectivist (or realist). Moral rightness as we conceive it is an objective property. Certainly it is normative, but it is also a genuine property not just the projection of our own emotional and prescriptive attitudes onto certain types of action.

Again he says, "Ayer's account of ethics would leave hardly anything left for moral philosophy, as traditionally conceived, to investigate."

The reason lies not so much in the emotivist analysis, as in the negative thesis which underlies it the denial of objective moral truth. For if there is no objective moral truth, then by and large, the traditional questions of moral philosophy become spurious. Whether we construe ethical sentences as assertoric nonsense or as expressions of feelings, moral philosophy has lost the greater part of its traditional subject-matter.[16]

It can be seen that emotivism is not a new theory presented by logical positivists. When the 'L.T.L.' by Ayer was published then it seemed that emotivists in ethics were everywhere. They had not converted by the book, it was their creed already. Thirteen years before Language, Truth and Logic came out, Ogden and Richords published their famous book 'The meaning of meaning'. They first introduced the word 'emotive' and used it in just the way that Ayer does. And their ethical theory, being derived from the same sources, and the outcome of the very same influences, is, even verbally, very close to his. One quotation from their book is, 'Good' is alleged to stand for a unique, unanalysable concept...... (which) is the subject matter of ethics. When so used the word stands for nothing whatever, and has no symbolic function. Thus, when we use it in the sentence. 'This is good' we merely refer to 'this' and the addition of 'is good' makes no difference whatever to our reference. .... it serves only as an emotive sign expressing our attitude to 'this' and perhaps evoking similar attitudes in other persons, or inciting them to actions of one kind or another.'[17]

Mary Warnock says, about logical positivists, that they were held actual responsible for the greatest evils of the twentieth century. Because, the verification principle entails the total dismissal of metaphysics, and with metaphysics has to go the propositions of religion. Even ethical and aesthetic propositions are said to be literally meaningless, people try to defend their most deeply held convictions. But no doubt the verification principle, as a theory of meaning, is grotesquely narrow and limited in its applicability.

Ayer presents his case for emotivism as, primarily, he desires to find an ethical theory which will not conflict with the general verification doctrine. He appears to reject what he calls absolutism on the grounds that to accept it 'would undermine the whole of our main argument.' The verification principle has to face a lots of criticism because of the mistaken belief that if it is refuted, there will be no reason for even considering an emotive theory.

Ross seems to regard the emotive theory as an attempt to 'discredit ethics' which would never have been undertaken if it had not been for the demands of logical positivism as a whole.

R. M. Hare against naturalism and non-naturalism, agrees with emotivists that ethical judgements are not factual or descriptive. But he does not agree with emotivists that these ethical judgements are primarily emotive as they just express and arouse the feelings.

He criticises the emotive theory. He says that the criterion of verifiability can successfully decide the meaningfulness of the factual statements but ethical judgements are not factual. They are not descriptive of anything. So, on the basis of this criterion, the meaningfulness of ethical judgements can not be decided.

Hare says that ethical judgements are rational statements which guide us about 'what we ought to do' or 'what we ought not to do', one can ask for reasons before following them. But according to emotivists, these judgements are used for affecting others feelings, but this view make these judgements as irrational and then we cannot differentiate between these judgements and mere advertisements, which do the same job.

According to Hare moral judgements are prescriptive. Prescriptivism is based on the use-theory of meaning. According to Hare, moral language is a form of prescriptive language, because its purpose is to answer our question that 'what we ought to do'.

It is said that Ayer fails to .distinguish between the functions of expressing feeling of one's own and attempting to arouse the feelings of others.

But Ayer, in the introduction to the second edition, denies that emotive theory is a mere corollary of the verification principle. And even if the verification principle is rejected, there are still good reasons for accepting an emotive theory of ethics.

As to the actual analysis which Ayer proposes, the emotive theory itself, this has great plausibility and appeal for any empiricist. Ayer is right to insist on his empiricist ancestry.

Berkeley, in the introduction to the 'Principles of Human Knowledge' distinguishes four different 'ends of language' and suggests that there are more. Besides the communicating of ideas, 'there are other ends, as the raising of some passion, the exciting to or deterring from some action, the putting the mind in some particular disposition.' The word 'good' may raise a passion without there being any particular characteristic which is referred to by its use.

The tradition of Hume is very important Hume insists that moral judgments are neither necessary and a priori, nor are they, descriptions of any actual feature of the world. Whereas we have actual sense impressions of the physical characteristics of things, their moral value is not among these characteristics. Hume says when, therefore, we use ethical or aesthetic terms, we are not directly referring to things in the world, but to our own attitude towards these things. Thus, we see that Ayer shares Hume's basic conviction that value is not part of the world.

C. L. Stevenson describes emotive theory as a kind of interest theory, that is, it is related to the theories of Hobbes and Hume. But whereas traditional interest theories assume that ethical statements are descriptions of existing states of interest, the emotive theory recognizes that 'the major use of ethical judgments is to create an interest.' It is the emphasis upon description, he says, which renders all the traditional theories irrelevant as analyses of the word 'good'. He explains, "the emotive meaning of a word is the tendency of a word, arising through the history of its usage, to produce (result from) affective responses in people."

Finally it can be said that the logical positivists are professionally interested only in scientific, fact stating discourse. They think that such discourse can be marked offence and for all from other uses of language, and they further think that these other uses, in so far as they often masqueraded as fact stating when they are not, are actually vicious. This explains why Wittgenstein in the Tractutus says that there can be no propositions of ethics. It explains, finally, why having roughly characterized ethical language as emotive. We can see that Ayer's purpose is negative. He wants to clear the field for significant discourses, and what is thrown out, provided it is shown to be truly non-scientific, is not worth examining very closely.

Stevenson, like Ayer insists that the function of moral philosophy is to analyse the meaning of ethical terms.

This is the fundamental feature of those empirical theories of morals which have had the most powerful influence in the twentieth century and whose most dramatic statement is to be found at the end of Wittgenstein's Tractutus :

"The sense of the world must lie outside the world. In the world everything is as it is and happens as it does happen. In it there is no value, and if, there were, it would be of no value. If there is any value which is of value, it must lie outside all happening and being so. For all happening and being so is accidental."

Marry Warnock says that, "the greatest part of moral philosophy in England for the next ten years may be divided into two-the first part being in sense the continuation of the work of Ayer and Stevenson, modified by an increase in subtlety and, sometimes, in sensitivity to the actual use of language, and the second part being perhaps more directly influenced by Wittgenstein."[18]

References

1. Hans Reichenback, 'Essential Readings in Logical Positivism', by Oswald Hanfling, p. 224.
2. Moritz Schlick, "Problems of Ethics".
3. Ibid, p. 19.
4. A. J. Ayer, 'Language, Truth and Logic', p. 102.
5. Ibid, p. 106.

6. A. J. Ayer, 'Philosophical Essays',
7. 'Philosophy of Science, Logic and Mathematics in the Twentieth Century', Ed. by Stuart G. Shanker.
8. A. J. Ayer, 'Language, Truth and Logic', p. 108.
9. Ibid, p. 108.
10. 'Twentieth Century Philosophy', Ed. by Dagobert D. Runes, p. 402.
11. G. E. Moore, "The Nature of Moral Philosophy', 'Philosophical Studies'.
12. A. J. Ayer, 'Language, Truth and Logic', p. 107.
13. Revolution in Philosophy, Ed. A. J. Ayer, p. 78.
14. C. L. Stevenson, 'Ethics and Language'.
15. Mary Warnock, 'Ethics Since 1900, p. 138.
16. John Foster, "Ayer", p. 82-84.
17. C. K. Ogden And I. A. Richards, 'The Meaning of Meaning'.
18. Mary Warnock, 'Ethics Since 1900', p. 119.

Conclusion

After having an idea of the logical empiricism of A.J. Ayer, we can say that Ayer is an important representative, in his own time, of the British empirical tradition, running from Hume through John Stuart Mill to Russell.

Empiricism has always been a main stream in the history of philosophy. We find it in Greek philosophy, especially in the philosophy of the Atomists and of the Sophists. In the modern age, empirical tradition continues with the philosophies of Locke, Berkeley and Hume. This traditional British empiricism, based on the psychological analysis of experience, takes the form of logical empiricism in Ayer's philosophy, which is based on logical analysis of experience.

As logical positivists have great respect for science and complete distaste for metaphysics, the same is with Ayer which leads him towards the elimination of metaphysics. Ayer takes metaphysics as a theory of reality lying beyond experience and condemns it as literally non-sensical by the application of verification principle, according to which either analytic, or empirically verifiable statements are meaningful. The statements other than these two classes are non-significant.

For Ayer, the rigors of verification were the antidote against metaphysics that was popular in Europe at that time. But, we have seen that verification principle could not be formulated successfully and faced fatal criticism. Though it got success, to an extent, in eliminating metaphysics, and, it is true that metaphysics has lost its former status, but the way it is done, is not satisfactory. Ayer condemns metaphysics not as being speculative, or even as being false, but as being literally non-sensical. Showing their non significance through a logical analysis does not satisfy those philosophers and even common men, who have a great respect for metaphysics as an attempt to describe the reality as a whole.

Again, this verification principle is just a criterion of factual meaningfulness, but it does not cover so many functions of the language other than describing the facts. So, it can not be considered as a proper criterion of meaning. And, therefore, we see that the 'use-theory' of meaning replaces it later.

We have seen that like other positivists, Ayer is much influenced by Wittgenstein's Tractatus, which establishes that philosophy is the clarification of our language, rather than advancement of any new proposals about 'the way the world really is.' Ayer too accepts that philosophy has a useful function to perform in analysing and clarifying the concepts which figure in the everyday life, and also in the scientific use. To avoid sceptic's claim about the physical world, he adopts reductionist strategy. His reductionsim, and especially the assumption that mental phenomena can be reduced, in some sense, to the vocabulary of the material or physical is, of a great importance. We see that with Ayer reductionism is redefined as an epistemological programme, aimed at completing the works of Ernest Mach, in formulating a descriptive, radically empiricist conception of science, seeking to eliminate metaphysical nonsense from scientific theories, any assumption of the unobservable. Ayer's idea that philosophical questions are largely questions of language, and, that theories of meaning are, therefore, of central importance, holds important place today.

We see that he draws the distinction between a priori and a posteriori, analytic and synthetic truths, in his own way and it has its own importance. The acceptance of verification principle makes it difficult to treat the a priori statements of mathematics and logic as statements of fact. Ayer refuces Mill's account of mathematical truths as empirical generalizations by saying that these are necessary truths because they don't describe the fact, they are analytic and true by definition. Ayer says that these analytic truths enable us to pass securely from one descriptive statement to another.

Again, Ayer disregards the question whether the propositions of mathematics are reducible to propositions of formal logic, in the way that Russell supposes. Thus he takes the truth of mathematics as well as those of logic to be tautologies. And, even if, it is technically impossible to transform mathematical into logical statements, the explanation of their necessity may be the same. Thus, in general, he accepts the Frege- Russell-Whitchead thesis that mathematics can be reduced to logic, but his view of a priori statements does not depend on this identification.

He defines probability as the degree of confidence with which it is rational to entertain a hypothesis. He does not specify criteria of rationality, but says they are conventional and vary through time. The significance of his brisk aside about probability is that it sustains the only solution, he admits, to the problem of induction. He finds it rational to be guided by the past in forming expectation about the future and no doubt the current practice of those, ordinarily described as scientists, is rational in that sense.

Ayer tries to solve the problem of personal identity in a logical manner. His Humean view of the self as a series of experiences contains wholly original element. Hume fails in finding a relation which can connect a series of experiences into a self. Ayer suggests that the experience of one self must all 'contain organic sense contents which are elements of the same body'. Ayer also ensures that no experience can belong to more than one self, which the resemblance and continuity, which Hume was inclined to favour failed to do.

Ayer consideres the statements of value as emotive. They are expressions of feelings, and are designed to express and evoke the feelings of others. Thus the verifiability criterion rules them out as meaningless because they are descriptive of nothing. But this view does not look acceptable. The judgements of ethics and theology have meaning in their own sphere. Since they are not supposed to describe any fact at all, so their meaningfulness can not be decided by the verifiability criterion, which is a criterion of just factual meaningfulness. But it can be taken as a development of the perfectly respectable logical point that normative statements are not derivable from descriptive statements, as Hume puts it, that, 'ought' cannot be deduced from 'is'.

Some of Ayer's main positions, such as verificationism and emativism in ethics, are still referred to as parameters within which discussions of particular topic, such as ethics or of science, are to be conducted.

It can be said that logical positivism had a considerable impact and influence in its heyday. It has an established place in the history and continuing development of philosophy. And Ayer's interpretation of the leading ideas of that tradition undoubtedly gives it a new lease of life. In an interview in 1979 when Ayer was asked about the main defects of logical positivism, he replied- 'I suppose the main important...was that nearly all of it was false.' But he later admitted that he still believed in 'the same general approach.' And in a number of ways, 'the same general approach' is still widespread today.

In the first post-war decades philosophy in Britain was dominated by Wittgenstein and Austin, one a genius, the other enormously gifted, but both execrable examples in many ways. Confronted by dire imitations of their respective styles of writing and reasoning, Ayer stood out as a marvellous champion of the best traditions of rational discourse.

Though many of the philosophical problems which he tried to settle still remains unsolved. But his greatest achievement is to help to introduce a new spirit into philosophy, to set a standard of logical rigour and intellectual responsibility. It can be said that if he had adopted a little liberal attitude while establishing his doctrines and criticizing others, perhaps, he would have been more effective.

Bibliography

I. Books by A. J. Ayer

1. Ayer, A. J. 'Language, Truth and Logic', Victor Gollancz, Penguin Books, London, 1936, 2nd Edn. 1946, Reprinted in 1990.
2. Ayer, A. J. 'The Foundations of Empirical Knowledge', Macmillan, London, 1940.
3. Ayer, A. J., 'The Problem of Knowledge', 'Macmillon, London, 1956, Reprinted in 1990.
4. Ayer, A. J., 'The Central Questions of Philosophy', Wiedenfeld and Nicholson, London, 1973, Reprinted in Penguin Books, 1991.
5. Ed., "Logical Positivism", Free Press, New York, 1963.
6. Ayer, A. J., 'Philosophy in the Twentieth Century', Wiedenfeld and Nicholson, London, 1982.
7. Ayer, A. J., 'Metaphysics and Common Sense', Macmillan, London, 1969.
8. 'The Meaning of Life and other Essays', Ed. Ted Honderich, Wiedenfeld and Nicholson.
9. Ayer, A. J., 'The Concept of a Person and other Essays', Macmillan, London, 1963.
10. Ayer, A. J., "Demonstration of the Impossibility of Metaphysics", Mind, 1934.

11. Ayer, A. J., 'Philosophical Essays', Macmillan, London, 1954.
12. Ed. 'The Revolution in Philosophy', Macmillan, London, 1960.
13. Ayer, A. J. and Copleston F.C., 'Logical Positivism- A Debate', Eds. P. Edwards and A. Pap. A Modern Introduction to Philosophy, Collier, 1965.
14. Ayer, A. J., 'Logical Positivism' Allen and Unwin, 1959.

II. Books by Others

1. Ackermann, Robert, "Theories of Knowledge: A Critical Introduction' , Tata McGraw-Hill Publishing Co. Ltd., 1965.
2. Aristotle, 'De Anima', Trans. W.S. Hett, Cambridge, Mass: Harvard University Press, 1936.
3. Austin, John, 'Sense and Sensibilia', Oxford Clarendon Press, London, 1962.
4. Bradley, F. H., 'Appearance and Reality', Oxford University Press, 1893.
5. Bhattacharya, S., 'Doubt, Belief and Knowledge', Indian Council of Philosophical Research, Allied Publishers.
6. Carnap, Rudolf, 'Logische Aufbua der Welt', Berlin, Trans. George D., 'The Logical Structure of the World', Routledge and Kegan Paul, London, 1967.
7. Castell A. and Borchert D. M., 'An Introduction to Modern Philosophy, Examining the Human Condition', 4th Ed., Macmillan Publishing Co. Inc. 1983.
8. Cassirer, H. W., 'Kant's First Critique', George Allen and Unwin Ltd., London, 1954.
9. Chatterjee, S.C., 'The Problems of Philosophy', University of Calcutta, 1946, 2nd Ed.
10. Dutta, D.M., 'The Chief Currents of Contemporary Philosophy', Calcutta University Press, Calcutta, 1970.

11. Descartes, Rene, 'Meditation VI', in Meditations on first Philosophy in the Philosophical Works of Descartes, Trans. Elizabeth S. Haldane and G.R.T. Ross, Cambridge University Press, Cambridge, 1911.
12. Foster, John, 'A. J. Ayer', Routledge and Kegan Paul, London, 1985.
13. Hume, David, 'A Treatise of Human Nature', Ed. by Selbybigge, L.A., Oxford, 1896.
14. Hospers, John, 'Introduction to Philosophical Analysis', Prentice Hall, 1967.
15. Kant, I, 'The Critique of Pure Reason', Ed. Smith, N.K., Macmillan and Co. Ltd., London, 1952.
16. Locke, John, 'An Essay Concerning Human Understanding', Ed. Compbell, Fraser, Oxford, 1894.
17. Macdonald, G.F., 'Perception and Identity', Macmillan, London, 1979.
18. Maurice Marleau-Ponty, 'The Structure of Behaviour' Trans. by Alden L. Fisher, Boston, Mass : Beacon Press, 1963.
19. Malcolm, N., 'The Verification Argument', N. Malcolm, 'Knowledge and Certainty', Cornell, 1963.
20. Muckerji, A.C., 'Self, Thought and Reality', Indian Press Pub. Allahabad, 1970.
21. Ed. by Oswald Hanfling, "Essential Readings in Logical Positivism', Basil Blackwell, Oxford, England, 1981.
22. Ogden C.K. and Richards I.A., 'The Meaning of Meaning', Kegan Paul, London, 1923.
23. Passmore, John, 'A Hundred Years of Philsophy', Duckworth, 1957, Reprinted in 1984.
24. Paton, H.J., 'Kant's Metaphysics of Experience', Vol. I, George Allen and Unwin, London, 1951.
25. Russell, Bertrand, 'The Problems of Philosophy', Oxford University Press, London, 1912.

26. Ryle, Gilbert, 'The Concept of Mind', Hutchinson, London, 1949.

27. Ramsey, F. P., 'The Foundations of Mathematics', Totawa, N. J. Littlefield, Adams, 1960.

28. Ed. by Runes, Dagobert D., "Twentieth Century Philosophy', Philosophical Library, New York, 1943.

29. Schlick, Moritz, 'Die Kausalitat In Der Gegenwartigen Physik', Trans. by Weinberg 'Examination of Logical Positivism.

30. Schlick, M., 'Problems of Ethics', Dover, 1962.

31. Shanker, Stuart G., 'Philosophy of Science, Logic and Mathematics in the Twentieth Century', Routledge History of Philosophy, Vol. IX, London, New York, 1996.

32. Stevenson, C. L., 'Ethics and Language', Yale, 1944.

33. Solomon, Robert C., 'Introducing Philosophy: Problems and Perspectives', Harcourt Brace Jovanovich, Inc., U.S.A., 1977.

34. Shoemaker, Sidney, 'Self-Knowledge and Self-Indentity', (Cornell University), Allied Publishers, New Delhi, 1971 (First Indian Reprint).

35. Strawson, P.F., 'Persons' in Minnesata Studies in the Philosophy of Science, Vol. 2, Minneapolis, Minnesata Press, 1958.

36. Shaffer, Jerome, 'The Philosophy of Mind', Englewood Cliffs, N.J.: Prentice Hall, 1968.

37. Sartre, Jean Paul, 'Existentialism as a Humanism', Trans. by Philip Mairet, New York, Philosophical Library, 1949.

38. Urmson, J.O., 'Philosophical Analysis', Clarendon Press.

39. Wittgenstein, L., 'Tractatus-Logico-Philosophicus', Trans. by C.K. Ogden, Routledge, London, 1922.

40. Warnock, G.J., "English Philosophy since 1900' Oxford University Press, London, 1969.

41. Warnock, Marry, 'Ethics Since 1900', Oxford University Press, London, New York, Toronto.

42. Windelband, Wilhelm, 'A History of Philosophy', Ist Ed., Vol. II, Harper and Brothers, New York, 1958.

43. Waismann, F., 'Synthetic A Priori Judgements', Reprinted from, 'Principles of Linguistic Philosophy', Macmillan and Co. Ltd., London, 1966.

III. Articles

1. Berlin, I., 'Verifiability in Principle', Proceedings of Aristotelian Society, Vol. XXXVII.

2. Blanshard, B., 'A Priori Knowledge', Reprinted from 'Reason and Analysis', La Salle, III, Open Court Publishing Co., 1962.

3. Carnap, Rudalf, 'Testability and Meaning', Philosophy of Science, III, IV, (1936, 1937).

4. Common Sense Versus Mr. Hirst's Theory of Perception', Proceedings of the Aristotelian Society, 1959-60.

5. Church, A., 'Review of Ayer's Language, Truth and Logic', Journal of Symbolic Logic, 1949.

6. Ewing, A.C., 'The Linguistic Theory of A Priori Propositions', Proceedings of the Aristotelian Society, Vol. 40.

7. Putnam, Hilary, 'Other Minds' Logic and Art, Essays in Honour of Nelson Goodman.

8. Quine, W.V., 'Two Dogmas of Empiricism', In Quine, 1953a.

9. Stace, W.T., 'Positivism', Mind, 1944.

10. Watling, John, 'Ayer on Other Minds', Theoria, Vol. XX.

Index

A

A absolute is lazy 36
A king had four sons 50
A pseudo-proposition 21
A treatise of human nature 69
An essay concerning human understanding 179
An inner process requires outward criteria 187
Absolute 205
Absolutist 203
Actual experience 52
All 33
Analysandum 83
Analysans 83
Analysis of the notion of a material thing 86
Analytic 133
Any state of affairs 21
Arsenic is poisonous 31
Author's feelings 206
Ayer, A.J. 13, 16
Ayer's
- analysis 58, 98, 194
- criterion of the synthetic 138
- distinction 124
- position 85
- reason 35
- theory 206
- view 43

B

Babylon 106
Bare particulars 73
Basic propositions 35
Behaviouristic 191
Behind 87, 190
Berkeley 6-7
Berkeley's
- claim 9
- idea 110
- later works 8
- own ideas 182
- position 8

Blue is a colour 148
Bradley's appearance and reality 51
Brothers are male sibbilings 88
Buddha-nature 181

C

Caesar is a prime number 25
Capleston's prediction has been verified 47
Category mistake 186
Cogito 66
Comte's
fundamental doctrines 11
ideal 11
Conceive 123
Conclusively verifiable 100
Construction 90
Consciousness 161, 182
Contingent 133
Convenience of measurement 97
Critique of language 71

D

Death 50
Deceitfulness 4
Definition in use 80
Dogmatists 63
Demonstrate 136
Density death fatherhood 50
Dictionary 37
Die Logik der forschung 32
Dogmatists 18
Dogs are faithful 41

E

Eggs 88
Ego-personality 181
Elementary propositions 102
Elimination of metaphysics 16
Empirical self 167
Ends of language 214
English speaking word 13
Entail 81
Entailment 36
Equivalent 81
Erkenntenis 13
Exist 159, 186
Experience 100
Experimential propositions 102
Explicit definitions 80
Eye-doctor 80

F

Facts 162
Factual meaning 46
Factually 27
Fatherhood 50
Fiction 165
First principle 67
Formal 133
Forms of life 52
Function 161
Function of philosophy 56

G

Games 52
Ghost in the machine 186
Give-up yourself 181
Give-up yourself identity 181
God 62
God exists 208
Good 197, 201-02

H

Having
  a body 160
  a mind 166
Hegelianism 8
Heidegger's statement 51
Hens lay eggs 88
Hesperus is phosphorus 126
Hilter's actions 200
History
  of philosophy 71
  of western philosophy 17, 60
Holism 146
Homo sapience 102
Human-nature 180
Hume's
  bundles 178
  empiricism 10
  forke 53
  sense 177

I

Idea 110
Ideal 41
Identical 161
Identical theory 161
Impossible 186
Imprinted by the senses 100
Inconceivable 128
Incorrigible 35
Independent of experience 133
Indeterminary of meaning 146
Initial principle 66
Inner 190
Instruction 101
Intellectual intuition 203
Inter-deducible 81
Introduction 33
Introduction for the forming of statements 100

J

Jealousy pronoun live 44
Jehovah is angry 209
John Stuart Mill 11
Jones 178
Judgement of ethics and theology 195
Judgement of value 200

K

Kantianism 8
Karst's
  basis of distinction 139
  theory of science 132

Keen 186
Knowing the
  analysis 88
  meaning 88
Knowledge 116
Knowledge of other minds 158

L

Language
  games 52
  going on holiday 52
  touches reality 102
  truth and logic 13, 119, 200
Law 87
Length 101
Literal meaning 46
Logical 13
  behaviourism 191
  empirical 107
  positivism 13
  syntax of language 105
Look beyond 186

M

Making something of yourself 181
Man 164
Marriage means responsibility 51
Martyrs
  exist 41
  suffer 41
Material 133
Material thing 87
Maximizing happiness 203
Meaning 24, 46, 49, 51, 87
Mental 161
Mentalistic theory 162
Metaphysical 27, 43
  reality 42
  sentence 27
Metaphysics 16, 43, 49
Method of verification 24
Moderate-sized specimens of dry foods 111
Modern philosophy 10
Moore's formula 203
Movement 12
Myself 161
Mystical intuition 52

N

Naming and necessity 126
Nature 62
Nature of philosophical analysis 78
Necessary 133
Necessary truths 128
New 14, 23
Non-cogito 66
Nol even in principle verifiable 51

O

Observation-statement 35, 102
Oculist 80
Ontological distinct 86

Operationism 101
Operation 101
Other premises 37
Ought 210, 220
Our knowledge of other people 191
Oxford 13, 125-26

P

Parmenides 17, 60
Particular 113
Perceives 111, 113
Perception, the problem of 109, 169
Per genus et differentism 80
Permanent possibility of sensation 12
Personal 164-65
Personal identify, the problem of 158
Phenomenalism 111
Philosophy 1
Physical world 109
Physiology 6
Picture 107
Principle of limited independent variety 70
Principles of human knowledge 214
Problems 75
Problems of
- knowledge 82
- philosophy 43

Proper task of ethics 197
Proposition 24
Prove the truth of 45
Pseudo-statement 14, 23
Psychology 6
Putative 24

Q

Queen Anne is dead 125
Quine propounds 145

R

Real 41
Reality 19
Reality as a whole 67
Red in a colour 149
Red shift 101
Reductive 83
Reduction 109
Relevant 34-35
Representation 110
Rest upon 38
Right 201, 206
Rose 105
Rose in a thing 105

S

Sees 115
Self 170
Sensation 110
Sensedatum 111
Sentence 24
Siffle hip brim 44

Simple entity 41
Solutions 75
Simply nothing 170
Small part 163
Some 333
Something is good 202
Soul 159
Soulless 182
Statement 24
Statements of value 199
Stealing is always wrong 201, 203
  money 205
  money is wrong 205
Strong 30
Substance 41
Substances 169
Synonymous 80
Synthetic 133

T

Terms — true/false 125
Test the truth of 45
Theory of meaning 52
Thinking things 160
Tractatus 78
Tractatus-logico-philosophicus 13, 21
Tragicomedy of Wisdom 2
Transcendent 17, 167
Transcendental unity of apperception 167
Truth 209
Truths of reason 132
Twar brilig and the slithy fores 25
Two dogmas of empiricism 145-46

U

Uncomfortably vague 34
Unicorns are fictitious 41'
Uniformity of nature 69
Universal 133
Unobserrable somewhat 170
Use theory 218
Using a meaning 24

V

Verifiable in principle 101
Verification principle 23
Verify or falsify 26
Vienna circle 12
Vorstellungen 110

W

Weak 30
Weakly 35
Western empiricism, a brief history of 1
Western philosophy, the history of 1
Wittgenstein's rejection of metaphysia 22
Wrong 206